MINILATERALISM

Economic diplomacy is changing. The big, multilateral organizations that dominated the last half of the twentieth century no longer monopolize economic affairs. Instead, countries are relying on more modest "minilateral" devices like trade alliances, informal "soft law" agreements, and financial engineering to manage the global economy. Like traditional modes of economic statecraft, these tools are aimed at both liberalizing and supervising international financial policy in a world of diverse national interests. But unlike before, they are tailored to navigating a post-American (and post-Western) world where economic power is more diffuse than ever before. This book explains how these strategies work and reveals how this new diplomatic toolbox will reshape how countries do business with one another for decades to come.

Chris Brummer is Professor at Georgetown University Law Center, C. Boyden Gray Fellow on Global Finance and Growth at the Atlantic Council, and Senior Fellow at the Milken Institute. He is the author of *Soft Law and the Global Financial System* (2012).

D1367290

Minilateralism

HOW TRADE ALLIANCES, SOFT LAW, AND FINANCIAL
ENGINEERING ARE REDEFINING ECONOMIC STATECRAFT

CHRIS BRUMMER
Georgetown University Law Center

CAMBRIDGE
UNIVERSITY PRESS

32 Avenue of the Americas, New York, NY 10013-2473, USA

Cambridge University Press is part of the University of Cambridge.

It furthers the University's mission by disseminating knowledge in the pursuit of education, learning, and research at the highest international levels of excellence.

www.cambridge.org
Information on this title: www.cambridge.org/9781107678569

© Chris Brummer 2014

First published 2014

Printed in the United States of America

A catalog record for this publication is available from the British Library.

Library of Congress Cataloging in Publication data
Brummer, Chris, 1975–
Minilateralism : how trade alliances, soft law, and financial engineering are redefining economic statecraft / Chris Brummer.
    pages   cm
Includes bibliographical references and index.
ISBN 978-1-107-05314-4 (hardback) – ISBN 978-1-107-67856-9 (paperback)
1. International economic relations.   2. Foreign trade regulation.   3. International finance – Law and legislation.   4. Soft law.   I. Title.
K3823.B78   2014
337–dc23   2013036428

ISBN 978-1-107-05314-4 Hardback
ISBN 978-1-107-67856-9 Paperback

Contents

Acknowledgments

The idea for this book first took shape over the course of daily conversations with Todd Henderson, Evan Lee, Amanda Rose, and Fred Tung during the summer of 2011 as Roger Traynor scholars in residence at the University of California, Hastings. Their thoughtfulness and rigor raised my ambitions for the project from an essay into a full-blown book project. I have since been privileged to receive input from some of the preeminent experts in their respective regulatory and economic fields, including Douglas Arner, Emilios Avgouleas, Randall Henning, Bob Hockett, Rosa Lastra, Francois Velde, and Yesha Yadav. As with virtually all of my work, I owe an enormous debt to my Georgetown colleagues Mike Gadbow, Anna Gelpern, John Jackson, Don Langevoort, Adam Levitin, Marilyn Raisch, Alvaro Santos, and Bob Thompson, who have been instrumental advisors and interlocutors during the process. Meanwhile, I would like to thank Fred Kempe, Fran Burwell, Garrett Workman, and Andrew Chrismer at the Atlantic Council's Global Business and Economics program for their unyielding support, and Ambassador Boyden Gray, whose kind and consistent encouragement of my work cannot be emphasized enough. I would also like to heartily thank Jim Barthes, Dan Gorfine, and Phil Swaegel, my wonderful colleagues at the Milken Institute's Center on Financial Markets, who reviewed parts of the book and were critical in its execution, along with Staci Warden, Paul Irving, and Mike Klowden for their generosity. Last, I am extremely grateful to my research assistants, the very able Anjali Garg, Josh Nimmo, Matt Smallcomb, Bodie Stewart, and Won Lee, and to my faculty assistant Jacquelyn Williams. All of you were simply outstanding.

Introduction

Rethinking Cooperation in a Multipolar World

Multilateralism just isn't what it used to be. Wherever you look, the big, global international organizations that dominated the postwar economic system appear to be suffering from middle age – and in some instances, irrelevance. The last major multilateral trade agreement was signed over 15 years ago, when 123 countries created the World Trade Organization (WTO) and crafted a new set of rules for international trade. Since then, attempts to conclude another big round of reforms have struggled, and goals for the latest Doha Round of trade negotiations have been watered down in order to salvage a much more limited deal. The United Nations, meanwhile, has played virtually no role in crafting international financial policy in the wake of the most recent crises – a significant departure from the 1970s when members launched radical policy initiatives redefining the very meaning of national economic sovereignty. And the International Monetary Fund (IMF) and World Bank, though retaining important resources for stabilizing the international financial system, have yet to recover from their highly controversial responses to the Asian Financial Crisis of the 1990s, and have been in many ways sidelined in crafting policy responses to the recent Greek, Irish, Portuguese, and Spanish debt crises.

Instead, the "global" multilateralism characterizing the last fifty years of international economic affairs has been supplanted by an array of more modest and seemingly less ambitious joint ventures – from regional clubs like the (shaky) European Union and (rising) Association of Southeast Asian Nations to more geographically diverse and less understood initiatives like the G-20, Basel Committee on Banking Supervision and Financial Stability Board. Like their predecessors, these institutions and forums seek to coordinate diverse sectors of the international economy and export shared policy preferences of member governments.

But unlike the multilateral institutions that have largely defined international cooperation in the wake of World War II, these institutions are markedly different – and less grandiose than their predecessors. More modest in size, formality, and even inclusiveness, they play small ball on the court of international affairs and embrace what can be described as distinctively *mini*lateral strategies of economic statecraft.

As such, today's economic diplomacy seems destined to disappoint the ambitious diplomat or international lawyer. After all, for more than a generation, the grand narrative of globalization has largely been one of ever growing economic cooperation. The story went that as countries, spurred by technology and free trade, allow the free flow of capital, goods, services, and ideas across borders, they also, inevitably, should come to cooperate more. Globalization shortens the distances for business and trade, allows for specialization and for countries to exploit their natural competitive advantages, and in the process makes countries depend on one another to an unprecedented extent. Indeed, many serious historians and economists – and yes, even law professors – presumed that trade wars (and indeed war itself) had become, if not obsolete, then highly unlikely insofar as global capital markets would not permit such disruptive, inefficient disturbances in the global economy. Global multilateralism – taking shape in cross-border institutions, treaties, and maybe even supranational democracies – would become ascendant in an increasingly interconnected world economy. "The end of history," which Francis Fukuyama famously proclaimed in 1989, would eventually arrive in the form of universalized capitalist democracy as both capitalism and democracy spurred others to trade, adapt, and evolve, all presumably for the good of the global economy.

In retrospect, these expectations seem quaint, if not altogether embarrassing in light of the increasing complexity of the global economic system, not to mention the myriad forms of domestic economic governance. Still, the power of globalization's narrative of cooperation and its seeming ineluctability – which has guided the decision making of a generation of CEOs and heads of state alike for more than two decades – provokes serious questions that deserve serious answers. Where exactly did the story of global cooperation go wrong, and what, if anything, did it get right? And, even more important, how should one understand and interpret the new, fractured, and seemingly chaotic economic orders? Can we even begin to describe the direction of global economic diplomacy, and for that matter the global economic system, as "good," "bad," or altogether something else?

Perhaps not surprisingly, pessimists have tended to dominate the punditry in recent years. For Parag Khanna, in today's globalized world, "islands of governance" tend to drive policy, as opposed to cogent global statecraft. Far from being connected, the world is "never more than a hair's length away from the symptoms of medievalism" – a disagreeable disease of "economic chaos, social unrest ... and wild expenditures." For Fareed Zakaria, the problem is even more basic, as the rise of emerging markets has made the world so complicated that it is impossible for countries to even articulate "grand strategies," or rules of thumb, for the conduct of their foreign affairs, economic or otherwise. Indeed, the very "doctrinal approach" to foreign policy, in which countries articulate guiding principles of foreign policy, "doesn't make much sense anymore. In today's multipolar, multilayered world, there is no central hinge upon which all ... foreign policy rests. *Policymaking looks more varied, and inconsistent,* as regions require approaches that don't necessarily apply elsewhere." International cooperation will thus have to do increasingly without single one-shot proclamations of national interests that explain state behavior. Fukuyama was wrong – we have plenty of history ahead of us.[1]

Inconsistency is, of course, in the eye of the beholder, but Zakaria's basic hunch is correct: ultimately, more varied approaches are not only common but also required in today's post-American world. Yet there are limits to how far the observation holds. Whatever its challenges, the increasing multipolarity of the international system is actually leading to *more*, not less, institution building and cross-border cooperation. But cooperation is arising very differently than it did in the past. Core tenets of postwar multilateralism – from big global forums, to formal rules of the road for economic relations, to U.S. dollar hegemony – are being supplemented, and in some instances replaced, with alternative mediums and diplomatic tools in order to respond to a world of more varied interests, preferences, and power constellations. These changes are not, however, beyond analysis. Indeed, today's tools of economic statecraft can be identified and even generalized. And once recognized, they help lend a good deal of coherence to what might otherwise come across as unbridled economic anarchy.

WHY WE CAN (AND CAN'T) ALL JUST GET ALONG

But before delving into details, let's stick with our puzzle for the moment. How – or perhaps better yet *where* – did so many people get the story of global economic cooperation wrong? Why hasn't globalization culminated in a seamless global (or indeed "world") government?

Part of the answer lies in the very paradoxical nature of globalization itself. Far from comprising a one-sided bailiwick for cooperation, globalization simultaneously makes cooperation more necessary and more difficult. This is because two conflicting dynamics ultimately undergird globalization. On the one hand, globalization generates greater demand for cooperation as countries, firms, and companies become more interdependent. Yet at the same time, as countries become more interdependent, and as influence and power become more dispersed, not only do the potential gains of cooperation increase, but so do the costs associated with achieving it.

Although this argument may seem a bit controversial, it is not an entirely novel one since, like most theories of cooperation, it finds its intellectual origins in the path-breaking work of economist Ronald Coase. In a famous paper entitled "The Problem of Social Cost," the future Nobel Prize–winning economist recognized as early as 1960 that rational actors will, when left to their own devices, engage in mutually beneficial (welfare-enhancing) transactions, so long as the costs of negotiating, monitoring, and enforcing their agreements are low.[2]

To underscore his point, Coase presented the now well-known example of a rancher whose livestock had the bad habit of wandering onto other people's property and destroying their crops. Coase queried under what circumstances a fence would be built to prevent future incursions, and who would pay for it. He concluded that if property laws were sufficiently clear, they would provide an answer, assuming one could put a dollar figure on the damage. If local statutes held that the cattle farmer was legally liable for the damage, he would have to erect a fence, have fewer animals, or negotiate a deal compensating the farmer for his cattle's occasional trespass. If local laws didn't hold the cattle farmer responsible for the actions of his animals, incentives would run in the opposite direction. It would be in the interest of the arable farmer, if he valued his crops highly enough, to pay for the construction of his neighbor's fence. But as long as the law was clear, the two farmers would reach an efficient solution in the sense that it wouldn't be possible to make one of the farmers better off without making the other one worse off.[3]

This observation may seem pretty basic, but it left an indelible imprint on a range of important academic disciplines, including international relations. International relations, a subfield of political science, largely bases its analysis on rational-choice models of state behavior. That is, it is assumed that states seek to maximize their own interests. As such, experts tend to apply the same invisible-hand presumptions about the efficient behavior of people to the behavior of nations and other international actors.[4] Countries are viewed as self-interested players in a chaotic, no-holds-barred world, seeking to maximize their own welfare, and driven by powerful incentives to enter into cooperative arrangements that, though potentially constraining, increase their economic welfare and security.

Applied to international relations, the Coase theorem implies that countries, too, are at least potentially capable of making efficient bargains and deals among themselves in the anarchic "market" for international relations. For such efficient bargaining to arise, the two conditions we see in the domestic context must hold here as well. Property rights would have to be clear as between countries, and the transaction costs associated with reaching an agreement would have to be low.

As between the two factors, property rights have been comparatively easier to establish in international economic relations, especially as they exist between countries. As Columbia law professor Louis Henkin observed, "[e]xcept as limited by international law or treaty, a nation is master in its own territory.[5]" This fundamental principle subordinates property to sovereignty and is problematic usually only when issues like border disputes and disputed territorial claims arise. The trickier problem is that of transaction costs. As Coase himself acknowledges, in the real world, the transaction costs associated with reaching an agreement are never zero. Indeed, they are often quite high. First you have to gather the information necessary to strike a deal. Parties have to identify opportunities for mutual gain and then find the best partner with whom to achieve the desired goal. But because information will rarely be perfect, there will inevitably be trial and error in both regards; people will not always identify good opportunities or good partners, leading at times to unproductive or inefficient outcomes that can prevent parties from achieving fully welfare-enhancing outcomes.[6]

On top of information costs, parties have to hammer out and negotiate an agreement. This means that financial diplomats not only have to figure out the preferences of other governments, but also have to invest time and energy into convincing others to accept a particular course of action. How hard this is depends on a variety of factors. The consequences of any new policy are obviously paramount. If lowering tariff barriers between China and the United States results in Hollywood movies popping up in Beijing theaters and decimating local movie producers, a deal might be tough for China to accept. Or if cross-border proposals for banks force European banks to restructure more than their counterparts in the United States, there will be considerable outcry. So policy decisions have consequences – and can take enormous effort to coordinate. Then again, if one country is bigger or more powerful than the other, it may be able to coerce or incentivize its smaller or less powerful partner to accept its rules and policy preferences, regardless of their fairness. Additionally, if a particular country's cooperation is necessary to achieve a particular goal, this country might be able to "hold out" on actively blessing or participating in any initiative until it has extracted maximum gains and concessions from other parties. But this kind of strategic action is, by definition, costly and can also add to negotiation costs.

Finally, in many circumstances, some enforcement and monitoring of agreements is required – a point acknowledged by Coase and masterfully illustrated by fellow economist Mancur Olson in his book, *The Logic of Collective Action*. In it, Olson shows that where individuals attempt to provide a public good – say, things beneficial for the environment, security, or global financial stability – each member of the group will have incentives to "free ride" on the efforts of others. So if, for example, a group of countries agrees to reduce greenhouse emissions, some countries may decide to allow other countries to adopt the stricter standards (and higher costs) of clean energy and permit local manufacturers to continue polluting in order to gain a competitive advantage over foreign counterparts. Similarly, if countries adopt rules for the regulation of banks, some countries may seek to underregulate or underimplement global regulations in order for their banks to operate with fewer (and less costly) restraints. Where this kind of behavior is tempting, mechanisms must be devised to monitor and potentially discipline those parties that backtrack or defect from their agreements. Without incentives to encourage participation, and disincentives for backtracking or dodging commitments, collective action is unlikely to occur – even where participants share common interests.

THE PROMISE OF INSTITUTIONS

Although transaction costs might stymie cooperation, virtually no one thinks that they are immutable and can't be changed. That is, under the right circumstances, transaction costs can be managed and even reduced in ways that enable cooperation. The secret, scholars have suggested, lies in institution building. Simply put, by wisely structuring repeating interactions of countries, people, and firms, one can enable cooperation by lowering the information costs, bargaining costs, and enforcement costs needed to achieve it.

Take, for example, the problem of information costs. We have seen that international cooperation can be difficult if you don't know where to go to solve a problem, if the preferences of others are unclear, or if you don't know with whom to team up in order to solve a problem. This can be a big challenge in the global economy where issues are complex and often require cooperating with different partners over varying areas and sectors. Institutions like the UN, WTO, and IMF can help lower these costs, however, by creating focal points for continuous interactions between countries. When a country has a particular problem, it does not necessarily have to search the world to find a proper venue or potential partners. Instead, institutional organizations and arrangements can provide go-to forums for resolving particular problems for the international community. And just as important, institutions can collect information about recurring problems and past responses, and in the process standardize basic definitions and understandings about issues of mutual concern when action is required in the future.[7]

Institutions can also lower some of the transaction costs of bargaining. Highly sophisticated organizations might provide administrative or back-office assistance for running meetings when diplomats meet. Or a more bare-bones institution might memorialize a set of rules and procedures for dealing with problems, minimizing the time and headache associated with negotiating basic process issues every time a problem pops up.[8] Furthermore, by bringing a wide array of countries to the table, institutions create at least the possibility that just one agreement in a particular area, whether in trade or monetary affairs, might be reached by signing one omnibus accord. One country need not seek out and ink agreements with all other 191 governments in the world. Institutions also create a kind of institutional knowledge that makes bargaining easier as time goes on. With each new round of bargaining, procedural problems can be resolved for then and for later, reducing in effect the cost of future iterations of negotiation should similar issues arise.

Third, along with helping their members communicate with one another, institutions also help facilitate the monitoring and even punishment of participants. Specifically, institutions help provide information about the "house rules" – and who complies with them. By providing explicit rules and terms of conduct – and optimally a monitoring mechanism and means of punishment for noncompliance – institutions give assurance to the parties taking on membership obligations or duties that the potential gains from cooperation will be realized. Countries know what to expect from their partners, and incentives to defect or backtrack from their commitments are reduced. Furthermore, by providing a focal point or forum for recurring interactions between members, institutions can also create reputations for members, which themselves can carry important consequences. Where a government does not follow through on its commitments, or consistently ignores "house rules," fewer countries will take its commitments seriously or will want to cooperate with it in the future. A chronic backslider can, as a result, find itself without friends or partners in the institution, or even excluded altogether, depriving it of the benefits of cooperation. On the other hand, a country that sticks to its word will have an easier time finding partners in the organization, and can retain its membership in the group.

Finally, depending on how they are structured, institutions can additionally act, in Coasian terms, as a kind of "superfirm" that makes decisions for participating countries in ways that promote efficiency and harmony. Institutions may, for example, play a role adjudicating disputes, such as by assigning property rights or clarifying legal obligations or responsibilities among nations. Or they can arise as supranational organizations where executive bodies or managers make decisions in the place of free-standing negotiations between far-flung and numerous members. But institutional complexes like these are not costless and can involve large administrative staffs operating with few institutional checks and limited accountability. Moreover, they are difficult to get up and running. Countries sometimes have to delegate responsibility to the organization and to bind themselves in advance to any future decisions. This kind of commitment can be hard to swallow for legislatures, which often see their job as protecting their country's rights of economic self-determination. Still, to the extent that such power is relinquished to an international actor, institutions can move the coordination process forward in ways difficult to do otherwise, or fill in important gaps when new decisions have to be made or disputes resolved.

THE HARD KNOCK LIFE ON THE PARETO FRONTIER

Now for the bad news. Institutions hold considerable promise, but they are not fail-safe, even where they bolster information sharing, negotiation, and enforcement. Indeed, they have very real limitations: sometimes parties have perfectly conflicting interests, and in such circumstances institutions will not be able to make countries cooperate. Similarly, even if two parties have overlapping interests, their ultimate policy objectives may be far enough apart that the bargaining required to reach a mutually agreeable solution may be too time consuming or complex to warrant investing the time and effort into hammering out an agreement. Getting to an agreement could involve complex institutional arrangements that are themselves costly to administer and on top of it all may not even work. In such circumstances, countries may be disinclined to even attempt to negotiate an agreement, especially where the prospects for reaching an accord are weak.

Furthermore, even when parties have similar interests (or similar problems), they may disagree as to just how to cooperate. Often, multiple solutions are available to solve any one given problem. So parties still have to agree on which solution is best – a process that itself involves negotiating how the potential "surplus" benefits generated by cooperation should be divided up. But cutting the proverbial pie can be difficult. Some political scientists, especially "realists" preoccupied with security and power, argue that agreements may be particularly difficult to reach where gains from cooperation are distributed in a manner that interferes "with any member's efforts to maintain its relative position within the international distribution of power."[9] According to this view of international relations, articulated most forcefully by the political scientist Joseph Greico, states are not so much concerned with welfare as they are with survival. And under no circumstance are they willing to see their relative position in the world fall. Thus, according to this line of reasoning, the major objective of states in any relationship is not to attain the highest possible individual gain or payoff. Instead, the fundamental goal is to prevent others from achieving advances in their relative capabilities. Indeed, states may even forgo increases in their absolute capabilities if doing so prevents others from achieving even greater gains.

Whether or not such "relative gains" considerations operate so simply in international economic affairs is, however, far from obvious. Unlike during the Cold War, when two countries vied for global supremacy, international economic law often involves negotiations with many countries gathered around the bargaining table. In such circumstances, the ultimate impact of any particular deal on the hierarchy of actors will be less obvious, especially over the long-term. Moreover, in economic contexts like trade- or services liberalization, benefits are diffuse enough that "relative gains" considerations center as much on liberalization's impact on politically connected special interests as they do on the relative power relationships among states.

Still, the intuition behind the theory of relative gains is useful insofar as it helps underscore the difficulty of agreement even where interests are ostensibly aligned. Coase suggested that all cooperative agreements are at least Pareto improvements. In other words, they constitute agreements where at least one party is better off, and no party is worse off. Yet this is often not enough to secure agreements in the world of international economics. Where cooperation entails one party sacrificing more than others, concerns of fairness or balance may preclude agreements from being struck, even where all parties may in fact benefit. Similarly, a country's support may be hard to get if it alone is expected to provide side payments to countries disadvantaged by a cooperative agreement, especially if it is receiving the same gains as everyone else. And, as mentioned before, cooperation can be particularly difficult where the gains can't be harvested exclusively by the cooperating parties, because countries not participating in the agreement may be able to free ride by enjoying the benefits of the public goods generated by the group.

These observations reveal that negotiating global agreements, even where they may produce global welfare-enhancing outcomes, can be tricky, and at times, impossible. Successful bargaining involves, as foreign policy guru Robert Cooper opined, employing diverse strategies of both distribution and production.[10] It is ultimately contingent not only on finding common interests, but also on negotiating an acceptable distribution of gains among participating parties. After all, in a world of steep domestic and international rivalries, even smart, serious actors won't necessarily agree about how to divide the bounties of cooperation, even where they are in constant (low-cost) contact and communication with one another.

POWER AND MULTILATERALISM: A LOVE STORY

How then did we *ever* get to have a multilateral system at all, especially for the vast global economy? The answer for most scholars has been, at least for the last fifty years, as American as apple pie – and, well, as America itself.

To understand why, it's first useful to recognize that today's multilateralism is itself a kind of rare historical fluke. The international system of countries is anarchic, and as such the extent to which cooperation is possible is finite. What does, however, tend to make broad scale cooperation possible from time to time is the presence of an overwhelming economic and military power – a so-called hegemon. Where such countries exist, and are willing to use their power and treasure, they are capable of creating "multilateral" systems of economic governance, usually characterized by extensive cross-border trade and finance between a wide range of countries. This has especially been the case of the world's most recent hegemon, the United States, although it was also the case in the British and Roman empires.

Why would a country enjoying such overwhelming power even want multilateral, broad-based rules for commerce and trade? Because it can quite literally profit from them. As the noted historian Immanuel Wallerstein has remarked, hegemony can in many ways be described as an economic "situation wherein the products of a given core state are produced so effectively that they are by and large competitive even in other core states, and therefore the given core state will be the primary beneficiary of a maximally free world market."[11] As the most competitive country, a hegemon benefits from multilateralism insofar as it provides the legal and political infrastructure through which its firms can exploit their competitiveness at a global level.

This is not to say that hegemons are always prone to creating free (or entirely fair) trade. Instead, hegemons tend to have a knack at creating or sponsoring systems that respond to their own policy preferences. Multilateral systems of empire, after all, cordoned off colonies from trading with the rest of the world in order to support metropolises like London and Paris, while today's global trading regime has created a range of carve-outs and exceptions that shield special interests and industries in the United States and Europe from broader competition with emerging markets.

The ability of hegemons to get their way is not without limits, however. A hegemon still has to deal with other countries that at least in theory can always rebel against its authority. That being said, a hegemon enjoys a range of game-changing options and tools with which to promote its interests and policy preferences. Sometimes the arrows in its quiver are quite literally that, arrows – or guns, or cannons. In the eighteenth and nineteenth centuries, the British Empire (along with other European powers) repeatedly resorted to gunboat diplomacy to resolve economic and trade disputes, and used military force to open ports and trade routes and ensure the flow of goods and raw material between far-flung parts of the world. Today, economic coercion is more common. Where countries refuse to lower tariffs on foreign goods, or fail to abide by multilateral trade commitments, powerful countries can and do occasionally threaten to reciprocate in kind. Similarly, in the financial context, the United States routinely blocks foreign companies from selling their stocks and bonds to U.S. investors when their governments have been deemed to be inadequately supervising their home financial markets.

Yet coercion is not usually the weapon of choice. As we'll see in the following chapter, using military force places a considerable strain on even a hegemon's resources, especially where it involves providing for global public goods – such as peace or safe waterways – that other countries can enjoy while free riding on the hegemon's efforts. Economic sanctions, too, are costly, especially given the dominant role of hegemons in global economic systems as international traders and financiers. Indeed, political scientists have long recognized that while coercion may be expedient and possibly even effective, "the application of sanctions nearly always imposes high political and economic costs on the international actors doing the sanctioning."[12] To the extent to which a hegemon closes its borders and effectively excludes a country from its markets, it almost invariably undermines its own economic welfare. There is always the possibility that the sanctioned country may retaliate with its own sanctions. And even where coercion is unilateral, a country may be keeping goods from domestic consumers who may have few alternative sources of supply. Imports may also comprise inputs necessary for goods to be exported. And without the necessary inputs, manufacturers may find their own ability to export compromised.

For these reasons, history has shown that leading powers do not always, or even often, resort to coercion in order to promote their economic policies. Instead, they seek out other more subtle means of control and orchestration. By dint of their stature – and the fact that meaningful international policies often cannot be effective without their participation – dominant powers frequently have the leeway of acting unilaterally in anticipation that others will follow. In this way, multilateral coordination can often arise after the fact, in the absence of an international agreement. Even where there is no single policy that is best for all players and from which no player has an incentive to deviate, hegemons are uniquely capable of creating a focal point around which players can coordinate their moves.

One way to think about this is to imagine a world where countries are trying to abide by common rules for the global system, like stopping at lights that are a certain color. One country could have rules where cars stop at blue lights, whereas other countries might have rules where cars stop at purple and green lights, and others at red. In theory, every country would prefer others to follow its conventions; but above all, each would probably want to avoid the ensuing chaos of all countries adopting such varying standards as to undermine the world's highway and transportation systems. So although any one country may not prefer to switch, it might well prefer switching over a global free-for-all. In situations like these, hegemons can be extremely helpful. Because of its prominence, a hegemon can provide a focal point for coordination by other countries, especially where some form of collective action can achieve, if not the best or most preferable outcome for all countries, at least outcomes that are not the worst. As the most important and dominant country in the international system, a hegemon can embrace a policy choice – say stopping at red lights – around which others can follow, thereby reducing the risk of needless conflict.

Hegemons can also, by virtue of the size of their consumer and capital markets, use incentives to motivate others to cooperate and adopt their unilateral policy preferences. Where, for example, the United States writes rules relating to how companies must raise capital, the rest of the world has at least traditionally followed suit and adopted similar or comparable standards. Why? Because most of the world's largest companies do business in the United States, and until somewhat recently have needed to tap its capital markets and stock exchanges. Once they began complying with American standards, they then tended to import them back home. Adhering to the highest common denominator allowed companies to streamline their operations across borders. Plus there were considerable positive "network externalities" associated with playing by U.S. rules. If you complied with its standards, even when operating overseas – by say, using U.S. GAAP accounting principles or using the same documents for communicating with investors as people do on Wall Street – you could rest assured that most people would understand what you were doing and even find your behavior acceptable. Not following the American standard, by contrast, could create significant costs to the extent that you might have to continuously translate or explain your practices to audiences that were less familiar with your policies, and by extension, more skeptical.

Finally, hegemons can help incentivize broad-based cooperation by subsidizing the multilateral systems they manage. Indeed, leading powers – from the merely "important" to full-fledged "hegemons" – are often required – and indeed expected – to shoulder a disproportionately large burden in making global institutions effective. Invariably, they are called on to maintain certain policies like low tariffs, positive trade balances, or strong consumer demand. Or they might be called on to provide financial resources for the operations of international institutions or emergency funding when participants in an institution encounter economic stress. And as they are often the most extensive participants in multilateral systems, they can provide critical information with regard to other members' compliance with international rules, and may help enforce discipline and respect of those rules through sanctions or other forms of pressure. In taking up these responsibilities, hegemons are especially well positioned to derive a range of special privileges of leadership, including the ability to effectively manage and direct institutions in ways that reflect their own policy preferences.

This quid pro quo for institutional leadership highlights the truism that even hegemons are not omnipotent. Even they must expend time and effort when pursuing their strategic objectives. There may be future rivals or other strategically important countries that need to be placated in some way in order for genuine cooperation to take place. Or bargaining may have to take shape over several distinct issues – with the hegemon lowering tariffs in one sector in exchange for a trading partner doing so in another. Hegemons thus routinely make concessions to other countries – sometimes explicitly, and at other times more discretely – in order to achieve what it believes are optimal outcomes for itself or allies. Such concessions are, however, often tactical preferences as opposed to absolute necessities. Even in the absence of agreement, hegemons routinely possess the ability to push through their priorities unilaterally, if necessary via sanctions or through their military, though the costs of such maneuvers may be higher than what decisionmakers would find politically, morally or economically acceptable.

GLOBALIZATION AND THE EROSION OF AMERICAN DOMINANCE

For the reasons outlined above, few people dispute that as a general rule, it's good to be a hegemon. You generally get what you want, if you want it badly enough. Yet for all of its advantages, hegemony comes with its own drawbacks and risks. Indeed, it is, as Karl Marx would likely observe, beset by its own "internal contradictions." Most important, the same multilateral systems hegemons routinely rely on to advance their interests can also facilitate and even speed their decline. This is in part because multilateral institutions are expensive enterprises to get off the ground, especially when one country, the hegemon, shoulders the burden of institution building. Then, once regimes are up and running, they tend to lull hegemons into making very bad policy decisions. Instead of leveraging multilateralism to bolster their own interests in lockstep with the rest of the world, hegemons tend to squander opportunities for leadership by using multilateral arrangements to finance costly wars or to hide their own poor economic management. Over time, allies become alienated and cooperation becomes harder to catalyze.

But bad habits and shortsightedness tell only part of the story. For the most part, multilateralism over the last two centuries has rested on some basic conception of free trade. This was largely because free trade enabled hyper competitive hegemons to prosper. Not only were their firms usually more competitive than those in weaker or less developed countries, but they also made it a point to negotiate agreements that favored their own manufacturers. That being said, even hegemons rarely captured *all* of the gains from multilateral agreements. No country is universally competitive across all sectors. Plus multilateral economic arrangements are frequently so complex that even the most powerful, thoughtful leaders are unable to predict and manipulate the full economic impact of liberalized trading arrangements. Thus even relatively weak trading partners have periodically been able to muster and deploy whatever competitive advantages they do enjoy, whether they be abundant natural resources or cheaper labor costs, and over time not only adapted, but prospered. All the while, hegemons routinely remain responsible for underwriting the international systems they create, even as their own power erodes – if not in absolute terms, then at least in relative ones – as other states make gains in the international economy. Economic wealth and power become more diffuse.

This story has been particularly relevant for the United States, the most recent hegemon on the world's stage, and to date the only one that has crafted a truly global system based on explicit global rules. Rich in natural resources and spared from the destruction of two world wars, the country emerged in the mid-twentieth century as the world's economic and military superpower. And as the world's superpower, America enjoyed both an absolute and comparative advantage in a wide range of activities, including the manufacture of goods and agriculture. But soon after the United States took the reins of global economic leadership, the rest of the world started catching up. In the two decades following World War II, Japan and Europe managed to rebuild their domestic industry. And in the last forty years, developing countries in Latin America and Asia began to implement market-driven economic reforms. Many of these emerging markets began to attract foreign investment, industrialize, and become more competitive players in the global economy.

Globalization has only accelerated this unprecedented rise of the rest. Not only do countries trade with one another to a far greater extent today than ever before – in part due to the multilateral system the United States and its allies developed – but globalization has also taken on a distinctly financial character as advances in information technology have spurred cross-border, outward investment. Innovations in information technology such as the Internet have enabled the transmission of virtually real-time information concerning securities traded on foreign capital markets. Earnings reports, government filings, and market developments can be disseminated via the web pages of issuers, financial advisers, the government, and online news services – along with near instantaneous quotations on most publicly traded securities. Equally important, the digitalization of information has brought instantaneous transmission, interconnectivity, and speed to the financial markets. Banks can provide billion-dollar loans to clients at the push of a button, and issuers now readily raise capital in multiple countries and jurisdictions. Through electronic trading, investors can purchase stocks and bonds in foreign markets in a matter of milliseconds. Not only are investors, companies, and financial services professionals mobile, with more choices than ever as to where to set up their operations, but they can also participate in far-flung markets virtually anywhere, instantly, regardless of national origin and boundaries. Emerging markets have generally been the big winners in this brave new world, and even now, as a supercycle of Asian economic growth comes to an end, GDP growth there and in the Global South still routinely outpaces that of developed countries, including the United States.

Most people would agree that this is by no means an undesirable development, especially when one considers the plight of the global poor, of which billions have improved their lot, thanks in no small part to globalized trade and finance. But the more equitable allocation of the world's wealth and economic power has not been without drawbacks for global governance. When countries become wealthier, they often become more assertive in expressing their own economic and financial interests, and they tend to seek a greater share of the "surplus" created by cooperation. Widespread agreement consequently becomes more difficult to achieve, even in multilateral forums embracing the virtues of universality and the global good. So as globalization has moved apace, it has not only created a greater need for cooperation as goods and capital flow more easily across borders, but it has also moved the balance of power out of equilibrium such that disagreements on policy are more likely to rise to the fore and create dissent.

THE MINILATERALIST'S TOOLBOX

So to recap, multilateralism, at least as it has been understood over the last half century, is under stress. The United States has become an economically less dominant player, at least in relative terms with the rest of the world, and more countries are rising with regards to their own economic prominence and influence. As this transformation has unfolded, multilateral bargaining has become more difficult as more countries, with more swagger and varied economic priorities, have to be consulted in order to get big global agreements done. Consequently, investing time and effort into multilateralism has become a less attractive strategy as prospects for failure around a big bargaining table have increased.

This all-too-apparent predicament has led politicos and policy wonks to ponder what is next for the global economic system. Many commentators have surmised that in the absence of strong multilateral platforms, cooperation will be more modest, or perhaps dry up altogether at the global level. Along these lines, globalization could shift into reverse, with once-leading powers adopting a more isolationist or unilateral posture, thus giving rise to a more chaotic world of ad hoc deals, broken promises, and even military conflict where economic diplomacy fails.

These fears are based on the presumption that international cooperation is an all or nothing venture. Either you get a big, ambitious, international agreement, or the global economic system unravels from discord. Yet the world of economic diplomacy does not operate along such simple dichotomies. In this book we will see that multipolarity in the international economic system is giving way to new, innovative modes of cooperation, which, like earlier modes of economic statecraft, are aimed at both liberalizing and supervising the global economy. These new modes are not, however, derivative of overwhelming American power or hegemony, but instead reflect a world of rising and competing sources of economic power. As such, the new financial statecraft is far less "big" than in the last half century. But even going small – and shifting from a *multi*lateral system of governance to varied "*mini*lateral" approaches of diplomacy – can nonetheless have a profound effect on both international cooperation and the global economic system.

Three key features characterize the new minilateral system. The first development is the accelerating turn away from global cooperation and toward strategic alliances in which countries attempt, as the renowned economist Moisés Naím has described in a similar context, to find the smallest group necessary for achieving a particular aim.[13] Of the three minilateral tools, this is perhaps the most intuitive. It is also dominant in what is the most familiar and advanced sector of international economic affairs, international trade. Instead of opting for laborious "global" accords geared toward reducing tariffs virtually everywhere in one big bang, countries have banded together in discrete clubs to reduce trade barriers. Originally developing along regional lines, these clubs have diversified in scope and ambition, and now routinely involve far-flung partners seeking to kick-start their economies without the procedural constraints of the multilateral system. Yet whatever their size, the number of parties ultimately affected by such accords can be deceiving, and as we will see even low-level bilateral agreements can have profound implications for global economy.

The second emerging coordination strategy involves a breathtaking turn from treaties – instruments that have for hundreds of years dominated international affairs – to informal, explicitly nonbinding accords. These accords, which I refer to as "soft law," are relatively novel tools of financial statecraft. Yet they are already leaving an indelible mark on international economic affairs, and especially international financial regulation. For one, their informality allows financial authorities to take risks on agreements where the outcome of cooperation may not be obvious or certain. It also reduces some of the transaction costs associated with more formal obligations. In contrast to treaties, which can entail months – if not years – of negotiation between heads of state, their representatives, and domestic legislatures, soft-law agreements can be struck between technocrats and administrative agencies, often with relatively little interference by political outsiders. Parties can also, because of the nonbinding nature of soft law, amend accords relatively easily. Soft law thus allows parties to experiment and, if necessary, to change direction when new information emerges or circumstances change. All the while, soft law can be backed with market and governmental enforcement mechanisms that can add bite to promises made by countries and their economic ministers or regulators.

Finally, governments, like the market participants they regulate, are increasingly inclined to resort to financial engineering as a critical component of their economic statecraft. New risks are building up in the international monetary system as the size of the U.S. economy relative to the global GDP wanes. Indeed, with growth moving to Asia, Latin America, and Africa, governments are finding it increasingly difficult to accept the dollar as an unrivaled source of liquidity. To accommodate shifts in the global economy, countries are actively exploring a range of dollar substitutes – from the euro and the Chinese RMB to synthetic currencies like the IMF's "special drawing rights" – all aimed at diversifying the world's monetary reserves and international transactions away from their dependence on the dollar. But pivoting even partially from the dollar, the long-standing "international money," is a costly business, and clubs and soft law can only get you so far. Thus, to effectuate new forms of monetary cooperation, governments are leveraging new financial tools, principles, and instruments alongside minilateral and multilateral strategies to catalyze changes in their monetary affairs. By embracing novel deal structures, such as swaps, special-purpose vehicles, and currency clearinghouses, finance ministries and central banks are experimenting with new strategies that at times make them look as much like hedge funds as conventional governmental bureaucracies.

Compared to the lofty ideals of liberal internationalism, minilateralism can seem unambitious, and perhaps even disappointing. By definition, the cooperative strategies embraced by diplomats are less inclusive than traditional multilateralism, less legal, and, at least ostensibly, offer less "compliance pull" or certainty with regard to obedience with cross-border rules and dictates. As a result, minilateralism's toolbox is often frowned on by internationalists, and rarely if ever identified as an effective route to eking out agreement between governments with at times very heterogeneous interests.

But for today's economic diplomats, minilateral diplomacy is not just popular, but is also often the best way to "get to yes" in international economic affairs. Alliances allow countries to circumvent governments that may seek to block even welfare-enhancing cooperation, and to engage both regional and global problems efficiently. Soft law allows for speed and flexibility where the costs of cooperation are ambiguous yet require large numbers of countries to pitch in. Plus institutions can be crafted that give even nonbinding accords bite. Financial engineering, meanwhile, helps parties hedge for the volatility that inevitably accompanies the dispersion of geoeconomic power by reallocating monetary risk and diminishing the switching costs of using new international currencies.

Indeed, in the following chapters we will see that the real challenge for minilateralism isn't really whether it "works" – for even small steps can have a big impact on global cooperation. Instead, many of the most pressing problems arise as a consequence of its *effectiveness*. Where, in short, minilateral diplomacy allows countries to sidestep some of the multilateral values of universality and due process, it generates big questions of fairness and democratic legitimacy, whatever good it may provide for economic growth and financial stability. Indeed, minilateralism is frequently exclusive – and even exclusionary – in order to cobble together efficient alliances and cooperative ventures. Some countries can participate in various trade, regulatory, and monetary arrangements, whereas others cannot. And to make things worse, plenty of minilateral agreements consciously evade long-cherished rituals like treaty ratification, and in the process sideline democratically elected parliaments and legislatures. All the while, minilateral accords can have a big impact on the global economy – from triggering lowered economic tariffs to forcing banks to lend less to creating new monetary hegemons (and "exorbitant privileges") for up-and-coming economic powerhouses.

Plenty of potential risks and rewards thus accompany minilateral statecraft, with much of the former arising where domestic traditions and democratic institutions can't keep pace or cope with the minilateral innovation reshaping the global economy. To the extent to which minilateral deals are perceived as unfair or biased, minilateralism can serve to fracture and even stymie the beneficial forms of cooperation and the financial supervision it makes possible. Accords reached among experts and financial authorities can unwind, backfire, or disappear altogether. To counter such risks, minilateralism must be used intelligently, and when necessary, individual strategies should not necessarily be deployed in isolation, but instead be coupled with other tools and even traditional multilateral programs in order to maximize claims of legitimacy and democratic consent.

A final note before we move forward. In the following pages, we will see time and again just how hard global governance gets in a world of increasingly dispersed economic power and interests. But this book isn't just about the erosion of traditional global governance. Rather, the book's bigger message is about the strategic *responses* to this development, and what these responses mean for economic statecraft. Each strategy has, to be sure, attracted a good deal of attention over the last couple of years from journalists, scholars, and practitioners of foreign affairs – and the term "minilateral" has been used colloquially for more than two decades (indeed, well before Mr. Naim's delightful article).[14] But, almost inexplicably, no one has tackled them collectively in one work, much less ventured a comparative analysis. This has led to undue tunnel vision when people talk about financial diplomacy – and for that matter, about trade, financial market regulation, and monetary affairs as well. So in this short little book, we will try to connect the dots. And by doing so, we'll see how minilateral diplomacy comprises a variety of distinct but often interdependent strategies that are fundamentally reshaping how countries navigate the new global economy.

1

Multilateralism's Rise and Fall

As much as people talk about economic "multilateralism," it remains very much an elusive term, in part because it is used loosely to denote two similar though distinct concepts. At its simplest, multilateralism often is described as cooperation between three or more countries. Still, most legal scholars tend to equate multilateralism with the forms of cooperation that have dominated the postwar story of international cooperation – highly ritualized "global" forums of cooperation where heads of state sign treaties that memorialize certain economic relationships, usually under the auspices of a formal international organization.

But before the mid-seventeenth century, countries rarely cooperated in the sense in which we are familiar today. This is in part because the very idea of a "state" was very much under construction. Countries did not always have the sophisticated governmental infrastructure, or even the territorial integrity, that we know today. Moreover, with poor communication and limited interactions among emerging nations, sophisticated economic arrangements were not always feasible. Instead, they became more popular only over time, as countries came into closer and more sustained contact with one another.

That being said, rulers have for millennia sought to manage and promote core economic activities within their realms. Perhaps the earliest priority – after taxing and taking tribute from conquered peoples – has been, quite literally, to make currency that could be used by both citizens and subjects. Indeed, even when land and livestock were the primary signs of wealth, local strongmen have sought to create a means of exchange for their territories that would facilitate trade in contexts where goods to be exchanged possessed nonequivalent value. In most parts of the world, societies turned to commodities as the means of making such transactions work. Gold, silver, and, to a lesser extent, copper had qualities that were attractive to societies seeking a means of exchange, or what we now call money: they were rare, durable, and, for the most part, easily transportable. Finally – and just as important – they could be fashioned into different sizes and shapes to denote different values. Not surprisingly, the most common form of money was the coin, an instrument pioneered by the Lydians in the seventh century BC.

For most of the history of commodity money, the popularity or prevalence of any particular coin was rarely the product of a refined economic strategy or decision, even though smaller countries or principalities occasionally embraced the coinage of their larger neighbors to lower the transaction costs of trading with them. Instead, the most important factor was conquest. The power to coin was the power to rule. Once territories were conquered, the right of coinage was often brutally enforced. The great emperor Darius, for example, considered fifth-century-BC attempts by Persian satraps in Asia Minor to strike their own coins a capital offense. Similarly, Athenian measurements and coinage techniques were forced on tributary cities as improvements in minting techniques brought more regularity to its coins.[1] And perhaps least surprisingly, as Rome came to dominate the Mediterranean in the hundred years prior to the birth of Jesus of Nazareth, it assumed absolute authority over mintage rights of precious metals in its territories. With a few notable exceptions like Egypt (whose separate currency nonetheless often sported Roman iconography), the empire generally imposed Roman weights, measures, and coins as the only enforceable legal tender.

The importance of conquest meant, of course, that losers in war usually lost their monetary systems. When the Roman Empire fell, various Germanic tribes initially maintained the Roman monetary system, having had no system of their own. But "little by little, tribal leaders, seizing the political debris, built up small states, lay and ecclesiastical, each of them claiming the sovereign power to coin money."[2] In the late eighth century, this monetary decay reversed as Charlemagne centralized the minting process and adopted the silver denarius as the official currency for the Holy Roman Empire. But after his reign, local warlords again began to assume control of the mints, and coinage licenses were granted to various nobles and bishops. Germany, in particular, saw an explosion in the number and diversity of local currencies as a result of the fragmented political and religious conditions that pervaded central Europe throughout the Middle Ages. The only common feature was the growing predominance of silver as money, because copper was too heavy and gold too light (and rare) for use as a mainstay currency, at least at the time.[3] Yet even with the gradual emergence of silver in the Middle Ages, there was little uniformity in the estimated value of precious metals, including silver, even within a single state or region. Bartering dominated the economy at the time, with metals playing only a subordinate role in facilitating economic transactions. Even feudal dues were often paid in produce, not coins.[4] There was, as a result, relatively little thought given to the exchangeable value of coins outside the local ruler's domain, and with precious metals being rare, economic observations and discoveries were few.

The hyper-localized nature of monetary authority evolved only over time. The London mint, for example, was established during the reign of Alfred the Great in 886, though operated alongside others in the realm. Two hundred and fifty years later, the unification of England had generated more pressure to systematize coinage across the kingdom. After creating the Exchequer to keep records of government finances, Henry I ordered all coins be cut in ways to show that they were not silver plated fakes. Then to secure confidence in the oversight and supervision of the coinage process – and satisfy the soldiers in his employ that they were receiving good money from their king – Henry ordered the castration of ninety-four mint workers as punishment for supposedly casting bad coins. But the real push toward interregional cooperation arose in the late Middle Ages and early Renaissance, as conquests both in Europe and abroad propelled greater monetary consistency. In the 1400s, banking families began to develop more sophisticated deposit-taking and capital-pooling strategies that brought disparate localities into closer financial contact than had been the case in centuries. Later, the conquests of the Americas by Cortes and Pizarro in the early 1500s greatly increased the circulation of gold and silver in Europe, making coinage both more practical and more challenging as precious metals flowed easily across borders. Attempts were thus made with varying degrees of success to coordinate between localized sources of monetary authority. In the *Muenzrezess* of 1667, for example, and the subsequent Leipzig Agreement of 1690, German principalities in the heart of Europe sought to coordinate exchange rates for the silver thaler and the Cologne mark, with the Holy Roman Emperor himself ultimately signing on in 1693.[5] Meanwhile, in the more politically consolidated, but technologically lagging country of France, Louis XIII installed coinage machinery in Paris and introduced new national coins in 1640.

NINETEENTH-CENTURY SYSTEMIC RISK

By the late 1850s, three different monetary policies began to congeal among the world's major economies. On one extreme were gold standard countries, which included Britain and Portugal. On the other were silver standard countries like Germany, the Austro-Hungarian Empire, Scandinavia, Russia, and China. Then, somewhere in between, a large group of countries including France, Belgium, Italy, and Switzerland adopted bimetallic standards, with both gold and silver coined at a fixed ratio of exchange established by law (and usually in relation to one another). Both metals were thus legal tender, giving people, at least in principle, the option of making payments in either gold or silver.[6]

Several factors contributed to the monetary diversity. First, the choice of currency was never made in a vacuum, and countries never considered the issue from the same starting point. Some countries tended to favor gold or silver because over the course of their histories they had large reserves of one or the other and therefore relied on it more than perhaps other countries did. Switching would require liquidating their reserves of one metal, usually at a discount, in order to purchase the other at a premium. Also, depending on the state of the local economy, some metals were more attractive than others. In the late nineteenth century, for example, many countries with large farming interests tended to favor silver. Farmers tended to incur serious long-term debts to finance agricultural production, and since silver was generally more prone to depreciation, a silver standard could reduce the amount that had to be repaid. On the other hand, countries with developed financial centers tended to favor gold, which was rarer and more likely to retain its value.

Switching also presented real practical costs. To be sure, certain taxes, or "seigniorage" revenues could be earned in forcing people to exchange their money. Sovereigns could (and did) require residents to trade in old coins with high precious metal content for new ones with less – and pocketed the difference. But adopting new currencies and coins was still expensive. After new rules were passed regarding the proper weight and thickness of a principality's money, coins had to be minted – a process that had evolved slowly since antiquity from hammering coins by hand to casting them. Only in 1817 did the process begin to enjoy significantly lowered production costs with the invention of a new type of minting press (the steam-driven "knuckle-lever" press) that made its creator, Diedrich Uhlhorn, internationally famous. And even then it took more than twenty years for the machine to find widespread adoption throughout Europe. So switching, even at the local level, took time and inevitably involved confusion among local peoples.

Monetary diversity also persisted, as it does even today, for reasons of national pride. As we saw earlier, European governments began to assume full control of the coinage process from local dukes, bishops, and authorities towards the end of the Middle Ages, and up through the nineteenth century. Through this extended and often hard fought process, national money became an increasingly important symbol of the state, and rulers were disinclined to sacrifice even a semblance of control over their countries' monetary affairs. This was especially the case in Britain, where the pound sterling had been associated with a particularly conservative (and successful) approach to monetary policy and had enjoyed a special, and indeed unique, position among the world's currencies.

But diverse monetary systems also created certain systemic risks for individual countries' payment systems and economies. Many of the continent's monetary systems relied on both gold and silver as valid means of discharging tax and contractual obligations. In these so-called bimetallic systems, a government mint stood ready to convert gold into gold coins and silver into silver coins at fixed prices; and each coin had a constant legal tender value. The idea was that markets needed multiple mediums of exchange, one (silver) for low-value transactions and another (gold) for higher-value transactions. Furthermore, it was hoped that the use of two coins could provide a modicum of monetary stability insofar as arbitrageurs would keep prices of the two in check. If one metal's legal value relative to the other was overvalued, or out of synch with the market, smart businessmen could exploit the mismatch through a series of simple trades, which over time would drive up demand of the underpriced metal and help to stabilize prices.[7]

This (helpful) form of arbitrage only works, however, if the bloc of countries adhering to a bimetallic policy is large enough to absorb fluctuations in the demand and supply of bullion for long periods of time. The economist Irving Fisher used the metaphor of a reservoir with a moveable membrane to describe the total money stock, with gold and silver on either side of the membrane, and the membrane moving around back and forth to absorb outside fluctuations. If the bimetallic bloc shrank for whatever reason, or an inflow of a metal was large enough, say due to the discovery of new gold or silver somewhere in the world, the stability of an official ratio could be undermined since there might not be a sufficiently liquid market to absorb the movements. Countries thus had to stick together and stand ready to coin the two metals at a fixed rate of exchange to make sure enough gold and silver were available.

Then there was the problem of the coins (or more precisely, "token" coins since most were not pure metal) themselves. Simply put, even solidarity wasn't enough to prevent at times disorderly forms of arbitrage where, as was not infrequently the case, countries used different coinage standards and ratios. A token with a certain amount or quality of silver, for example, might be hoarded if another foreign coin with less or lower quality silver participated in the same currency system and could be used to purchase just as much. At the extreme, a government's high quality coins could disappear from use altogether in a country and find themselves replaced by lower quality foreign coins.

This particular risk to payment systems had been an annoyance since the Renaissance, when merchants for the first time began to use gold instead of silver to settle large-scale cross-border transactions. But in the mid-nineteenth century, arbitrage became a much bigger problem as unprecedented cross-border trade was coupled with experimentation by newly independent European principalities operating distinctly interdependent bimetallic systems. Across Europe, as monetary systems diverged, "bad" coins with lower levels of silver would be spent in lieu of "good" or more valuable ones. France and Italy, for example, had adopted higher-quality coinage standards than Switzerland, which shared the franc system with them – and as a result soon found Swiss coins circulating domestically. Meanwhile, French and Italian coins were exported, melted, and recoined in Switzerland at a profit. This then created a monetary race to the bottom, threatening to drive out of circulation the money needed for smaller economic and business transactions. When Italy saw foreign currencies displacing its domestic money, it responded by lowering the quality of its smaller coins, creating pressure for an exasperated Belgium to do the same.

THE FIRST DRY RUN AT INTERNATIONAL MONETARY COOPERATION

Europe's increasingly chaotic monetary system eventually convinced many of the continent's leading financial authorities that only by coordinating their coinage could they provide a deep enough reservoir for gold or silver to absorb market fluctuations. And just as important, coordination could help stymie the flow of foreign coins across borders if all countries adopted the same or similar monetary standards.

On November 5, 1865, the French Emperor Louis Napoleon convened an international monetary conference in Paris with representatives from France, Italy, Belgium, and Switzerland, all with the purpose of harmonizing coinage practices. At the conference, an agreement was reached to create a formal monetary union between participating countries – one of the first of its kind, and backed by binding legal obligations. In the resulting treaty, officials agreed on specifications in weight and diameter that mirrored French monetary regulations – all in an effort, in the words of the treaty's preamble, to "remedy the inconvenience to trade between their respective countries resulting from the diversity of their small silver coin."[8] Furthermore, to promote their new standard internationally, the treaty provided that any other country could join the union as long as it abided by the agreement's terms. And to be sure, other countries would ultimately opt into the club, including Greece in 1868, and even more would follow its conventions informally, including Romania, Bulgaria, Venezuela, Serbia, and San Marino.

Part of the LMU's initial success was due to the sheer tenacity of its promoters. Successive international conferences were convened in 1867, 1878, 1881, and 1892, all to lay "siege to the citadel of monetary diversity" and increase "commerce and exchanges of every description among the different members of the human family."[9] Nevertheless, the LMU ultimately proved a short-lived experiment. In many ways, it was ill-equipped, despite its grand ideals, to operationalize monetary cooperation in a world of disparate geostrategic interests. For its part, France liked the plan not only for what it would do for the human family but also for what it would do for France. France would largely escape the cost of adopting new rules because the regime was based in large part on its domestic monetary system. By contrast, Great Britain and the quickly rising United States would have to refit all of their local mints and modify all outstanding contracts according to the new French regulations if they wanted to join. Countries also had different risk appetites and perceptions about the wisdom of silver as a commodity money. For many economists, silver seemed overvalued, and a number of countries, including Germany – ironically the leading silver standard country of the day – saw in the LMU an opportunity to switch to what they believed was the more promising gold standard. With economies like France focused on supporting a bimetallic standard – and, by implication, silver – gold, it was reasoned, was probably undervalued. The smart policy would thus be to turn from silver and switch to gold before others in order to capture the appreciation of gold when the market eventually corrected and other governments switched to the more stable precious metal.

Yet the most important factor that would stifle successful cooperation – and nearly kill off silver as a credible monetary standard in Europe – was the Franco-Prussian War in 1870. The war was a disaster for France and as a condition to ending the hostilities, France was required to indemnify Otto von Bismarck's young German empire with five billion gold francs in five years – a bounty that would be used to help Germany switch from its then-prevailing silver standard to a new gold standard. Once stocked with sufficient gold reserves, Germany withdrew more than one billion marks worth of silver coins from its domestic market, and within three years of its victory over France, it passed a law providing for the minting of new gold coins. Berlin then sold off much of its silver holdings on the market. Germany's silver dump in turn created a cascading set of systemic risks for the continent, including hyperinflation for silver-standard and bimetallic countries. Responding to the threat, Belgium and Switzerland passed various laws limiting the amount of 5-franc pieces that could be coined. And France, the great defender of bimetallism, switched from a bimetallic standard to a de facto gold standard, where silver remained legal tender but was not freely coined. By 1878, only gold would be freely minted.

GREAT BRITAIN AND THE CLASSIC GOLD STANDARD

The LMU's failure increased incentives for countries around the world to adopt the gold standard. Gold had already been popular as a reserve currency and store of value. It was also the commodity money embraced by Great Britain, then the world's leading economy and the largest provider of trade-related services like merchant banking, insurance, and shipping. With Britain at the center of the global economy, foreigners had to either acquire its gold-backed currency – the sterling – or gold stocks in order to settle balances with their British counterparties.

But once Germany, Europe's second-largest economy, effectively abandoned silver to join Great Britain, pressure was ramped up even higher for other major countries to follow suit. Up until that time, the existence of major gold, silver, and bimetallic monetary blocs had created some balance in demand conditions for the different metals.[10] However, when Germany shifted full tilt to gold, the new and expanded bloc of gold countries upset the prevailing equilibrium. Demand for gold spiked just as interest in silver plummeted. This meant that for a central bank at the time, maintaining a silver standard was fraught with risk. Just keeping silver as a reserve currency meant risking the very solvency of your country as demand for the metal fell. Not surprisingly, a number of powers such as Denmark, Austria-Hungary, and the United States followed other countries onto the gold standard, with mostly colonial states whose capital markets were ill-positioned to compete for gold opting to retain a silver standard.[11]

The gold standard, in its purest form, was anchored by three main principles – a point illustrated by the economist Barry Eichengreen in his many leading works.[12] First, the currency had to be valued in terms of a certain amount of gold, underpinned by the commitment of the monetary authorities to buy or sell any amount of gold at a fixed price. Second, the money in domestic circulation consisted only of gold coins with the appropriate weight and fineness. Third, the government would not impede the exportation of coins to other countries. These rules created a system that assured people in a transparent way that the government would not tamper with the value of the currency; if it did, people were free to convert their banknotes into gold and, if they wished, export it. The system gave the government what it wanted most – a monopoly on the issuance of money – but it also gave people the right and the means to protect their financial interests by melting down and exporting their gold, if the government failed to maintain the value of the currency against gold – a standard of value for people across the globe.

The advantage of the gold standard was that it provided a mechanism that automatically regulated the rate of monetary creation or contraction, based on natural market forces. When the price of gold in the private markets fell below the price fixed by the government, indicating that a contraction of the money supply had taken place, people would sell their gold to the government in return for currency. This would cause an expansion of the money supply, which in turn would generate inflation, which in turn would increase the price of gold until it reached the redemption price set by the government. When the market price of gold moved above the government's price, people would buy gold from the government with currency, thereby reducing the supply of money, inducing deflation, and pushing the market price of gold back down toward the government's price.[13]

The system also had built-in mechanisms to ensure international equilibrium. Suppose that a country had a trade deficit with another country. The deficit would be settled with the deficit country paying out of its gold reserves, leading the country's money supply to fall. This reduction in the money supply would then create deflation. Deflation would cause a reduction in the price of domestic goods and services in the country, which in turn would make the country's exports cheaper. With cheaper exports, the country could sell more goods to the rest of the world, and the trade balance could be restored.

That being said, in practice, gold standard countries in Europe often had access to a number of levers with which to facilitate adjustment without resorting to immediate gold shipments from their treasury. Interest rates were the most important tools. When governments started to lose gold due to a payments deficit, central banks could raise interest rates which, in effect, constrained the money supply (because the cost of borrowing increased) and put downward pressure on prices. This helped make domestic goods and services more competitive vis-á-vis those of foreign competitors. Thus by manipulating interest rates, balance of payment deficits could be addressed without resorting to gold payments.[14]

The cornerstone of the pre-war gold standard was the priority governments attached to maintaining convertibility. In the countries at the center of the system – Britain, France, and Germany – there had to be no doubt that officials would ultimately do what was necessary to defend the central bank's gold reserve and maintain the convertibility of the currency.[15] Britain, in particular, was under the spotlight. London banks provided liquidity for the world financial system. They lent money to the world in sterling, and required that borrowers use sterling to likewise repay their debts. Additionally, sterling bills issued and backed by the British government were used by central banks as reserves alongside gold, and merchants relied on them as a means of exchange and tradable securities. As the sterling achieved gold-like status, the global economy would come to depend at least in part on Britain's monetary and fiscal wits. International financial stability would ride on the country's ability to manage its monetary and fiscal policies properly—and on its capacity to project an air of competence and reliability.

Fortunately for Britain, by the time London came to dominate the global economy, the country had built up a wealth of credibility with regard to its commitment to the gold standard. It was one of the first countries to adopt the gold standard, and only abandoned the regime once to fund the Napoleonic wars. Moreover, when hostilities were over, the government underscored its continued commitment to gold by reintroducing the redemption of gold in 1819 at virtually the same prices that had prevailed prior to conducting military incursions into France. The government had also taken periodic steps to highlight its own prudent monetary and macroeconomic stewardship. As the British financial sector grew, the Bank of England was given a monopoly over the issuance of bank notes in order to curb the provision of credit and reduce inflation. Meanwhile, commercial banks, although constrained in their ability to issue their own bank notes, were permitted to take deposits from the public and recycle those deposits as credit on to others. Eventually, these deposits would form the basis of Britain's enormous financial power. In the second half of the century in particular, Britain had the highest savings rate in the world, and the country's massive resources were leveraged to finance commercial activities in virtually every part of the globe.

FREE TRADE MERCANTILISM

Britain also bolstered its economy through state-supported, or "mercantilist," trade policies. Under mercantilism, the dominant economic philosophy of the seventeenth and eighteenth centuries, governments sought to promote international commercial interests through the state, and in turn, state interests through the market. The idea was that although local or domestic commerce might enrich some people individually, it would not necessarily galvanize a nation's economy as a whole. Instead, a country could still find itself a pauper state, and effectively borrowing from the rest of the world to finance domestic economic activities. The thinking went that in order to really improve the welfare of a country as a whole, a country would have to successfully trade with other nations – and in the process accumulate wealth (and in particular – gold reserves). Therefore the government should do whatever it takes to make sure its trade relationships are successful, and if necessary, intervene directly in promoting exports.

With this in mind, colonialism became a defining feature of mercantilist economic strategy. Empire offered – quite literally – a captive supply of producers and consumers, thereby ensuring a positive trade balance. Colonies provided cheap raw materials for English industrialists, and could colonists be required to purchase comparatively more expensive manufactured goods made in London. So, not surprisingly, Britain regulated its trade relationship to its empire with at times near scientific precision. For over two hundred years, intermittent laws were passed, occasionally banning colonies from shipping commodities such

as tobacco and sugar to anywhere but England.[16] Furthermore, manufacturing activities in the colonies were banned altogether, such as the
construction of new rolling and slitting steel mills in America. Even
transport was regulated, and under the so-called Navigation Acts, all
trade with Britain had to be conducted on British ships.[17] Meanwhile,
exports from colonies that competed with British products were often
banned, such as cotton textile imports from India in the eighteenth
century – regardless of whether they were superior to and cheaper than
British counterparts.[18]

Eventually, however, mercantilist ideas gave way to greater "free trade"
beliefs and policy, especially in England. This was attributable to both
political and economic necessity. Mercantilism was, for one, extremely
expensive. A range of Napoleonic tariffs on foreign grains, called the
Corn Laws, stuffed the pockets of powerful rural interests, propping up
cereal prices and limiting competition from abroad. Similarly, the protection of sugar and tobacco plantations in the colonies caused prices
across agricultural sectors to rise. In most cases, the benefits of such policies seemed remote at best for the average British citizen.[19] Instead of
advancing vital national interests, the agricultural subsidies and foreign
taxes appeared to favor a small landed gentry and to divert resources
from urban priorities such as transportation and infrastructure that
were becoming increasingly important in the wake of industrialization.
In 1845, frustrations reached a boiling point with the onset of the Great
Famine, when a potato blight left the United Kingdom with insufficient cheap agricultural imports to feed its population. Riots broke
out, and as the prospect of civil war increased, Parliament repealed the
Corn Laws, as well as a variety of tariffs on manufacturing goods.[20] The
Navigation Acts were then repealed just three years later as part of an
ongoing effort to reduce the cost of food and ease wage inflation.

British policymakers followed up on their unilateral actions with
negotiations aimed at eliciting additional reforms from neighbors.
Most important, the famous Cobden–Chevalier treaty was concluded
in 1860, committing Britain to reduce its duties on French spirits in
return for France reducing its tariffs on British manufactured goods.[21]
The accord was then followed by a series of bilateral trade agreements
with other European countries that sought similar concessions. All
the while, many concessions were "multilateralized" to the extent
to which the treaties included commitments – termed most favored
nation ("MFN") treatment – that required signatories to extend the
benefits of the trade agreements to any other country with which

they had signed a treaty. By extending benefits to third parties, MFN clauses created a network of legal obligations that became pivotal in reducing tariffs throughtout Europe and her colonies during the 1860s and 1870s. By "the mid 1870s, most prohibitions on trade had disappeared and average tariffs on manufacturing stood at low single digits in Britain, Germany, the Netherlands, Sweden and Switzerland, and in the low teens in France and Italy down from levels that were a multiple of these rates."[22]

Not everyone was offered the opportunity to bargain for a better trade relationship, however. Indeed, as was common for the time, what was good for Europe wasn't necessarily good (or allowed) for the rest of the world. Instead, gunboat diplomacy often accompanied economic negotiations, especially with non-European powers. As early as 1838, Britain had signed a treaty with the Ottoman Empire that forced the country to restrict import duties to a maximum of 5 percent and to abolish import prohibitions and monopolies. The British also fought the so-called Opium War with China from 1839 to 1842 in order to open up China to imports of opium and other British exports.[23] Such reliance on military prowess persisted even as colonization became more regulated in the wake of the Berlin Conference of 1884 and 1885, and the British navy, the most powerful in the world, was repeatedly relied on to ensure that British investments abroad were protected and foreign government debts were repaid.

THE END OF BRITISH HEGEMONY – AND DE FACTO MULTILATERALISM

Several forces conspired to end this first modern wave of economic globalization. Free trade may have been a boon for Britain, but not for all of its trading partners. Between 1873 and 1896, recurring business crises and persistent deflation drove the major economies of Europe into what was at the time one of the most severe crises in history, ultimately causing Germany in 1879, and France in 1881, to abandon free trade. Both hoped that by raising tariffs they could spur employment at home and jump-start their economies (a tactic that, at least for Germany, proved somewhat successful). Britain, however, continued to embrace free trade unilaterally. Part of its tenacity derived from the country's largely unwavering belief in liberal trade. But it was also a natural outgrowth of its own hegemony. Britain imported less than it exported, so it had less to gain from retaliating against trade partners because imposing tariffs on such a tiny base of imports would have little punitive power.[24]

It would instead take a fundamentally game-changing event – World War I – to unhinge Britain's embrace of liberalism. With the outbreak of hostilities in 1914, universally recognized forms of commodity money like gold and silver were needed to produce and purchase the weaponry for conducting military operations in European and African theaters. In order to finance acquisitions of arms, European governments, including Great Britain, imposed regulations prohibiting convertibility in the absence of specific licenses, effectively creating floating exchange rates between national currencies. Moreover, when revenue-generating schemes like higher taxes and government bonds proved inadequate to meet the necessities of conducting the war, governments began to circulate bills that were no longer backed by gold to pay soldiers and purchase domestic supplies.[25] By the end of World War I, European industrial countries had spent nearly half of their GDPs fighting the war and were effectively bankrupt.

Nevertheless, Britain didn't give up easily on the gold standard, which had embodied its unique brand of tight macroeconomic management and served the country well over the previous two hundred years. Instead, after the war, in 1925, Britain worked to restore the gold standard – at the prewar rate of convertibility – since floating rates proved susceptible to speculation and wild currency valuations. The idea was that by returning to old monetary policies, it could relive the success seen under the Resumption Act a hundred years before, when the country returned to the gold standard after waging war against Napoleon. It was a risky bet, since gold required a credible commitment to convertibility. But in the minds of British authorities, a gold standard would provide a signal to the world that Britain was back in business and ready to reassume its traditional place in the heart of the international economy.

Unfortunately for Britain, the gamble failed. In contrast to its earlier return to the gold standard, when its economy was ascendant, Britain's post-World War I peg came at a time when its economic might had been diminishing for over a half century. The United States, which had emerged relatively unscathed from the war, was widely recognized as the world's largest economic power. And even in Europe, both France and Germany were nipping at Britain's heels for dominance. The old peg did not reflect this realignment, and the sterling was overvalued relative to other currencies.

Then came Wall Street's 1929 crash, making a gold peg all the more unsustainable. As America's premier stock market plunged, the availability of U.S. capital investment in Europe dropped, along with the worldwide demand for goods. Britain's trade balance also plummeted, as did its earnings from tourism, receipts from financial services rendered to foreigners, and dividends on foreign investments received by the Bank of England.[26] In the face of a looming balance of payments crisis, the Bank of England raised interest rates, a tried and true technique in the past that helped shore up its balance sheet. It was hoped that by raising rates, and offering foreign investors a better return on their capital, Britain could attract more capital and gold to its shores, and thus improve its current account.

But again, things had changed in the world since the country's nineteenth-century heyday. Interest rate hikes usually help ward off crises when investors believe governments will take on the painful adjustments necessary to make their economies competitive – like allowing wages to fall where domestic industries become less competitive. In the past, there was little doubt among investors about the government's commitment to do whatever necessary to ensure the sterling retained its strength even as the country borrowed. However in twentieth-century Britain, investors had become much more skeptical. They knew that the electorate had grown precipitously over the last hundred years. Workers had gained the right to vote and had organized successfully as unions. Politicians were, as a result, accountable to more people than ever, and to a far greater number of well-organized interest groups. Depressing wages was no longer as feasible as it was in the past, when wealthy aristocrats and industrialists dominated politics – and would risk the ire of the country's growing middle class.[27]

In short, the country's new political environment meant that it was unlikely that any legislator would introduce policies that could trigger bouts of deflation or widespread economic pain on the growing electorate. Instead, investors guessed that the opposite was true – and that the British government would eventually abandon the gold standard (and tradition) to free up its own monetary policy and domestic spending, all to the detriment of creditors. So they started to bet against the sterling. And once that happened, the already limited capacity of the government to sustain the gold link collapsed, prompting a self-fulfilling prophecy. In 1931, Britain abandoned the gold standard. The pound would ultimately lose more than a quarter of its value.

Britain's exit from the international monetary stage sent shockwaves through the global economy. In just a matter of days, other countries with close trade and financial ties to Britain, including Denmark, Finland, Norway, and Sweden, likewise permitted the depreciation of their currencies relative to gold. And in December, Japan followed suit.[28] As the pound depreciated, making U.S. exports less competitive, Franklin Roosevelt ordered all gold coins and certificates be exchanged for other government-sanctioned money, effectively taking America off the gold standard. This in turn encouraged other countries, including much of Central America, to similarly abandon gold.

The global trading system unravelled alongside monetary relations. In order to enhance the competitiveness of local manufacturers in domestic consumer markets, many countries adopted a premeditated policy of raising tariff walls.[29] In 1930, the United States imposed the highest tariffs in its history under the now infamous Smoot-Hawley Tariffs. The British Parliament then responded in kind a year later with the Import Duties Act, which levied a general tariff of 10 percent on all imports except foodstuffs and raw materials.

Meanwhile, countries that were still clinging to the gold standard – including Germany and France – found their currencies overvalued, and in response adopted a range of defensive measures to counter other countries' currency devaluations. Trade was the weapon of choice. Remaining gold club members could not resort to other tools, such as interest rates cuts, because cuts would make it less attractive for foreigners to deposit their gold in the country and thus undermine the ability of national governments to defend gold parity. So instead, they resorted to trade tariffs in order to shift domestic consumer demand away from what had been cheap foreign imports. To offset the sterling's depreciation, for example, France quickly imposed a 15 percent tariff on British goods and adopted quotas restricting the amount of goods to be imported. Canada and South Africa followed by adopting antidumping duties aimed at British imports, and the German government imposed "equalizing" tariffs on goods produced in countries with depreciated currencies. Even the Netherlands, which had long espoused free trade, raised tariffs 25 percent to offset foreign currency depreciation.[30]

Within just sixteen months of Britain's devaluation, the 1933 League of Nations World Economic Survey estimated that twenty-three countries had imposed general tariff increases.[31] Customs duties had been increased on individual items or groups of commodities by fifty countries, and thirty-two countries had adopted import quotas, prohi-bitions, licensing systems, and other quantitative restrictions. Import monopolies existed in twelve countries; milling or mixing regulations were in place in another sixteen. Export duties or prohibitions had been adopted in seventeen countries, with export premiums being paid in nine others. Although at the time trade had only composed about 9 per-cent of the world economy, these measures collectively dealt a serious blow to global trade, with the volume of world trade falling 16 percent from 1931 to 1932.[32]

As the decade concluded, free trade was a distant memory – and was becoming even more so every day as the prospects of a new world war increased. Nazi Germany began to identify and select trade partners that were within its sphere of influence and most subject to control in order to ensure sufficient raw materials for its industrial and military mobilization. Bilateral agreements were signed with countries along Europe's eastern and southeastern periphery, and by 1938, nearly half the trade conducted by Yugoslavia, Hungary, Romania, Bulgaria, and Greece would be with Germany, which would export manufactured goods in exchange for raw materials. Similarly, the U.S. government, under the direction of Franklin Roosevelt, reaffirmed more govern-ment control of trade policy to ensure sufficient production of wartime goods. Allied armies were financed through the Lend-Lease program between 1941 and 1945, and with the outbreak of World War II, domes-tic production was diverted from satisfying consumer demand toward meeting the needs of allies, as military victory, not trade, became the primary objective of the government.

THE UNITED STATES TAKES CONTROL

World War II had essentially the same effect on the global balance of economic power as World War I – but to an even larger degree. The continent of Europe lay in ruin, and for the most part, bankrupt. Meanwhile, the United States emerged from the war as the wealthiest country in the world. Not only was it physically unscathed, but it was also economically strengthened by wartime industrial expansion, such that it enjoyed both absolute and relative industrial advantages in pro-ductive capacity over both its allies and its enemies.

In contrast to the interwar years, however, when the United States jumped headfirst into self-serving (and short-sighted) protectionism, postwar America sought to reestablish the multilateral trading system that had collapsed in the preceding two decades. Deeply shaken by two world wars, U.S. political leaders had come to embrace the ideals of international economic cooperation, as well as the value of the common good, in hopes of averting future conflicts in Europe. Furthermore, the promotion of Western capitalist democracy was seen as essential in checking the threat of Soviet economic and military expansion. Trade provided the incentives for ensuring that Europe and Japan followed U.S. policy priorities and prescriptions, even as America's relations with the Soviet Union deteriorated in 1945.

Growth was also paramount. During the war effort, the U.S. economy, like others, had been restructured in order to prosecute the war, and in the process was lifted out of the stagnation wrought by the Great Depression. Now that peacetime had returned, these industries, and the economy more generally, had to be converted back. But for this to happen quickly, and without harming growth, changes in economic policy would have to be taken abroad. Trading partners would have to adopt their own reforms, such as lowering tariffs and abolishing special bilateral payment arrangements. Meanwhile, declining European powers such as Britain would have to reduce or eventually eliminate altogether imperial trade preferences to ensure a broader flow of competitive goods and services.

For this to happen, the United States sought a much more formal system for international economic relations than had been available under British hegemony, and one more overtly based on postwar ideals of inclusiveness and order. Instead of exclusive, low-level bilateral arrangements with special trading partners, U.S. leaders sought open and at least comparably more "global" accords, in which virtually any country espousing free market capitalism (or at least U.S. perceptions of it) could participate. Second, in contrast to de facto, and often ad hoc, "follow thy neighbor" habits of coordination seen in the past, more explicit, rules-based moorings of international governance were established. The hope was to spell out in advance the expectations and appropriate conduct for all countries in international economic affairs.

To make this happen, the United States set about herding support for a truly institutionalized international economic order – backed not only by staunch policy pronouncements, but also by market disciplines, sanctions, and the power of international law. The framework for this new world of economic multilateralism was hammered out in 1944 in a hotel in Bretton Woods, New Hampshire, where representatives from nearly forty-four nations, led by Harry Dexter White and

John Maynard Keynes, would spend three weeks contemplating the future of the international economy.[33] From the conference, two pillars would come to ground the new, liberalized international order: an international law of money, associated with the IMF, and a burgeoning regime for international trade, which would eventually be based on the General Agreement on Tariffs and Trade (GATT). Meanwhile, a third organization, the World Bank, would play a supporting role by helping finance development and reconstruction in Europe – and later the developing world.

AN INTERNATIONAL LAW OF MONEY

The framers of the Bretton Woods system knew from their own personal and professional experience that trade and monetary policy were inextricably linked. Without monetary oversight, efforts to regulate trade could be upended altogether. As Keynes himself acknowledged, it would be "extraordinarily difficult to frame any proposals about tariffs if countries [were] free to alter the value of their currencies without agreement and at short notice."[34] It was thus incumbent on any new rules-based system to tackle currency valuations and provide stability and predictability in international monetary affairs.

With this in mind, the cornerstone and founding economic pillar of the Bretton Woods conference was the IMF. Its mission was to help promote international trade and global economic growth by establishing a regime for exchange rate stability and monetary cooperation. As part of its mandate, it was charged with overseeing and supervising a multilateral system of payments for current account transactions between countries, and where necessary, provide lender-of-last-resort financing for countries experiencing balance-of-payments crises.

The IMF's founding documents – which were considered to be the memorialization of legally binding commitments by member states – established what was known as the par-value system. Simply put, IMF members would maintain a par value for their currencies, either in terms of gold or the U.S. dollar. To the extent to which currencies fell below or above the specified ratios by more than 1 percent, countries were expected to intervene in capital markets by purchasing or selling their currency. Participants also agreed to refrain from the currency devaluations that plagued the monetary system prior to World War II, except when a correction of the exchange rate was required due to fundamental shifts in the country's competitiveness. And even then, the IMF's blessing of the par-value adjustment was required under the organization's Articles of Agreement. If a member did not comply with the exchange-rate requirements of Article IV, that country could be barred from drawing on the Fund's resources in the future.

Under Article IV(4)(a) of the original Articles of Agreement, the forty-four original signatories also committed to collaborate with the Fund to promote exchange stability. Pursuant to these and other IMF obligations, members were required to make contributions to a common pool of money that would be accessible to countries having balance-of-payments problems. The amount each member was expected to contribute reflected its size and relative importance in the global economy. The larger a country's GDP, the more it was expected to contribute. At the same time, the larger the contribution, the more any particular member would be permitted to draw in times of crisis. One-quarter of each member's contributions were to be made in gold, and the balance was to be paid in a country's local currency. Since most countries did not have convertible currencies at the time of the IMF's creation, dollars were the money of choice for cash-strapped governments. Because dollars were convertible and widely accepted forms of payment, countries under financial duress could effectively borrow dollars from the Fund and use them to settle accounts and repay foreign debts.[35]

As such, the IMF stood as a major innovation of the times. During the era of British hegemony, international cooperation had been uncoordinated and mostly ad hoc. International monetary cooperation only took place when central banks felt that one another's commitment to maintaining the gold system was serious – and thus any loans extended would be repaid – or when some kind of bailout was absolutely necessary because of the size or importance of the country. The IMF of the 1940s and 50s would serve, by contrast, to systematize cooperation in hopes of bringing more order to the international system. Rules of the road were laid out in advance for all countries to obey. And in times of crisis, each member would be permitted to borrow from the IMF several times the amount it paid in via its subscription, or to tap other additional lines of credit.

The IMF also ushered in a new era of monetary discipline in international monetary affairs. As with the gold standard, profligacy would be punished. Exchange rates were required to operate within predetermined and multilaterally agreed-upon rules. Not only would irresponsible governments face possible capital flight from speculators if they failed to control spending and their currencies, but the IMF, too, could exert additional pressure and sanction members who failed to comply with agreed-upon monetary policies. Rescue packages for cash-strapped countries would also depend on compliance with negotiated policies with IMF members and the United States, which backed the system. As such, emergency access to IMF resources would often be contingent on countries undertaking painful government and market reforms demanded by the Fund.[36]

LEGALIZING FREE TRADE INCREMENTALLY

Trade composed the second important pillar of the postwar multilateral system. Protectionist measures on foreign goods had built up since the 1930s, and the United States and its allies sought to dismantle the overhang in order to restart the global economy. The solution was to be an International Trade Organization (ITO) whose charter would include provisions concerning commodity price stabilization, international antitrust measures, and fair labor standards.[37] A dispute resolution mechanism was also contemplated whereby disagreements could ultimately find themselves settled by the International Court of Justice.

Tariff negotiations started in 1946 with twenty-three countries agreeing on nearly $10 billion of trade-related concessions, which at the time constituted nearly one-fifth of the global commerce in goods. Together, the tariff concessions and rules became what is today known as the General Agreement on Tariffs and Trade (GATT), an agreement that entered into force in January 1948, and which was intended to be a precursor to ITO.[38] Soon, however, it became clear that the ITO Charter, which had been agreed on at the United Nations (UN) Conference on Trade and Employment in Havana in March 1948, was not going to be ratified by many national legislatures – including the U.S. Congress. And without U.S. support, a global trade organization was a fairy tale.[39] From its earliest days, multilateral trade liberalization comprised a classic coordination problem: countries could only import more if they exported more, but this was possible only if other countries lowered trade walls as well – especially the United States, which at the time made up 80 percent of the world's GDP.[40] But many members of Congress found the ambitious and comprehensive organization too radical and unnecessary for promoting trade, and President Truman abandoned efforts to ratify the Charter once the Korean war began.

With the ITO stillborn, the provisional GATT – which the U.S. government had secured by means of a narrow writ of authority Congress had granted the executive branch to enter into reciprocal trade deals – remained the only vehicle for the development of international trade, and for nearly fifty years it would serve as the primary instrument for global trade reform. Similar to British treaties before it, the GATT espoused MFN, such that in Article I, all parties pledged to apply the same regulations and tariffs to all like goods from GATT signatory countries, without regard to the origin of goods. Furthermore, the GATT went a step further than most treaties of the day by prohibiting states, under national treatment obligations, from discriminating between domestically produced and imported products in areas identified in the GATT. Finally, through a series of provisions, the GATT restricted a range of other forms of governmental restraints on trade, including quotas on imports and licensing schemes.

Importantly, the GATT's purpose was never to eliminate all trade barriers between all countries in one fell swoop. Instead, it was just a provisional agreement aimed at dismantling some of the protectionist measures that had built up over the previous two decades. It was also limited in scope, and left a wide range of sectors untouched – from financial services to construction to, perhaps most importantly, agriculture.[41] GATT's enforcement powers were also, in the eyes of many, embarrassingly weak. GATT provided for panels of experts to adjudicate disputes between members, especially when one country thought that another was violating its treaty commitments. But any panel determinations required that all GATT representatives sign on to and agree with the decision. In practice this meant that the consent of every country, including the country that had been accused of violating GATT commitments, was required.[42] As a result, GATT panels had limited disciplinary power beyond stigmatizing countries as noncompliant with their treaty obligations.

What GATT was particularly good at was getting countries used to the notion of free trade via an incremental, though recurring series of negotiations. Eight successive rounds of multilateral trade negotiations managed to reduce tariffs from their postwar highs, and the agreement's MFN commitments ensured that all signatories benefited from lower tariffs on the exports, regardless of how powerful they were or to what extent they participated in negotiations.

The creation of the World Trade Organization (WTO) in 1995 was a culmination of the success of earlier rounds, as well as a reflection of changing perceptions of the overall advantages of free trade. As Dani Rodrik notes, over the course of thirty years of an increasingly free market and consistently rising global GDP, many policymakers and politicians came to view the growth in the global economy as the result of multilateral trade liberalization.[43] The WTO presented the opportunity to not only cure the defects of the GATT, but also to achieve a modern day version of the ITO. Agriculture and services, which were untouched in 1945, were brought squarely into its sights. New institutions were also developed to lend more discipline to trade commitments. GATT's ultimately dysfunctional and highly political systems for dispute settlement were replaced with a rules-based and procedurally sophisticated infrastructure sporting legally enforceable decisions. In a reversal of past practice, arbitral decisions were final in the absence of all members collectively overturning them.[44] And the WTO also had teeth: to the extent to which countries that were found to violate their obligations failed to change their policies, the WTO could authorize injured states to retaliate by suspending their favorable treatment of the violating countries' exports.

Both the IMF and WTO would come to symbolize a more institutionalized model of multilateral economic governance than had been seen under British hegemony. As opposed to an ad hoc system of international economic governance, with leading countries plotting policies intermittently, formal institutions were launched for coordinating policy, memorializing commitments, and in some cases, even disciplining countries that defaulted on these commitments. The IMF, for its part, would in its early years establish rules-based exchange rate stability, a multilateral system of payments for current account transactions, and, where necessary, make available the IMF's resources when countries fell into crisis. The GATT, meanwhile, would create a platform for steadily lowering tariff walls, and as it evolved into the WTO, would provide an increasingly effective mechanism for monitoring, adjudicating treaty disputes, and disciplining members who failed to live up to their commitments.

DOLLARS, DEFICITS, AND (RELATIVE) DECLINE

Academics tend to see the weakening of Bretton Woods–era multilateralism as a consequence of the gradual loss of U.S. hegemony in international economic affairs. Ultimately, however, even this development was not so much a cause but rather a consequence of two decisive, historic developments: the rise and persistence of acute global macroeconomic imbalances in the global economy on the one hand, and the globalization of financial services and investment on the other.

The first development relates to the not so extraordinary fact that twentieth-century multilateralism, despite its broad-based institutional moorings, relied not only on U.S. support, but also on the maintenance of certain trade and current account surpluses. At the time of the Bretton Woods Conference, the United States was the only country with gold reserves large enough to commit to convertibility and provide liquidity for the global economy. And because the United States was committed to developing greater world trade, it did so – at the price of $35 an ounce. In the process, the status of the dollar was elevated to a virtual gold substitute – both practically and implicitly under international law. But by committing to convertibility, the United States had to commit, at least implicitly, to the maintenance of its current account, or balance sheet. In other words, the United States had to retain gold reserves large enough to meet its convertibility requirements, and had to remain the overwhelmingly dominant market for goods. Over the long-term, the only way to do this was to keep a positive balance of payments – in short, making sure that more money came into the country than left it, through exports or investment dollars, so as not to necessitate drawing down its gold reserves.

The laws of economics did not jive well with America's big postwar foreign policy priorities, however. In order to speed the reconstruction of Europe and Japan, and finance cold war allies including the Greek and Turkish governments, the United States had to actually encourage the *outflow* as opposed to the inflow of dollars from 1947 until 1958. Later, in the 1970s, spending jumped with the escalation of the Vietnam War, causing the country's gold position to deteriorate by nearly 50 percent, and forcing the once-financier of the gold standard to abandon convertibility. In its place, a floating system of currency valuations was developed based on the relative value of the world's currencies to the dollar.

Once the United States abandoned the gold standard, the IMF's role in monetary affairs necessarily had to change. Its regulatory mandate to oversee and impose specific rates was eliminated. Virtually all restrictions on countries' ability to manage their currencies were removed, save a lasting ban on currency manipulation.[45] Formal multilateralism would be superseded by a reassertion of national monetary sovereignty. That being said, the IMF's responsibilities in promoting surveillance and information sharing between its members would receive new emphasis because the newfound monetary flexibility enjoyed by countries would enable risks to build up in countries' balance sheets. In order to oversee the new international monetary system and its effective operation, each member of the IMF was required, under a rewritten Article IV(3) (b), to provide the Fund with information necessary for carrying out surveillance, and to consult with it when requested.[46] The IMF was also endowed with enhanced lender-of-last resort powers. The progressive reorientation of the international monetary community away from top-down regulatory policies has meant that the IMF has assumed inter-mittent responsibility for stepping in to provide liquidity when financial markets fail because of teetering state coffers or beliefs by investors that loans extended to a government will not otherwise be repaid. So the expansion of the IMF's financing portfolio coincided with the decline of the Fund as an international supervisory institution.

Chronic U.S. fiscal and trade deficits would not have the same prob-lematic implications for the international trading system, at least not at first. As we've seen, even during an age of Western profligacy – and indeed perhaps spurred by it – periodic rounds of trade negotiations were successfully completed, with the most recent culminating in the creation of the WTO. And with the wind at their back in 2001, confi-dent trade negotiators announced in Doha, Qatar, that a new round of talks would be launched, aimed at making trade rules fairer for devel-oping countries.[47]

Over the last two decades, however, the multilateral trading system has frayed in startling ways. In the late 1990s and early 2000s, the United States and Europe both began to sour on global trade and to question its benefits. For some experts, the trade deals struck in the preceding two decades were responsible for catalyzing a yawning trade deficit that continues today (see chart below), reflecting the inflow of millions of low-cost foreign imports. Moreover, multilateralism was increasingly viewed as unfair for middle-class wage earners. Advances made by emerging markets were not so much the product of waning American or European competitiveness, but instead were enabled by poor labor, welfare, and environmental standards that cheapened the price of developing-country exports. Labor and human rights activists on both sides of the Atlantic argued that global trade was not designed to pro-mote human welfare, but instead put economic interests over other key priorities such as safe workplaces, food safety, and the environment.

At the same time, emerging markets were drawing a line in the sand. Rising powers such as China, India, and Brazil became more asser-tive in promoting their national economic interests. They began to take more uncompromising stances with regard to concessions they expected from the European Union and the United States in areas

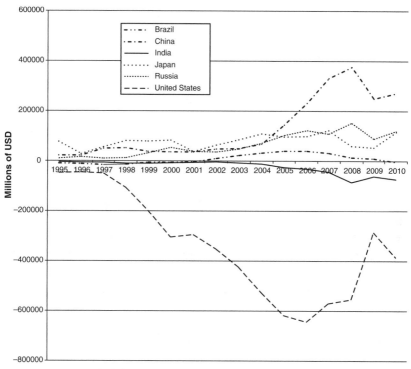

FIGURE 1. Trade balances, current prices and exchange rates, 1995–2010.

such as agriculture, which had been protected. Looking at the chart mentioned above, you might find this a bit surprising, to say the least, since emerging countries have benefitted disproportionately from globalization and the systematic reduction in global tariff barriers. But for leaders of the Global South, their diplomatic postures since the 1990s have just been making up for lost time: the rulemaking in the IMF, World Bank, and WTO had, after all, been dominated by the West for over a half century, either as a result of their membership, rules for voting, or informal influence – and multilateral policies reflected this dominance. So it was high time, they argued, to rebalance the global trading rules, and emerging markets voiced a new willingness to walk away from multilateral negotiations if their demands were not met.

In 1999, frustrations reached a boiling point. Fed up with what they saw as an uncaring, multilateral system driven by corporate interests, and predicting that the talks would ultimately work against the interests of the global poor, activists and rioters from around the world coalesced in the streets of Seattle, Washington, to protest (at times violently) any expansion of the global trading system, just as the terms of the Doha Round were being negotiated.

The riots did not end negotiations immediately, but they did ruin prospects for agreement in Seattle and in Washington, D.C., the following year during IMF and World Bank discussions. They also poisoned the water, so to speak, just long enough for new irritants to derail discussions. Just as perennial quagmires such as agricultural tariffs and subsidies complicated increasingly polarized multilateral discussions, new irritants such as carbon emissions and Chinese currency interventions gained political traction. Negotiations floundered for years, causing Pascal Lamy, the WTO's former director general, to ruefully describe his organization as lying in a state of "paralysis." Eventually, with no consensus in sight, experts and academics around the world declared one by one, both publicly and privately, that the Doha Round, at least as it had been known, was "dead." Only a watered down agreement, or a series of shallow pacts of limited economic significance, would be possible.

With such declarations, even among trade advocates, it's perhaps not surprising that there is a good deal of cynicism concerning the future of the multilateral trading system. Still, the gloom and doom might be a bit overblown. After all, WTO rules are not inconsequential – countries are still expected to abide by their commitments, and the very existence of a multilateral trading system is largely credited with helping avoid an upsurge in protectionism following the onset of the Great Recession in the wake of the 2008 financial crisis. Moreover, cases continue to be brought before the WTO, and adjudicated before its powerful panels. That being said, it is indisputable that there is little movement forward in the formulation of new global trading standards. To be sure, limited side deals are possible, along with important rulings of arbitral panels and trade officials. But the multilateral trading system's golden age appears to be coming to an end – and prospects for a new, game-changing round of global trade negotiations may not be forthcoming for years, if not decades.

THE MISSING PILLAR: INTERNATIONAL FINANCIAL REGULATION

Pragmatic as it was, the Bretton Woods system focused on the problems of its time – namely restoring global commerce through revived international monetary and trade policy. As such, and quite understandably, few efforts were launched to regulate or coordinate financial market regulation during the 1940s. Cross-border capital flows at the time were limited, and subject to the control and supervision of national regulatory authorities. And for much of the postwar period and up through the late 1980s, the objects of financial regulation – banks, the buyers and sellers of securities, and insurance companies – were primarily domestic actors. Not to mention, self-help was available, at least to the few countries that hosted world-class capital markets. With a relative dearth of places to raise capital, foreign companies had to come to your shores to raise money, so you could simply regulate them through domestic channels. This meant that regulators like the United States Securities and Exchange Commission didn't need to regulate the world directly, but could do so simply by regulating the New York Stock Exchange, where foreign companies sold their stocks to local investors.

But as international trade linkages have deepened with advances in technology, so have financial ties, to the point that capital now flows even more freely across borders and across greater distances than goods do. Billions of dollars can be committed across the globe, far beyond the United States, with just a click of the mouse.

For the last two decades, economic theory has not been shy about the perceived benefits of this free-flowing democratization of capital. Indeed, economists have consistently trumpeted the dramatic changes in global financial markets, largely on the basis that they allow the world's savings to be directed toward their most productive uses, regardless of location.

Yet during this same period, globalization has demonstrated – with ever more apparent consequences – that the breathtaking growth in international finance is not without its own significant drawbacks. Besides potentially opening the floodgates to cross-border Ponzi schemes and accounting fraud, financial globalization can facilitate and even encourage nasty asset bubbles and other systemic risks. When capital becomes more readily available, banks and other financial institutions start to compete as lenders chasing borrowers and investments – which is the opposite way healthy financial markets should operate. When that happens, they can't demand a premium from borrowers for using their capital. So to maintain their profits, banks and other firms may enter into riskier transactions, where they can charge higher interest rates. But if the loans and investments don't pan out, an institution may find its balance sheet destroyed and facing bankruptcy. If the bank is big enough, its failure could threaten the economy of the country in which it is based—as well as others.

Collectively, these risks – which bedeviled emerging markets in the 1990s and now preoccupy policy leaders in the United States and Europe – have placed serious strains on economic multilateralism. Their very existence highlights to just what degree financial market regulation falls beyond the core competency of the postwar Bretton Woods architecture. The World Bank's mission, for its part, has centered on economic development. Meanwhile, the multilateral trade regime has focused on liberalizing the provision of cross-border financial services, rather than regulating it. Indeed, only the IMF's responsibilities plausibly involve some degree of financial market surveillance. But even here, its mission has historically been extremely limited since the IMF was never meant to assume the role of a global financial market regulator. Instead, its mandate lay in preventing balance of payments crises.

BACK TO THE FUTURE – OR THE MIDDLE AGES?

The erosion of U.S. hegemony, along with the challenges facing the IMF and WTO, have underscored what many economists and political scientists have been noticing for years – that economic power and risk is becoming more widely dispersed than at any time since the 1940s. This awareness has become all the more pronounced since the 2008 financial crisis – when the United States, instead of providing an anchor for economic security, effectively exported financial chaos through mismanaged monetary and housing policies and poor financial market supervision. Even before the crisis struck, America, saddled with stubborn trade and fiscal deficits, struggled to maintain a dominant voice on global economic policy. In the wake of the crisis, its influence has waned even further, as unemployment has hobbled growth, and the country has been forced to focus on its own economic and financial problems, occasionally at the expense of global economic leadership.

Instead, other countries can, and routinely do, bring their opinions to bear on issues of global import. This isn't necessarily a bad thing. A greater diversity of actors now routinely shapes global policy agendas, and in the process probably helps ensure a more equitable distribution of gains from international cooperation. Plus it is at least possible that an evolving international order will leave room for more policy experimentation better tailored to meet the specific needs of local markets and citizens.

Still, the decline of U.S. hegemony presents quandaries for global governance. Whatever its shortcomings and recent policy mishaps, the United States has played what by most accounts has been a productive role in underwriting the international system and assiduously promoting the values of open, global trade. It has historically been the largest contributor to the IMF and World Bank, and has for the most part complied with the rulings of the World Trade Organization, whether they be in its favor or not. All the while, the United States has supplied the world with liquidity, both through official spending channels such as the Marshall Plan and by dint of its long-standing role as "consumer of first resort" for the world's export markets.

What will come after such a benign and largely productive era of U.S. leadership remains very much in question. For optimists, rising powers will readily assume the reins of governance alongside traditional powers and continue to promote global economic trade and cooperation. According to this view, emerging economies have an obvious self-interest in retaining and maintaining the rules-based, nondiscriminatory systems that enabled their rise. Multilateral institutions clear the way for trade and investment and also enable the transfer of technology and human capital necessary for development. Plus they provide rising powers with a measure of insurance for the gains they have already captured. After all, as emerging markets continue to grow, other slower growing countries – including possibly Western economies – might choose to impose protectionist and discriminatory policies in order to advance their own interests. A strong multilateral system inhibits such tactics and would serve as a bulwark for nondiscrimination, and perhaps even smooth what would otherwise be turbulent interstate relations.[48]

Pessimists, on the other hand, suspect that the diffusion of economic power is likely to exacerbate tensions between the established and the rising powers – and between emerging powers themselves. Economic relationships involve aspects of both partnership and rivalry.[49] Countries cooperate and compete with one another simultaneously. For example, governments may, in one instance, cooperate on issues of financial market reform in order to avoid cross-border shocks to stock exchanges, but in other deliberations develop rules that give their national banks competitive advantages over their foreign counterparts with whom they transact abroad. Moreover, even when countries agree in principle to cooperate, they may have varying, and indeed rival, conceptions of what cooperation means. Emerging powers in particular are increasingly skeptical of the sustained dominance of Western countries in multilateral institutions.[50] As their importance in the global economy has grown, many countries believe that they are entitled to greater weight and respect in global institutions. At the same time, even as countries seek to enhance their clout, it is *not* necessarily the case that they desire more global governance. Thus even as countries in Asia, Latin America, and Africa have sought larger roles for themselves in global financial institutions, few have pushed for greater roles for, or interventions by, multilateral forums and organizations.

As a result, some observers see serious risks in the return to what can be described as the international economic "Middle Ages" – a dynamic, multi-civilizational world in which every country, city-state, dwindling hegemon, and rising superpower looks out only for itself.[51] Under this scenario, multilateralism is relegated to the dustbin of history. And in its place, the international system comes to resemble a Hobbesian state of nature. No country will be able to trust the other in the absence of coercion (economic or military), and the relationships often necessary for deep, sustained forms of coordination won't exist. Countries might, as a result, be entirely unable to make any of the key collective decisions necessary for sustaining economic growth and stability – whether it be safeguarding free trade, regulating cross-border financial markets, or providing sufficient global liquidity for the world's consumers and firms. All we have ahead of us is an indefinite period of economic stagnation, crisis, and ruin. Happy times, indeed.

Turning from the past to the present (and ultimately the future), we'll see that neither view is entirely correct. There will always be some residual reliance on multilateralism, if for no other reason than to provide some context for understanding the new forms of economic diplomacy now populating international affairs. But alternative forums and instruments of economic cooperation *will* proliferate away from the traditional multilateral model. These changes are not leading – at least not in every instance – to economic pandemonium, however, even when they reflect a decline in American hegemony. Instead, a new toolset for economic statecraft is being developed that attempts to navigate a multipolar world in an orderly way. In doing so, today's diplomacy strikes new institutional configurations attempting to achieve multilateralism's aims of predictability, stability, and discipline on the one hand, while responding to new economic and political configurations of financial power on the other. Understanding the interplay of these forces, and the evolving policy responses to them, is the focus of this book.

2

Playing the Numbers in Trade

One of the central ironies of today's financial statecraft is that "global governance" isn't always, or even mostly, about the "globe." Instead it's about groups, and the interaction of groups. This shouldn't be entirely surprising. As we saw at the outset of this book, multilateral bargaining traditionally corrals countries with diverse economic philosophies and strategic interests, and that are at vastly different stages of development. Crafting a deal of any real import can consequently be difficult, especially when governments are expected to make complex sacrifices and commitments. For every additional party you put at the negotiation table, an exponentially greater number of issues potentially have to be haggled over, as each country will want to maximize its welfare. Thus smaller negotiation groups can be, and indeed often are, quite attractive.

Of all the arenas of international economic law, no other domain has seen the power of small numbers more than international trade. Trade deals of all sizes and natures increasingly populate interstate economic relations, and to such an extent that they are steadily decreasing the importance of the multilateralism embodied by the WTO. For many economists, this is a truly disconcerting phenomenon. Free trade, at least as it has been traditionally conceived, works to the advantage of all countries by lowering barriers to the flow of goods, insofar as each is able to exploit its own competitive advantages. Along these lines, countries that grow the best-tasting, most delicious bananas should be free to sell those bananas to the world, instead of consumers in other countries getting stuck with second-rate bananas just because they live across a border. Meanwhile, other countries can focus on what they do best, whether it be cattle ranching or producing planes. Free trade should be *global* and allow "each country to concentrate its productive efforts in ways that will give it the most return (and reciprocally, ensure the same maximum return to its trading partners)."[1] In that way, increasingly sophisticated divisions of labor give rise to ever greater "welfare" gains to society.

Why then is *mini*lateralism an important, if not defining, feature of today's international trade agenda? For one, unlike some economics professors, practitioners of financial statecraft are not always (or even usually) concerned with the "absolute" gains of free trade. This is because free trade may be good from a "global" standpoint, but it is not necessarily good for everyone, all the time. When a country reduces its barriers, its consumers may benefit, but domestic producers might suffer. A country might be able to import better tasting bananas, but local farmers may go broke as business shifts to other countries. Or in order to meet the challenge of lower import walls, a country might have to adjust to new competition in ways that its citizens may not like – such as becoming more efficient by closing warehouses and slashing salaries, or adopting weaker environmental or child labor regulations that may be popular or acceptable in competitor economies. So to avoid as much pain as possible, countries are often picky about with whom they trade, and under what circumstances.

Crafting sound trade strategies can nonetheless be challenging for governments – especially over the long term. Losers today, even in seemingly uncompetitive industries, might be winners tomorrow. This might seem somewhat intuitive nowadays, but it was not always thought to be the case. Classical trade theory tended to view a country's comparative advantage vis-á-vis others as an outgrowth of its natural endowment, and as somewhat static.[2] Countries in certain climates will be better at agriculture. Others, by contrast, might be better at raising livestock. Yet others still might be best served by focusing on manufacturing. In today's modern economy, however, comparative advantage is as much about technology and information as it is about tangible productive resources. Farmers can learn to improve the quality and bounty of their produce, as well as the cost of growing it, and potentially become competitive even in the absence of a favorable geography. Furthermore, in knowledge-driven economies, countries can move up the value chain. Toymakers today might be airplane manufacturers or the inventors of the next Facebook tomorrow.

That said, trade has historically lent itself well to international deal making. Although trade barriers can (and increasingly do) take on a variety of hard-to-detect forms – including subsidies, technical standards, and administrative policies – most obstacles to the free passage of goods have traditionally taken shape as tariffs, or taxes on imports. As such, trade barriers have often been highly observable, and their impact relatively easy to quantify or at least estimate. If I'm an exporter of nails, I can gauge pretty effectively how duties will affect the competitiveness of my nails in the German marketplace. I can look at my customs invoices, assess the customs charges applied to my nails, and then take a flight over to Germany and walk down the aisle of a hardware store to figure out the cost of similar nails in Germany. Presto – by comparing the two, I can begin to gauge the impact of the tariff on the competitiveness of my nails.

This relative transparency has made trade an especially attractive target for striking narrow, minilateral, cross-border accords. Unlike some other areas of international economic affairs – such as financial regulation, a topic we will explore in the next chapter – trade does not inherently require broad multilateral cooperation in order for it to be effective. And where there is sufficient information as to one another's trade barriers and the costs and benefits of liberalization, countries can often hammer out an agreement that accommodates the strategic objectives or concerns of negotiating governments. Bargaining becomes pretty easy between any two parties: we can lower tariffs in sector Y, where your manufacturers are competitive, if we can also lower tariffs in sector X, where my manufacturers are competitive.

For similar reasons, trade agreements, especially when conducted by more than two countries, have tended to take shape among countries that are geographically proximate. Neighboring countries tend to have more information about one another – what kinds of products the other makes, how competitive those products are, and what kind of market there will likely be for one another's goods. They also tend to have long-standing political relationships, even when peppered with military conflict. So once deals are made, countries are often in a better position to monitor one another's commitments as well as police compliance and follow-through with regard to those commitments. Think of it as the "awkward neighbor" theory of economic cooperation: I may not like you, but we live next to one another, and I know more than anyone else about you, for better or worse.

Therefore, it should be expected that regional trading organizations are far from novel phenomena. And to be sure, regional deals have been key stepping stones to many of today's most successful nation-states. In

1789, for example, the U.S. Constitution barred individual states from levying duties on trade with other states, effectively creating a free trade area, just as provincial borders were wiped out in France, creating a customs union between newly formed regional departments.[3] Almost three decades later, eighteen German provinces would unite to form the Zollverein to manage common customs and economic policies, a coalition that would pave the way for German unification in 1871. A similar series of events would play out in Italy and Switzerland, as beneficial trade alliances morphed into states.

Modest deals like regional accords are more than just convenient, however. In some circumstances, they can contribute to a more efficient trading system. The "coalitions of the willing" strategy inherent to regional pacts can make it a lot easier for like-minded countries to strike a deal in relevant sectors of their economies and avoid the kind of holdups that increasingly inhibit the global trading system. Moreover, minilateralism can unleash competitive forces that can spur even inward-looking states to cooperate with others. As we will see a bit later in this chapter, once trade agreements are struck, they can generate enormous pressure for countries on the sidelines of the global economy to enter into their own custom-made alliances in order for their domestic industries to stay competitive with foreign rivals. As such, minilateralism can catalyze a wholesale dismantling of trade barriers – and in the process generate changes in policy that go well beyond the comfort zones of many naturally protective countries and governments. In doing so, minilateralism represents a very different model for global trade than the WTO-driven multilateralism of the postwar period, one built on choice as well as strategic coercion.

THE INTERNATIONAL MOORINGS OF REGIONAL TRADE

Although regional trade deals are far from recent phenomena, in today's world they can't be taken for granted, at least when one considers the legal operations and values of the multilateral system. At its core, the multilateral trading system is based on the principle of Most Favored Nation (MFN) treatment in which all WTO members pledge to treat imports from all other signatory states the same.

MFN rests on the notion that a good should be purchased on the basis of its price and value, not where it was made. It thus prohibits countries from discriminating against one another selectively and demands that a country treat all of its trading partners the same way. In doing so,

MFN promotes trade on the basis of efficiency, not politics. It also helps to "multilateralize" trade relations to the extent to which concessions granted between any two countries are extended to all others to which MFN treatment has been awarded. Deeper levels of liberalization are pushed forward just as principles of fair play and a level playing field are institutionalized in trade relationships.

MFN treatment, like regionalism, has a long history in international affairs. Its origins date back nearly a thousand years to the eleventh century, when European merchants strove to access foreign markets.[4] When Italian merchants sought to establish monopolies on certain trading routes, French and Spanish traders along the Mediterranean coast petitioned Arab princes of western Africa to issue franchises to their respective merchants. These franchises would accord the French and Spanish the same treatment as those granted to the citizens of Venice and later to those of Pisa, Genoa, Ancona, and Amalfi.[5] By the seventeenth century, the clause had started to become more popular. But it was often used by powerful nations as a political lever to compel less powerful states to grant their citizens and firms the same trading rights accorded to others.[6]

In the eighteenth century, European states began to differentiate political treaties from commercial treaties, and the MFN commitment began to take its modern shape. That said, MFN treatment had a distinctly conditional character, and was largely dependent on prospective trading partners granting reciprocal market access.[7] The conditional form of the MFN clause was, however, virtually abandoned with the conclusion of the Cobden–Chevalier treaty between Great Britain and France in 1860, and it did not reappear until after World War I, which severed treaty relations between the warring nations.[8] Years later, after World War II, the GATT sought to return to the prewar order, and the MFN clause was reinstated as an unconditional commitment among trading partners with the aim of tearing down the protectionist barriers that had been erected with the arrival of the Great Depression.[9]

Yet MFN, even in its modern day incarnation, is no panacea. Even though it can multilateralize agreements, it can potentially stymie trade negotiations as well. This is because MFN can reduce the incentives of countries to continue lowering their tariff walls on their own once they've secured an agreement with an active trading nation. Assume, for example, that Finland enjoys MFN with all countries in the world. Assume further that every country has high tariff walls vis-á-vis all others. Under these circumstances, how much incentive does Finland have to negotiate trade treaties? Well, it depends. If Finland knows or suspects that other countries are planning trade negotiations, not much. In theory, Finland could sit back, let others do all the hard work, and reap all the benefits of the trade deals they strike because of the MFN status it enjoys. Meanwhile, if all countries have the same tactic – and look to free ride on others' efforts – there could well be an under-negotiation of treaties as everyone sits around waiting for others to make trade deals. Or, precisely because gains are multilateralized, countries may be less inclined to strike deals because of the unknown consequences of extending the benefits of trade liberalization to all other MFN-wielding countries.

The framers of the GATT were not oblivious to these strategic problems, and provisions were included under Article XXIV of the agreement to permit less-than-multilateral agreements that could liberalize trade beyond GATT commitments without triggering MFN obligations. That way trade alliances could be struck without having to extend a club's trade benefits to all other GATT members. But these more limited accords are permissible only under certain conditions. Most important, any country seeking to deviate from multilateral norms is not allowed to selectively liberalize sectors with alliance members, but instead must accept the full, at times bitter, pill of free trade. The GATT thus requires that any minilateral accords cover "substantially all trade" between participating countries and that they implement terms in a "reasonable length of time," though interim agreements are permitted. Additionally, the GATT prohibits collectively raising tariff walls on nonparticipating countries or imposing tariffs that are on the whole more restrictive than the duties in effect prior to the formation of the trade alliance.

Taken together, these conditions embraced the idea that trade alliances were fine so long as no one was made worse off, and that local deals were just a stepping stone to greater multilateral cooperation. Still, most policymakers had assumed that any resort to Article XXIV would be limited. Under its terms, countries would have little leeway to craft regional agreements escaping deep structural adjustment for inefficient domestic industries. And most countries were not in a position to seriously consider broad sectoral liberalization, especially in the early years of the GATT. Indeed, even wealthy countries would have to at least ostensibly undertake painful reforms of their less competitive industries where they entered into regional deals.

These restrictions on regional pacts were expected to be taken seriously, and to underscore the point, a special WTO body, the Committee on Regional Trade Agreements, was created in 1996 to monitor compliance with these provisions.[10] But in practice, they have ended up being rather hollow. For one, they didn't apply to all regional deals. Regional services agreements secured under the General Agreement on Trade in Services (GATS) – a counterpart to the GATT, geared toward everything from tourism to financial services – weren't covered. Neither were agreements reached under the "Enabling Clause" to the GATT, which allows developed countries to offer one-sided preferences to developing countries.[11] Moreover, even when the GATT did apply, it was notoriously difficult to put into practice. As the famed Columbia economist (and critic of regionalism) Jagdish Bhagwati has observed, the agreement provided very little instruction on how to decide how much time was considered "reasonable" or at what point duties for "substantially" all trade were eliminated. Plus, ambiguity abounds as to which parties have to notify the WTO about their accords. Indeed, many governments only provide notification after agreements have been negotiated and implemented, making WTO processes appear like "futile ex post-bureaucratic [exercises]."[12] And because of the technical and broad-based nature of the analysis, years can pass before WTO officials can complete even a preliminary factual examination of a regional accord, and the WTO rarely even publishes a final examination report.[13]

As a result, despite intermittent calls by academics to shore up and elevate the WTO to the sole forum for trade liberalization, countries have continued to have free rein to ink regional deals. Not only that, noncompliance with GATT dictates is widespread. In some of the most egregious cases, regional clubs go so far as to require participants to raise tariffs to outsider countries in order to monopolize the gains of liberalization and block nonparticipants from enjoying what had been relatively low barriers to member markets. Nevertheless, despite a widely held consensus that more than a few regional accords run awry of GATT rules, the WTO has yet to find a single agreement in violation of Article XXIV. And by extension, it has never formally sanctioned members of a regional pact. Meanwhile, the WTO's famed dispute panels have shied from providing any guidance or oversight on the issue, and on occasion even ruled that Article XXIV provides a valid justification for measures that could otherwise be illegal under the GATT.[14]

A PRIMER ON THE VARIETY AND TYPES OF TRADE ACCORDS

It is always hazardous to carve the world up into neat conceptual slices, but ultimately three basic types of minilateral agreements populate the world of international trade: preferential trade accords, free trade agreements, and customs unions.

The loosest type of arrangement is a preferential trade agreement, where members agree to give one another special access to their domestic markets. Under this kind of agreement, tariffs are reduced for certain imports, although tariffs are not scrapped altogether. This kind of arrangement can be appealing for plenty of countries, especially developing countries seeking closer economic ties with bigger, more advanced neighbors. In such instances, a government may want better access to a neighbor's markets, but have concerns that its developed neighbor may host industries that are so competitive that in the absence of at least some tariff walls its own domestic or nascent industries could be wiped out.

Some countries go a step further and eliminate most (and in some instances virtually all) tariffs under a free trade agreement. Participants "pay to play" the game of regional trade by opting into a system of reciprocal preferences and tariff reductions that can culminate in a common market of free-flowing goods, services, and other factors of production. As with preferential trade agreements, however, each member may retain its own policies with regard to the tariffs it applies to nonparticipating countries. Consequently, outsiders to free trade agreements must negotiate their own deals with each member in the free trade bloc in order to secure similar concessions and benefits.

Third, regional agreements can take the shape of customs unions. As such, signatories to a trade agreement agree to apply to nonparticipating countries the same external tariffs on goods. Under the dictates of the Treaty of Rome, for example, all participants in the European Union (EU) are required to apply the same tariff rates on imports coming into the community from other parts of the world. Similarly, participants in Mercosur, the occasionally fractious trade bloc in South America, have a shared tariff scheme that all members are expected to apply to imports. As such, customs unions hold ambiguous implications for free trade. On the one hand, they can minimize the potentially quilt-like complexity, expense, and inefficiency that arise when countries independently enter into different free trade areas and alliances.[15] They also allow countries to negotiate as a bloc with the outside world.

Nonetheless, customs unions also restrict members' ability to unilaterally enter into economic relationships on their own. Participants have to agree on specific tariff schedules and on the treatment of subsidies, foreign investment and rules of origin, just, as they would with a typical preferential or free trade agreement. But if they don't agree with one another, you potentially don't get any kind of deal at all – whether on an individual or regional basis.

Restraints of this sort can be very difficult for countries to swallow, especially when they have very different trade relationships with the outside world. If, for example, Ghana and Senegal wish to adopt a common external tariff, it could be challenging if each enjoys and participates in different tariff schemes with their former colonial rulers, Britain and France. Their preferences with regard to how they should treat each European power could differ dramatically, even if the two neighboring West African countries have growing or robust trade with one another. The same problem could arise where countries like the Dominican Republic and Haiti may neighbor one another, but enjoy different levels of development, and thus have different policy and trade preferences.[16]

As a result, most customs unions are highly imperfect organizations. Indeed, few organizations besides the European Union, the South African Customs Union, Mercosur, and the Caricom in the Caribbean are even acknowledged as such. And many are riddled with a range of debilitating opt outs and exceptions that collectively undermine the mission of regional economic integration. Take the Andean Community, a group of countries that comprises Bolivia, Colombia, Ecuador, and Peru. In 1994, three members adopted a common external tariff for the purposes of creating a customs union. But their "common" policy turned out to be only partial, as underlying differences among member states in the level and composition of foreign trade made it difficult to agree on a common external tariff. Bolivia – the only landlocked Andean country, subject to rules Chile imposed on the use of its ports, cargo handling, and other important matters – maintains its own tariff, although how it is applied is subject to coordination with the Andean Community.[17] Peru, meanwhile, which initiated economic liberalization in 1992, has generally avoided the common tariff altogether. Because it set out on the path of liberalization later than the other members, it has opted for steeper liberalization programs in hopes of spurring faster development, and thus did not want to restrain its ability to continue advancing its own free trade priorities.[18] Eventually in 2004, the bloc lifted restrictions barring members from negotiating with nonmember countries, and Columbia and Peru entered into their own free trade deals with the United States. Because of the Swiss-cheese nature of the common external tariff, it combines features of both a free trade agreement (FTA) and a customs union.

THE FIRST WAVE OF REGIONAL INTEGRATION

Regional clubs have popped up in clusters, the first arising in the quarter century following World War II, and the second, more recent wave in the 1990s. They all exhibit very different characteristics, both with regard to their scope of membership and their commitments by members. But there is, to be sure, no better place to start understanding regionalism than in the European Union. The oldest and by far the most familiar regional organization, it is credited with growing from a fragile coalition of war-torn states into an expansive twenty-eight country colossus whose successes and failures regularly dominate the financial headlines.

European regionalism was born of political necessity. After two disastrous World Wars, the continent's leaders agreed – even in an atmosphere of lingering distrust – that deeper political integration was necessary to prevent another European conflagration. The focal point for such integration was trade among the future member states. Countries that traded together, stayed together, it was believed – or at least would not fight each other to the death if they were economically interdependent. Plus, it was hoped that a common market could help realize lasting economies of scale and productivity gains for the recovering continent. The first sectors of emphasis were the coal and steel industries. In 1951, France, West Germany, Belgium, Luxembourg, and the Netherlands signed the Treaty of Paris. In it, they created a first of its kind organization, called the European Coal and Steel Community (ECSC), which would pool key raw materials for industry and reduce countries' perceptions of their own military vulnerability. Then in 1958, the Treaty of Rome was signed, which provided for the establishment of a common market, a customs union and other shared trade policies under the umbrella the European Economic Community (EEC).

Together, the two initiatives would yield impressive economic payoffs. In the eight years following the ECSC's formation, iron and steel production rose by 75 percent, which in turn helped fuel industrial production, which rose 58 percent. The EEC, meanwhile, chipped away at intra-regional barriers to goods and services, and by 1968, tariffs and custom duties were abolished, helping to generate an 80 percent increase in trade. New nontariff barriers managed to spring up in the 1970s, however, as EU members sought to shield their domestic markets and industries from global (as well as intra-European) competition. But in the 1980s, the community made a comeback, and introduced plans to launch an upgraded European single market, and initiated a process of reform that, although formally concluded in 1992, in many ways still continues today.[19]

Europe's early successes encouraged countries elsewhere to try their own luck at regional trade deals throughout the 1960s. Although some modest efforts were launched in Africa, most were centered in Latin America. Economists have offered a range of explanations as to why. Unlike Africa, Latin America is dominated, with the significant exception of Brazil, by one language: Spanish. Additionally, most of the region's countries had roughly similar colonial and postcolonial experiences, leading to a greater familiarity with one another's economic stages of development and ultimate political aspirations. Latin American regionalism departed, however, from the espoused best practices of European regionalism in several important ways. Perhaps most significantly, it actively embraced member-country policies that aimed to spur industrialization by substituting foreign imports with regional goods. Regional integration schemes also took occasionally harsh stances on the treatment of foreign direct investment, which had been viewed as too often promoting the interests of far-flung governments over those of the countries hosting the investment. Countries would instead focus on helping manufacturers import capital goods necessary for production, often through special state-centered plans and aggressive monetary policies.

Latin America's initial steps toward import substitution were grounded in the necessity and chaos wrought by the Great Depression. In the 1930s, most Latin American countries exported agricultural products and raw materials, while they imported manufactured goods. This model proved unsustainable with the onset of the Great Depression, however, when the region's exports to the United States plummeted. The problem was then exacerbated by World War II, when Latin American countries were foreclosed from U.S. consumer markets as funding the war effort took priority over trade with the Southern hemisphere. In response, Latin American countries learned to be self-sufficient throughout much of the 1930s and 1940s, and local factories sprouted up across the continent to satisfy domestic demand. As World War II eventually wound down, heads of state decided to continue building up their domestic manufacturing capacity as a means of promoting development and consolidating power over their local economies.

As such, import substitution was based in part on clear-eyed self assessments concerning the international competitiveness of Latin American firms. Opening up nascent industries to global competition was largely disfavored because many firms were ill-positioned to compete against their more advanced counterparts in Europe and America. Indeed, free trade would, in the eyes of many so-called "Third World" elites, do little to improve local competition because few local firms would survive the onslaught of rivalry from abroad. So instead of opening the floodgates to global competition, political and military leaders sought to harness the demand of their own (collective) domestic markets as a source of growth.

This more protective approach to managing economic development was not without precedent. Governments throughout South America, especially in Argentina and Brazil, looked in part to Italy (and even New-Deal America) as inspirations for state-backed industrialization to ease the pain of foreclosed consumer markets. Later, as regional models for import substitution developed, Europe itself became a model of sorts, especially with the highly protective agricultural subsidies embraced by EU member states. Indeed, even the World Bank had endorsed various forms of "modest intervention" by governments, aimed at kick-starting local industries.

But import substitution is a hard game to play well. Above all else, it depends on there being sufficient demand from partners to substitute for the demand generated by exports elsewhere. To put things in perspective, suppose for the moment that Bolivia wanted to take on import substitution by itself and replace imported cars with cars manufactured in Bolivia. For Bolivia's program to work, it would have to make sure there was sufficient domestic demand to support a national substitute producer for the foreign imports. The problem, however, is that the smaller the market, the harder it is to establish capital or labor-intensive industries. In order for industries to be successful, they have to be able to exploit economies of scale, which is especially difficult for developing countries. Local industries consequently tended to have higher costs of production – and higher prices.

Regionalism, not surprisingly, was seen as a means of addressing this challenge. By cooperating with neighbors in forums like the then-named Latin American Free Trade Association and Andean Pact, a country could theoretically expand its export markets – and its sources of demand for domestic goods. Larger regional markets could in turn provide scale economies for firms, which presumably enable efficiency gains. So if Bolivia did not have the local demand to support the production of certain goods, it could potentially secure them, along with economies of scale, through strategic minilateral (albeit inward-looking) cooperation with neighbors.

Yet regional import substitution proved difficult to put into operation across the continent. Even at the regional level there was often insufficient demand to generate the economies of scale and scope necessary to modernize local industries and ensure their global competitiveness. Moreover, with import substitution managed by government officials and party bosses, industrial policy was not always, or even usually, based on scientific market analysis. Instead, political priorities guided policy decisions. Consequently, resources were routinely directed toward inefficient and noncompetitive sectors. Protected industries, meanwhile, could charge super-premiums for the (often subpar) goods they produced because of the relative absence of competition. To finance their operation, governments largely indulged themselves in expansionary monetary policy – printing money out of their respective central banks or borrowing money from abroad. These monetary policies in turn created inflation, and tended to hike the price of protected products even more as money poured into the economy.

Macroeconomic forces did not help. Easy credit extended by resource-rich emerging countries in the 1970s pumped recycled petrodollars to developing and developed countries alike. Later in the 1980s, relentless interest rate hikes by Paul Volcker, the U.S. Federal Reserve chairman, would inadvertently stymie growth in Latin America by strengthening the dollar, and by extension, raise the price of dollar-denominated oil imports throughout the region.

Eventually, debt-fueled growth took its toll on the largely inward-oriented economies. Borrowing for expensive social projects outpaced earnings from exports, creating chronic capital account deficits. And over time, the costs of servicing loans began to exceed the value of exports in countries such as Argentina and Brazil. As the prospect of Latin American countries repaying their loans became dimmer, investors began to reduce their lending, a trend that accelerated with the onset of economic recession and stagflation in the late 1970s. Interest rates skyrocketed, and when the well of global finance had run dry, Latin American governments, without recourse to foreign currency

from exports, found themselves in a bind, unable to access the foreign currency required in order to service their debt or to fund their
slow domestic industries. Out of options, both banks and governments
across the continent had to restructure their debt and undertake economic reforms that would come to redefine the relationship between
the state and industry.

THE GREAT REFORMATION

The 1980s would prove the beginning of the end for most regional
import substitution schemes. As the economist Dani Rodrik notes,
"The state went from being a handmaiden of economic growth to
the principal obstacle blocking it."[20] Part of this ideological transformation is attributable to gradual political change as military dictator-
ships slowly gave way to democracies toward the end of the decade
and throughout the 1990s. A new generation of political leaders rose to
power, trained in the United States and skeptical of the supposed benefits of strong governmental involvement in the economy. They had
instead come to embrace various tenets of the so-called "Washington
Consensus," a set of prescriptions regarding international development
that advocated free market prescriptions for global economic relations
and domestic governance.

As leaders revised their preferences with regard to the role of the
state, the character and purpose of many regional agreements changed
as well. Instead of being seen as a means of cordoning off markets from
the outside world, regionalism was reconceived, and in some instances
relaunched, as a means of greater international economic integration.
The European Union's single market program was started, and new
efforts were introduced to remove nontariff barriers that had become
significant obstacles to trade as the European economy became more
complex and highly regulated. Meanwhile, old preferential trade
areas (PTAs) were relaunched in Africa. The Union Économique et
Monétair Ouest Africaine replaced the Communaute Économique
de l'Afrique Occidentale, just as the Common Market of Eastern and
Southern Africa was resurrected, the Preferential Trade Area for Eastern
and Southern African States expanded, and the Union Douanière et
Économique de l'Afrique Centrale revamped.[21]

Still, the most dramatic changes were in Latin America, as countries
throughout the region wanted back in to the global economy. Country
by country – and club by club – Washington Consensus policies were

adopted at both the local and regional level. As part of the process, import substitution schemes were superseded by more neoliberal policies. The continent's primary regional organization, the Latin American Free Trade Association, gave way to subregional blocs like Mercosur, which vigorously promoted a broad-based free trade area among its members, and eventually entered into free trade negotiations with other blocs, including the European Union. Similarly, the Andean Community evolved from a moribund Andean Pact, and in its new institutional guise pushed a range of reforms both at the individual country and regional levels aimed at reining in government spending and increasing foreign direct investment. Across the region, countries offered increasingly robust safeguards for foreign investors (including protections against expropriation) and reduced a range of local content requirements that indirectly taxed investment dollars directed to the region.

It's hard to overstate just how much these reforms represented a 180-degree turn from the previous development policy.[22] Throughout the 1960s and 1970s, Latin American leaders were extremely sensitive to the long-standing systematic exploitation of their countries. To the extent to which local industries had engaged in international ventures, they did so not as winning industries, but as relatively underdeveloped cogs in a larger supply chain of production. Instead of, say, finishing products, local firms were designed only to extract raw materials as cheaply as possible, and then to transport those materials to Western centers for refinement. Finished products would then be resold at a profit to countries at the periphery of the global economy, just as they were during the colonial era. Not surprisingly, there was a profound interest in breaking this cycle, and simply carrying on with business as usual seemed to be a losing proposition. Instead, import substitution appeared to offer a winning hand in the otherwise rigged game of global trade.

But as democratic movements began to take shape on the continent, experts and political leaders began to look elsewhere for models of economic reform. And by far, the most attractive one came from Asia. Although eschewing regionalism at the time – in part as a result of the diverse economies and stages of economic development in the region – Asian countries had long adopted, on an independent and at times unilateral basis, export-oriented models of growth. This approach embraced targeted strategies of sometimes significant protection, but did so in order to groom their local companies for eventual international competition. By the 1980s, this strategy had begun to pay some hefty dividends. In their now canonical paper, economists Jeffrey Sachs and John Williamson showed that in the 1960s and 1970s, East Asia increased its growth of exports nearly fourfold relative to GDP through a selective combination of protectionist and export promoting policies, whereas Latin America's exports remained flat given its overwhelming reliance on protectionism.[23] This was in part because as Japan's economy started to take off in the 1970s, causing domestic wages to rise, South Korea, Taiwan, Singapore, and Hong Kong all began to lower tariff barriers to attract Japanese companies to their shores and establish bases for the manufacture and assembly of Japanese products.[24] Rather quickly, a novel, export-driven model of regional development started to take shape, built around supply-chain economics. And over the next decade, the rising tide of the Japanese economy would lift, if not all, at least many boats in the region.

Success stories in Asia inspired both developed and developing countries alike. In developed countries, multinational companies increasingly started to rethink their own supply-chain economics. Since the Ford assembly line, generations of managers presumed that the most efficient process for manufacturing goods involved centralizing activities in one location, usually the country in which goods were ultimately sold. But with advances in information technology and transportation, smart MBAs started to figure out how their supply chains could be decomposed such that parts could be sourced from multiple locations in the same region and in ways that were more efficient than centralized operations.[25] Developing countries, meanwhile, began to seek renewed trade relationships with local industrialized economies in ways specifically targeted toward attracting foreign capital, while also locking in their domestic policy reforms. Doing so required rethinking not only the purpose of regional integration, but also the fundamental concept (and content) of a trade treaty. Instead of seeking access in another country's markets based entirely on one's own competitive advantages in particular sectors, such as agriculture, the primary objective is to secure foreign direct investment from the partner country in order to service the production capacity of the larger economy.[26] Think of it as the "if you can't beat them, join them" theory of international economic relations.

This strategy was exemplified in Mexico's approach to the North American Trade Agreement, the first preferential trade agreement negotiated under Article XXIV that involved developed countries (the United States and Canada) and developing countries (Mexico), and the first clear deviation from multilateral trade usually embraced by the United States. For many experts, the fact that Mexico was at all interested in free trade was at the time surprising. Mexico had, like many of its peers in Central and South America, followed an economic policy of import substitution throughout the 1960s and 1970s. As part of this policy, a range of controls was imposed on foreign direct investment, including performance requirements whereby foreign investors were obliged to purchase a minimum amount of the goods for their manufacturing operations from Mexican companies, even when they were highly inefficient. The lodestar was the automotive industry. In the early 1970s, the Mexican government banned the importation of cars, as well as many engines and auto parts. Vehicles were instead subject to a 60 percent local value-added requirement on vehicles assembled in Mexico, plus foreign companies were limited to a 40-percent stake in auto parts plants, all in an effort to kick-start the local economy.[27] The government also borrowed aggressively to fuel economic growth through a range of infrastructure projects, which in turn attracted foreign car companies to set up experimental industrial facilities, including Nissan, Volkswagen, and the U.S. "Big Three" automakers, Ford, General Motors, and Chrysler.

These policies had only a limited impact on sustained growth, however, as local content requirements eroded the efficiency of the plants, and restrictions on foreign direct investment prevented foreign companies from achieving economies of scale to reshape the automotive industry.[28] Poor decisions would catch up with the country in the early 1980s, when Mexico experienced what would turn out to be the first of several financial crises in Central and South America, as interest rates spiked along with inflation, and the government began to have problems servicing its debt.

To stem its economic slide, which was exacerbated by the country's inability to attract investment and compete internationally, Mexico embarked on a rapid and sweeping process of economic liberalization. Besides reducing content requirements for joint ventures and restrictions on foreign investment, Mexico sought to secure economic agreements with the United States that would preserve, and perhaps even increase, American investment in the country. Early unilateral liberalization efforts had already reaped considerable rewards by the mid-1980s. Foreign car companies in particular ramped up auto production in the region. General Motors, for example, relocated its production of wire harnesses and upholstery, and by 1990 the company had thirty export assembly plants near the U.S. border. Ford similarly expanded its stamping and assembling facilities as well as its production capacity for engines, and moved most of its assembly operations of the compact car model Fiesta from Germany and South Korea to Cuautitlán Izcalli.[29] Similar moves were made in the electronics and household appliances industries.[30]

Encouraged by these developments, Mexican officials hoped to speed the trend by securing a bilateral trade deal with the United States. It would serve as a kind of insurance policy. Although considerable investment had been made in Mexico, there were few guarantees that investment dollars would stay. In 1988, the United States signed a unique free trade deal with Canada, in which tariff rates would be lower than they were between the United States and Mexico. There was, as a consequence, the prospect of a potential redirection of U.S. investment dollars away from Mexico to Canada. Additionally, instability in Mexico's domestic political scene offered few assurances that the turn to liberalization by the country's ruling party, the PRI, would be a lasting one, given its historically statist bent. A trade treaty offered the opportunity for Mexico to consolidate its early gains and to credibly commit to a long-term policy of liberalization and economic engagement. By entering into a treaty, Mexico could provide the United States government with certain guarantees and protections with regard to foreign investment, as well as offer U.S. manufacturers a long-lasting, stable base for the manufacture of goods by a lower cost and educated workforce.

This kind of reasoning has its risks, and consistently rustles the feathers of more progressive-minded development economists. By their very nature, trade agreements between a rich country and its poorer neighbor almost always consist of terms that are most favorable to the wealthier participant. And to be sure, Mexico did not negotiate seeking to secure concessions in sensitive areas of the American economy, such as better agricultural access. Instead, the government hoped the country's geographic proximity to the United States could be leveraged to attract investment from it and other countries seeking to establish manufacturing bases for goods destined for America. In that way, Mexico could potentially move up the value chain as the country developed its own skilled labor force, technology, infrastructure, and capital markets. Still, when a country negotiates with a partner that is overwhelmingly more powerful, it can "give away the store" with few reciprocal trade concessions in return. Additionally, if a country hitches itself to the wrong economy, where all of its industries are less competitive or where its labor force is a poor fit for the kind of investments the country is seeking to attract, a country can experience jarring unemployment and economic disruptions.

For that reason, the North American accord serves as an interesting case study of minilateral cooperation. Did NAFTA work? The jury, even two decades later, is still out, although for many experts, the numbers suggest that the gamble paid off. From an economic standpoint, Mexico is a much stronger country than it was two decades ago: Between 1993 and 2002, the total two-way trade between Mexico and the United States grew from $81 billion to $231 billion, and Mexico reversed what was a modest trade deficit into a $37 billion trade surplus in the ten years following the deal.[31] Moreover, Mexican exports to the United States have quadrupled since NAFTA's implementation, from $60 billion to $280 billion per year.[32] That being said, American exports to Mexico increased sharply as well, more than tripling as Mexico's economy has grown. Furthermore, unemployment has remained consistently high, even as the poverty rate has declined. Overall, however, most experts have concluded that trade liberalization has had positive consequences not just for Mexican business interests, but for everyday citizens as well.[33]

HOW NUMBERS CAN BE DECEIVING

The fact that trade deals can have an impact on the competitiveness of a country's firms means, by definition, that a deal between any two parties can have external implications for other countries – even those that do not participate in the negotiations. This is because once a country gets preferential access to a market, its firms escape tariff charges or other barriers, lowering the price of their goods relative to outsiders.

Although consumers will enjoy the lower price, economists have long held that a partial reduction of tariffs among potential suppliers of goods may not always be optimal. On the positive side, trade can be enhanced, and higher quality goods may find their way to store shelves.[34] Plus increased trade can, and often does, lead to more foreign direct investment. But it is also possible that regional goods, because of their tariff advantages, could displace imports from the rest of the world, even where they are not of the highest quality or made at the lowest cost. In such cases, regional trade would result in a "diversion" of trade away from more efficient (non-regional) producers.[35]

How Preferential Tariffs Create Trade Diversion

	Price with Identical Tariffs	Preferential Tariff Applied
UK Goods	$2.00	$2.00
France	$2.50	$1.50

So to put things in perspective, imagine a situation in which Germany applies a $1 duty on all imported nails (usually tariffs are applied to the declared value of goods, but we'll keep our example simple). Assume further that firms in the United Kingdom manufacture nails with a sale price of $1, and firms in France manufacture nails with a sale price of $1.50. If Germany applies the same tariff to both, say $1, UK firms will beat out French firms because their nails will sell for $2, as compared to the French nails at $2.50. If, however, Germany and France enter into a free trade agreement, and Germany removes tariffs on French nails, but not on UK nails, then French nails will have a price of $1.50 versus a sale price of $2 for UK nails. Consumers will thus likely opt for the French nails, even though they are less efficiently produced than the UK nails, creating a "wasteful" allocation of resources as less competitive firms enjoy the greater business.

Pinpointing trade diversion is, however, rarely so straightforward. Often, it requires divining what trade would have looked like had a deal not been reached. As such, a determination must be made that partner-country costs are out of line with the prices from outside the trade club. This will normally not be the case where partners have had low trade barriers and face international competition – although this can be a problem in some regions, such as Africa, where countries commonly have high walls against most products, whatever their origin.[36] So where, say, Namibia and Senegal enter into a preferential trade agreement that reduces tariffs or significant trade barriers, the degree of diversion may be considerable, even if consumers may pay less for goods under the new trade regime. So the facts and circumstances of regional deals matter a lot – and make modeling the welfare effects of regional trade deals notoriously difficult.

Complicating things is the fact that trade diversion is only really possible to the extent that one takes a long view of global economic relations. As the Asian experience shows, protection today can lead to competition tomorrow. If you're a rising developing country, you might have some of the fundamentals with which to become a leader in a given sector. Maybe you're like India, with a large domestic consumer base, and a highly skilled information technology labor force. Or maybe you're like China, with a large domestic labor force and the scale economies to make environmental technology, such as solar power, cheap. But nascent industries take time to develop and gain the size and scale necessary to compete against more experienced or established firms in industrial countries. So you may opt for protection – either tariffs, subsidies, or even import quotas – although in the future, by launching globally efficient companies, you may drive up competition (and global welfare) in the long run.

So where would one at least *expect* to see trade diversion? Often, it's associated with customs unions, and for good reason: member countries gain special access to one another's markets, and escape the club's external tariff regime. But in practice, trade diversion can be just as significant, and perhaps even greater, in free trade areas, which can also create "club" benefits that are foreclosed to outsiders. The primary means of doing so, in the absence of a common external tariff, are "rules of origin" that dictate under what circumstances a product should be deemed to emanate from a state participating in a preferential trade area. Rules of origin are attractive because, among other things, they prevent a company from a nonparticipating country from cherry-picking a member state with the lowest tariff rate, setting up a nominal presence there, and then exporting the product to members of the trade club. Instead, rules of origin require goods exported between members to derive a certain proportion of value or undergo certain production processes in a member state in order for the good to obtain preferential or duty-free treatment in the other member states. If products are thus deemed to be manufactured or having added value in a member state, then they can be shipped across borders in the club under a reduced tariff schedule. If the goods do not meet the threshold of having sufficient value added in the member state, they are subject to whatever regime would apply to their original home country.

Again, NAFTA provides a good example worth considering. As we saw earlier in this chapter, Mexico's unilateral reduction of various import tariffs induced various automotive firms, including the U.S. Big Three, Nissan, and Volkswagen to set up engine and automotive assembly plants there. NAFTA raised the prospect of more tightly integrating North American production capacity, at the regional level, for the increasingly global firms. However, U.S. automotive and electronic suppliers were concerned that a free trade agreement might enable firms from other parts of the world to set up a minimal presence in Mexico in order to export goods such as auto parts, electronics, and even textiles to the United States under the reduced tariff system.

To prevent this kind of trade arbitrage, and to placate special interests, NAFTA doubled down on what were already significant rules of origin that had been in place in an earlier Canada-U.S. Free Trade Agreement.[37] For example, a value-added test for automotive parts required that more than half of the value of automotive parts receiving preferential treatment be created within the free trade area. At the time, Japanese firms were importing cheap component parts from Japan to use in their production processes in Mexico, and there was a concern that they would use this supply chain to infiltrate U.S. markets. NAFTA changed the business model of these firms, however, and Japanese manufacturers began to incent suppliers to produce component parts in the United States and Mexico.[38] This strategy was brought to bear on other industries as well, requiring, among a host of other things, that the tubes in color televisions be of North American origin, prompting Japanese and South Korean firms to establish new factories in North America over other locales in Southeast Asia.[39]

The policy justification behind rules of origin is that they grease the wheels of negotiation. Trade deals are hard to negotiate. Even in win-win situations, where all parties experience economic growth, there will be losers. Inevitably, some firms will lose business to foreign competitors – which in turn can translate into lost jobs. Furthermore, in more one-sided negotiations, during which a country inks an ambitious trade deal with a vastly more efficient or productive competitor, liberalization can imperil broad swaths of a country's exports, creating current account and trade deficits. So governments won't take on the process of ratification and the possible social and economic dislocation accompanying liberalization unless they can be assured that their efforts will at least bring forth positive net benefits that will accrue to a wide range of domestic interests. Rules of origin, embodied in formal treaty arrangements, help provide such assurance. Governments (and their special interests) can rest reasonably assured that they will get something out of restructuring their economies, from greater productivity and international competitiveness of local firms to inroads into foreign markets. Rules of origin also prevent third parties from free riding on the negotiations of others as is possible with MFN. If you want to enjoy the fruits of a trade deal, you have to bring something to the table. But rules of origin, like other mechanisms aimed at creating club benefits for friends and allies, come at a cost. Although perhaps helpful in "getting to yes," and securing agreement, they *are* distortive, and can create or empower special interests, often at the expense of consumers. Thus over time, they can raise barriers to future international cooperation just as much as reduce them over the immediate or short-term.

WHY PREFERENTIAL TRADE IS CONTAGIOUS

The fact that trade deals have systemic consequences for the global economy is critical to understanding just how economic statecraft continues to evolve. The possibility of trade diversion introduces another economic motive for regionalism, namely the possibility that countries strike minilateral trade deals defensively – either to prevent trade diversion because of other parties' arrangements, or to confer losses from trade diversion with new gains or inroads into other markets.

Defensive considerations have been at play in the formation of many regional agreements, including NAFTA. As we saw above, the signing of the Canada-U.S. FTA in the mid-1980s put Mexico under enormous pressure to negotiate its own bilateral deal with the United States. Head-to-head competition between Canadian and Mexican suppliers was, despite their different stages of development, intense, as both countries depended on machinery and transportation equipment for nearly half of their total U.S. exports.[40] After the Canada-U.S. free trade pact entered into force, however, the tariffs on Canadian exports to the United States began to decline, while tariffs on Mexican exports remained unchanged. This spurred Mexico to enter into trade negotiations with America and secure a deal for itself. But then the prospect of a Mexico-U.S. bilateral agreement compelled the Canadian government to trilateralize the arrangement lest Canadian exporters risk losing their competitive position in the U.S. marketplace. Thus the prime motivation for both countries was not so much the prospect of mutual gain as much as the fear of exclusion from regional and bilateral accords arising around them.[41]

Yet NAFTA did not simply shift the status quo for the parties. Instead, it too catalyzed other actors, in particular the European Union, to enter into their own deals. Indeed, the mere prospect of North American trade collusion prompted EU members to complete their Single Market Program in 1992 and secure a rival trade bloc. Then once NAFTA was completed, the Europeans negotiated their own free trade accord with Mexico. Since then, the European Union's trade policy has been driven in many ways by U.S. decision making. Virtually all of its enacted or proposed FTAs – with Central America, Chile, and South Korea – followed or anticipated similar moves by the United States. It has also sought to gain advantage over the United States by entering into agreements with countries – such as with the Mercosur bloc – where U.S. efforts have failed.

Asia, too, caught the trade bug.[42] The EU's 1992 Single Market Program, along with NAFTA, heightened fears throughout Asia that, in the words of Indonesia's foreign minister, Asian economies would be left alone in an "inhospitable jungle, where the rule of the strongest would be the rule of the day."[43] Thus in 1991, the once-sleepy Association of Southeast Asian Nations (ASEAN) agreed to upgrade what had been moribund trade relations with an ASEAN free trade agreement designed to reduce tariffs on regional trade to between 0 to 5 percent by 2008. At the same time, the Asia-Pacific Economic Cooperation (APEC), an informal consortium of twenty-one Pacific Rim countries, was launched, which would by 1994 adopt a range of goals aimed at securing free and open trade and investment in the Asia-Pacific by 2010 for industrialized economies and by 2020 for developing economies.

Even China has played the free trade game. Following its WTO accession in 2001, in itself a remarkable achievement after years of heavy negotiation, China entered into free trade agreements with Hong Kong, Macao, Australia, New Zealand, South Africa, Chile, India, and the Gulf Cooperation Council. It also signed a Framework Agreement on Comprehensive Economic Cooperation with ASEAN in 2002, which was implemented in 2010.

In the wake of these and other efforts, more than 175 new agreements have been put into effect and 70 more are under negotiation or awaiting implementation. Tariffs, not surprisingly, have fallen by more than one-third in just the last fifteen years. And the next decade has the potential of being active as well, and could even spark a spate of regional deal making reminiscent of the 1990s. Just as North American trade ignited fears in Europe about being excluded from future commerce in the region, Asian trade accords sparked concerns in the West, and especially the United States, of being "locked out of Asia."[44] But instead of starting from scratch with new negotiations, the United States joined talks involving what had been known as the Trans-Pacific Strategic Economic Partnership Agreement. This accord originated as a negotiation aiming to eliminate tariffs among Brunei, Chile, New Zealand, and Singapore. But after Vietnam indicated its potential interest, the United States sought to engage as well, and declared in 2008 its intent

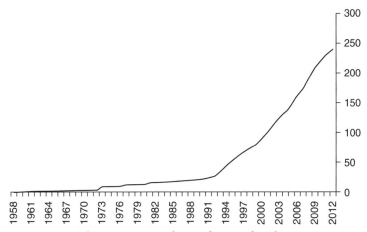

FIGURE 2. The growing popularity of regional trade agreements.

to secure a "21st century" expanded version of the agreement that would incorporate labor and environmental standards, as well as intellectual property rights. Dubbed the Trans-Pacific Partnership (TPP), the agreement would include more country participants and also address crosscutting issues such as rules of origin, supply-chain management, competition policy, state-owned enterprises, government procurement, technical barriers to trade, regulatory coherence, competitiveness, and expanded opportunities for small and medium-sized enterprises.[45]

Because of its breadth and scope, the TPP has catalyzed interest from unlikely quarters. For years, Japan had for the most part refrained from trade deals with countries beyond the region, largely due to an interest in protecting its own domestic agricultural interests. Its reluctance was, however, becoming costly as trade agreements were being concluded in its backyard without its involvement. Especially discomforting for Japan were two South Korean agreements concluded with the United States and the European Union. Japanese exporters increasingly lamented their exclusion from lucrative trade pacts that could facilitate local supply chains and trade with the outside world, and saw South Korea's meteoric rise as the result, at least in part, of a shrewd liberalization strategy. So when the United States jumped into TPP negotiations, and welcomed additional participation from countries like Vietnam and Australia, Japan eventually followed suit. On November 11, 2012, the Japanese prime minister, Yoshihiko Noda, announced his country's intention to join America and the other negotiating parties of the TPP. And with his announcement, the TPP was decisively transformed from a modest agreement with a series of minor powers into one that had the potential of redesigning wholesale trade relationships in Asia and beyond.

With Japan and the United States seriously engaged, the geoeconomic chessboard changed for even far-flung economies in North America. Mexico had already seen in the TPP a means of potentially serving as a bridge between U.S. and Asian trade. Meanwhile Canada, which had been highly skeptical of the TPP because of decades-old quotas for domestic dairy, egg, and poultry farmers, saw a new urgency in trade reform – or at least trade negotiations once the nascent trading bloc began to take shape.[46] In particular, when the United States joined, and Japan expressed serious interest in the initiative, Canada recognized that it needed to be at the table to protect its economic interests.[47] The United States was Canada's most important trading partner. Meanwhile, Japan was Canada's fourth most important merchandise export market.[48] Not to mention, Japan accounted for 21.6 percent of Canada's meat exports in 2010.[49] Consequently, Canada quite literally couldn't afford to be left out of talks that could potentially alter its economic relationship with key partners. Nonetheless, several negotiating governments, skeptical of Canada's ultimate interests in abiding to all of the terms of the TPP, publicly expressed their desire to "see clear evidence of a matching commitment" by Canada "to attain a high-quality agreement across all chapters, including the most sensitive matters" before joining in negotiations.[50] As New Zealand's trade minister Tim Groser colorfully noted, "there is a very strict dress code involved and we are going to be stuffy and old fashioned in enforcing it. When our Leaders said 'eliminate' tariffs and other direct barriers to imports, they meant it." Canada, for its part, has meanwhile mentioned the tariffs as bargaining chips up for negotiation.

Whether or not the TPP will eventually win adoption is as of the writing of this book anybody's guess. TPP negotiators were given a tight deadline to hash out an agreement and success could depend on whether a reluctant (largely Republican) Congress grants President Obama (a Democrat) trade promotion authority. Nevertheless, as should by now be expected, the mere prospect of a TPP has increased incentives for non-participants to strike their own deals – especially the European Union. Indeed, Europe saw in the TPP an accord that could one day expand to include all of APEC, a regional forum for Asian economic cooperation, and possibly even China. It would also allow participants to take advantage of both lower tariffs and new business opportunities that first movers are in the best position to exploit when significant trade barriers are reduced. So matching again the United States, the EU concluded an accord with South Korea in 2011, and has been active in its own pan-Asian negotiations with Singapore, India, Indonesia, Malaysia, Japan, and Vietnam.

Furthermore, the TPP seems to have also helped spark interest in an EU-US trade agreement – which both historically and economically is a big deal. For decades, groups on both sides of the Atlantic have called for a U.S.-EU free trade agreement, but parochial interests and protectionism stymied serious efforts to make it happen. Now, however, both governments' pivots to Asia, along with stubbornly slow growth in Europe and the United States since 2008, have focused minds. Certainly the logic for an accord is strong: Most large European companies operate in the United States, and collectively European companies employ more Americans than any other country – just as U.S. multinationals employ more Europeans than even upstarts like Brazil and China. But plenty of impediments complicate transatlantic trade – from tariffs to conflicting governmental regulations – even when a company deals with its own affiliates. Removing these impediments, some economists predict, could add real growth to both EU and U.S. gross domestic product. With this in mind, and after a series of ministerial meetings between EU and US trade negotiators, President Barack Obama announced in 2013 America's intention of entering into a "Transatlantic Trade and Investment Partnership" (or TTIP) with the European Union. As with the TPP, negotiations are far from guaranteed – more due to persistent U.S. skepticism about liberalizing trade than intractable disagreements between negotiators on individual trade issues. But if successful, the pact would create the largest-ever bilateral trading bloc in terms of global GDP and commerce.

MANY-LATERALISMS

The fact that bargaining in small numbers can have big consequences for the global trading system does not answer the underlying question as to whether or not, from an economic standpoint, regionalism is better or worse than traditional multilateralism. Some economists, of course, view regionalism with disfavor. Liberalization is not, as it were, strictly "on the merits." Free trade isn't just free; it's also preferential, because not all countries are playing on a level field. Countries that hold competitive advantages in providing a particular service or in manufacturing a particular product won't necessarily offer the lowest prices, creating inefficiencies, or as Jagdish Bhagwati describes it, "termites," in the international trading system. Plus preferences create special interests that block future attempts to liberalize trade relations with other countries – both at the minilateral and multilateral levels.

But minilateralism can certainly prove to be an important stepping stone to broader multilateral cooperation. This is because countries' interests in trade are not fixed – a point often overlooked by economists and political scientists alike. Since Adam Smith, free trade proponents have envisioned countries as possessing relatively static natural advantages of climate and location, but in today's world, where technology is just as important as natural resources, that is no longer the case. Indeed, with proper planning and a little luck, a country can bounce up the economic value chain and compete with other, more developed countries. From this perspective, minilateral accords can be helpful tools in making the transition. Global agreements can be risky and difficult to evaluate, especially for a poor country concerned with the possibility that opening its doors to the world could wipe out its nascent local industries. But a minilateral accord with familiar trading partners is more likely to be able to bridge immediate circumstances with long-term competitive priorities. So even as regionalism creates inefficiencies, development itself will spark a greater interest in taking on the world through multilateral forums.

And even if you're a more traditional free trader seeking broad-based liberalization early on, minilateralism still impresses. In the real world, multilateralism is, despite its theoretical advantages, unlikely to achieve deep and consistent integration. Because it requires broad-based buy-in and consent, any member can, for whatever reason, prevent a rule from going global simply by objecting to it. So not surprisingly, when agreements are reached, they often include finely detailed (and innumerable) carve-outs and exceptions pasted to the back of trade deals in annexes, codes, and reservations. Thus even at the global level, trade deals can and often do introduce trade distortions of varying sizes and consequences as exceptions swallow rules.

By comparison, minilateral deals are often more comprehensive than their multilateral counterparts, even though they may not necessarily enjoy multilateralism's breadth of participation. The freedom to opt into minilateral arrangements allows any country – from the weakest to the strongest – to create its own trade relationships that depart from the universalist model reflected in the GATT and WTO. Of course, minilateralism isn't fail-safe. Indeed, even negotiations between small groups can and do regularly fail. But small groups have advantages over big ones, and allow individual countries to work with others that share overlapping interests, which can include everything from reducing trade barriers for greater efficiency to enhancing geopolitical stability and relations between neighboring countries (and even far flung ones). Plus you don't have to worry about pesky holdouts blocking widely shared consensus on key matters. Consequently, sticking points in multilateral negotiations, like tariffs, are routinely eliminated in regional free trade accords, just as bilateral agreements often liberalize trade relations even more so than regional pacts.

But the story doesn't end here. Once deals are made (or even the mere prospect of a deal arises), greed and fear kick in among trade ministries and political classes in countries that are not participating. Where any two or more countries defect from the multilateral system to make their own deal, the incentives for others to do the same rise. Outsiders try to lock in their own deals with the defectors, or among themselves, driving liberalization forward. One-upmanship, for its part, creates incentives for countries to cooperate in order for their firms to get better deals in prized markets. At the same time, the proliferation of accords creates pressures for fence-sitters and would-be free riders to actively negotiate trade deals in order to mitigate the possible trade diversion generated by other nations' cooperation. Countries have strong interests in avoiding being left out from or disadvantaged by liberalization taking place elsewhere. It's not a pretty process, but it gets results, sometimes dramatic, and at other times incremental – and almost always where the multilateral system cannot. And in some cases, it can be leveraged to generate ever wider coalitions for trade liberalization.

Minilateral trade as such presents a very different model for global trade when compared to the WTO-multilateralism of the postwar period. It is on the one hand built on choice – both of partners and the level of commitments any country ultimately undertakes. As such, minilateralism is a highly strategic mode of financial diplomacy. But it is also a system frequently infused with coercion. Big countries have more leverage to not only liberalize, but to also strategically protect their markets. Moreover, once trade agreements are struck, they can generate pressures for the innocent bystanders to opt into the fray of selective liberalization, either as participants or as promoters or founders of different alliances. These dynamics depart from the WTO's global rulemaking scheme. Although big economies have the most leverage, they must still extend to even the smallest countries the concessions they grant to larger and more powerful members. Everyone conceivably gets to benefit from any series of WTO pacts and negotiations. The pressure for alliances arises not when deals are struck, but when they aren't – and when members decide to go beyond the consensus reached under the WTO to secure even deeper levels of liberalization.

From this perspective, it shouldn't be surprising that despite the shortcomings of regionalism, interest in rolling back opportunities to play the numbers in trade have been paltry. It's safe to say that for most heads of state, regionalism presents an *opportunity*, not a problem, and for the most enthusiastic, a *solution* to the problem of stymied multilateralism. With the WTO's ever greater size and diversity, and the increasing complexity of trade relationships, the advantages of thinking small have never been greater.

That said, just how trade minilateralism will be practiced in the future is still very much up for grabs. Take the example of technical regulatory standards, one of the growing number of "non-tariff" barriers minilateral agreements are increasingly trying to tackle. Many goods, when traded across borders, face different regulatory regimes. A country that imports apples may require that all apples allowed across its borders be newly harvested, or treated with only a certain kind of pesticide. Or our nails discussed at the outset of the chapter may only be permitted to be sold in a particular country if authorities there can certify that the head of each nail has a certain diameter or shape. In principle, two or more countries may seek to harmonize these kinds of standards in order to simplify cross-border trade – indeed it is a subject both the European Union and the United States are actively considering in their recently proposed transatlantic trade accord. But if the group opts for exclusivity, they may end up undermining instead of promoting the very standards they are embracing. Why? Because countries left out of the deal may create their own regulatory clubs – and go so far as to adopt *weaker*, as opposed to stronger, standards. Environmental standards might be low, or manufacturing, agricultural, or labor rules loosely applied in order to attract foreign companies to large international trading areas with the promise of low regulatory burdens and costs.

It is thus conceivable that as trade negotiators tackle a broader array of impediments, multilateralism's core values of nondiscrimination will become more critical than ever. By keeping alliances open, and at least offering the potential of enhanced access to allied markets, minilateral trade alliances can spur nonparticipants to adopt higher standards. Closing clubs off, however, can drive nonparticipants to create clubs that potentially undermine high-quality social standards. Nondiscrimination can thus provide a powerful pragmatic tool for exporting policy preferences.

A full-scale reversion to WTO-led multilateralism is highly doubtful, however – even as the organization's values may come to have more pragmatic and strategic salience. Recentering the WTO as the focal point for global trade negotiations could still lead to the same bottle-necks that led to the slow, painful death of the Doha Round. Policies embodied in the TPP or TTIP would probably have little chance of becoming reality on the global negotiating stage, even though, as mini-lateral instruments, they might collectively impact 70 percent of world trade. Moreover, stricter WTO control over regional and bilateral deals could easily require unwinding existing deals and eliminating noncon-forming provisions, scaling back both the scope and depth of regional commitments.

Not surprisingly, WTO members have thus been reluctant to chal-lenge the legality of even those regional accords from which they are excluded or left out for fear of opening a Pandora's Box of international trade litigation that could ultimately unravel their own valuable trade deals.[51] Instead, minilateralism has remained an enduring feature of trade negotiations – and arguably its most important guise.

3

Soft Law in International Finance

Groups can help solve problems where holdouts stymie multilateral cooperation – and groups can be especially popular where allies don't have to share the benefits of their cooperation with others. Opting into groups won't solve all of the problems inhabiting international economic coordination, however. Some kinds of problems need and require everyone to chip in, and the lowest amount of effort put forward by one person determines the benefits or welfare for everyone else.

UCLA economist Jack Hirsheifer explored this particular kind of problem in a series of famous papers, in which he explored under what circumstances public goods like safety and security would be voluntarily provided by private individuals. Among his many important observations, Hirsheifer found that a particular subset of problems are of such a nature that all relevant stakeholders have to cooperate in order to address them effectively. Moreover, in order to achieve optimal results, everyone who is affected by the problem has to cooperate at a high level to address it. If just one person slacks off, that person can rob the entire group of the benefits that their cooperation is supposed to make possible. It's the Three Musketeers theory of economic cooperation: one for all, and all for one. Or else.

To illustrate his point, Hirsheifer invents Anarchia, which he describes as a low-lying island with a flat topography. On Anarchia, each inhabitant is required to pitch in and build a dike alongside owned property if he or she wants to prevent flooding. Together, the dikes provide protection against rising tides. The plan is simple enough, but here's the catch: in Anarchia, if any person fails to protect her property, or if any one dike turns out to be poorly constructed, the island could be completely flooded. The island's ultimate protection against flooding will thus be determined by the contribution and efforts of its laziest inhabitant, or the "weakest link." Small alliances of go-getters won't necessarily work – instead, everyone that owns property has to pitch in, cooperate, and build an effective dike.

Alliances may also be of little use where there is a lot of what can be described as "extreme" policy uncertainty. Groups, big or small, are hard to herd together where people do not know the consequences any particular policy route may have for financial markets, businesses, or the economy. In this kind of atmosphere, coming up with formal obligations can be tricky, if not downright impossible, no matter how many or few countries are negotiating. Finally, even in small groups, some agreements can take time to memorialize, and even after heads of state or trade representatives come up with agreements, it can take months and even years for legislatures to ratify them. In many countries, supermajorities are needed for agreements to become formal legal obligations of the state, leaving internationally negotiated accords in legal limbo for years until the political circumstances are right for politicians to consent to them.

International financial regulation has to navigate both hurdles. On the one hand, failure to regulate even smaller markets can upend the global financial system. Market disruptions in Greece, Cyprus, or Thailand can potentially infect economies worldwide. As a result, broad cooperation among supervisors of the world's financial centers is necessary for financial stability. At the same time, international financial regulation is plagued by plenty of uncertainty – what rules and regulatory proposals may mean for local financial systems, the competitiveness of domestic market participants, and the protection of investors. Markets are moreover constantly subject to change and innovation, making cross-border governance especially difficult to maintain.

To address these challenges, financial diplomats have veered from traditional economic multilateralism and instead relied on very different instruments to coordinate supervision and rule making. As with trade agreements, these kinds of accords aren't always global in scope, although they aspire to involve all countries whose markets are relevant (or "systemically important") to the regulatory task at hand. But what makes international financial agreements *really* special is how they are created and what they represent. Instead of binding treaty commitments ratified through legislatures and executives, regulators use explicitly nonbinding administrative accords to support cross-border regulatory action. Meanwhile, financial authorities don't convene meetings or promulgate rules via formal international organizations, but instead work through institutions with ambiguous legal status and arcane designations like the Basel Committee and Financial Stability Board. Yet despite their informality, these so-called soft law accords are charged with a serious mandate – to provide focal points for addressing highly technical and fast-moving problems that can undermine international financial markets and global prosperity.

International financial coordination nevertheless gets a bad rap from commentators. For some, it is ostensibly antidemocratic and avoids any semblance of political or legal legitimacy. Meanwhile, for others it seems useless or totally ineffective. What, after all, is the value of nonbinding international accords in the first place? In this chapter, we demystify the phenomenon.

FROM TRADE TO FINANCE: A TALE OF HYPER-GLOBALIZATION

International trade has captured both the attention and popular imagination of people around the world as new institutions have popped up to push the trade agenda forward in novel and unexpected ways. As we have seen in prior chapters, the GATT's evolution into the WTO has enhanced the international trade regime's legitimacy and importance, as new institutional organs sport unprecedented powers of adjudication and dispute resolution. And a new generation of regional agreements, starting with NAFTA, has helped achieve historic reductions in cross-border trade barriers that advocates have applauded – and which many dissidents to economic liberalization have ruefully lamented.

But arguably the most important developments in globalization have not really been in trade, but in the more obscure world of finance. Since the early 1980s, the world has experienced an unprecedented expansion of cross-border financial transactions. This phenomenon, routinely referred to as financial globalization, has reshaped the global economy such that the global trade in goods and services is now dwarfed by the size and volume of cross-border capital flows.

Three key developments have driven this escalation in cross-border capital flows: deregulation, technology, and financial innovation. The first factor, deregulation, was the key to making investment abroad even possible. Prior to the 1990s, many countries restricted foreign investors' ability to convert currency and expatriate profits. These restrictions made investing in their countries unattractive and costly. If you were a large American company, it was risky investing in, say, Brazil, if the country limited your ability to convert profits earned there into U.S. dollars or prohibited you from repatriating your profits back home for shareholders. In the 1990s, many countries sought to ramp up foreign investment in order to spur development, and a common course of action was to ease rules on currency convertibility, facilitating the ability to repatriate capital and in the process lowering the risk of investing inside their borders. Other additional reforms included helping "sophisticated" foreign firms invest in domestic capital markets, as well as raise capital, free of intrusive governmental interference.

The second big development has been the centuries-long evolution of technology epitomized by today's explosion in information technology. Foreign investment relies, in short, on timely and accurate information exchange, especially when capital is deployed over long distances. In the past, this was a major factor constraining cross-border investment. Consider, for example, the challenges of investing in a foreign stock exchange in the 1860s. If you were in New York and wanted to invest in the Marseille Bourse, you would have to worry about not only differences in custom and culture, but also about whether or not you had up-to-date information about the French stocks you owned. Bad news about one or more of the stocks in your portfolio could pop up, but take days to reach you. In the meantime, local investors in Marseille could sell the stocks before you would even get a whiff of what's happening. Distance thus made investing a lot riskier, adding to the cost of investing abroad.

Over the last century, and especially in the last two decades, technology has dramatically reduced some of these risks. The invention of the telegraph, followed by the eventual laying of the transatlantic telegraph cable in the 1860s, cut the time involved in long-distance communications and information gathering from weeks to a single day. The telephone and fax then reduced the time to minutes. Today the Internet allows nearly instantaneous transmission of information around the world. You don't have to remain in the dark about where your money is, or about how well your investments are doing. Investors can ask management questions, review up-to-date prices of stocks and bonds, and sell their holdings to far-flung counterparties, all on increasingly virtual facilities and via trading screens with little more than laptop computers. Money can flow anywhere, at any time, regardless of national origin and boundaries, and once-exotic foreign markets have been able to dramatically increase their attractiveness as destinations for capital.

Financial innovation has also worked over time to reduce the information asymmetries and risks of investing abroad. In the nineteenth century, at the height of the first great modern age of globalization, financial firms developed an intricate web of collaborative relationships and affiliated companies to channel investment flows across borders. Allied firms in a broad array of locales would help acquire information on investment opportunities for firms in London, as well as provide a "boots on the ground" judgment about the creditworthiness of borrowers for potential lenders. The seven leading London merchant banking houses each established a North American counterpart, for example, to execute deals locally and evaluate potential market and investment opportunities.[1] British insurance companies, meanwhile, channeled the savings of frugal English workers to invest in foreign stocks, and in the process acted as some of the first transatlantic middlemen. More recently, in this century, innovation has helped divvy up and reallocate risk in ways scarcely imaginable even a generation ago. With techniques like securitization, otherwise illiquid loans like real estate mortgages can be pooled locally and then sliced into new securities to be sold to investors anywhere in the world. Loans bundled in Idaho can be diced up and portions purchased by a commercial bank in India. Similarly, securities firms and banks can contract with one another to make future purchases of anything from bushels of apples to oil, and then trade the contracts on exchanges all over the world via cell phones and laptops.

Collectively, these developments have transformed capital markets in ways that have rendered financial globalization the most potent force in global economics. In the 1990s, while trade flows increased by 63 percent, gross capital flows surged 300 percent between advanced industrial countries. And while cross-border finance dipped after the 2008 crisis, by 2010 the stock of foreign investment assets reached $96 trillion, ten times levels in the 1990s, and international bank lending totaled $31 trillion, rivaling levels in 2007.[2] By virtually any measure, capital not only flows more easily across borders than goods or the provision of services, but also flows in greater amounts and with enormous implications for the health of national economies.

WHY DEMOCRATIZING CAPITAL ISN'T WITHOUT DOWNSIDES

For the most part, economists lauded these developments in the name and spirit of global growth. Interconnected financial markets, many argued, allow the world's savings to be directed toward their most productive uses, regardless of location. This development allows businesses and companies that would not otherwise have access to funding, given the limited resources of their home countries, to secure financing for growth. Furthermore, financial globalization has allowed for the diversification of risk. No longer are investors from one country precluded from investing in another, with the consequence that country-specific risk is diminished.

Yet during this same period, globalization has demonstrated – with ever more apparent consequences – that international finance is not without its own significant drawbacks. The highest profile challenges have been those related to financial crime. The same instruments that make international investment possible facilitate international fraud. Fraudsters from one country, for example, can solicit unwitting investors from thousands of miles away through telephone calls or email. Ponzi schemes, fake investment opportunities, and services can all be launched via the Internet into millions of homes.

Moreover, just as the distribution system for the sale of financial products has gone global, so have fraud and other deceptive practices. With today's information technology, fraudulent accounting statements, bankbooks, and investment prospectuses travel easily across borders – leading to an increasingly international array of victims. This isn't entirely a novel idea, and many people almost instinctively turn to the Enron and WorldCom scandals in the early 2000s as obvious illustrations of how accounting fraud can wreak havoc on global capital markets. But even individual acts of deception can have enormous international implications. Bernie Madoff's $65 billion Ponzi scheme cost Nomura Holdings, a Japanese company, $300 million; Union Bancair Privee, a Swiss private bank, $850 million; Banco Santander, a Spanish bank, $3.1 billion; and Benbassat & CIE, a Swiss private bank, $935 million. Meanwhile, 75 percent of Allen Stanford's (worthless) securities were sold to Latin American investors through offices in Venezuela, Colombia, Mexico, and Ecuador. The stakes were so large that when the fraud was discovered during the financial crisis, Venezuelan President Hugo Chavez was forced to announce that his government would back all losses in order to stymie an ensuing bank run. Stanford's fall from billionaire to prison inmate was only triggered when he was caught selling fake certificates of deposit from his offshore bank in Antigua.

Traditionally, when countries have faced financial instability or lapses in market integrity, they have resorted to regulating domestic actors that were potential troublemakers or sources of financial market risk. If banks were undercapitalized, national bank regulators would order local banks to raise more capital. If you saw fraud, or a heightened potential for it, you would enhance your disclosure and surveillance of domestic firms, and make arrests.

Under this territorial approach, entities operating in a designated geographic space (usually coterminous with national borders) and seeking to access that area's investors, capital, or market intermediaries are deemed subjects of regulation. For banks, this means that they become subject to regulation once they set up operations and take deposits from customers. In the case of securities law, territorial control arises when investors sell stocks or bonds to the public or make use of an infrastructure that physically exists in a particular jurisdiction (such as stock exchanges or other centralized trading venues). Once jurisdiction applies, certain regulatory requirements take effect. In the case of banks and insurance regulation, the consequence is that foreign banks must comply with capital reserve requirements and periodic examinations. And securities firms, along with issuers, must register with the host country's national securities regulator or, in the absence of a national regulator, with the relevant stock exchange authorities, meaning that periodic disclosures must be made.

Territoriality makes a lot of intuitive sense, and reflects long-standing international values that we saw in the early pages of this book. It inherently recognizes and embraces the principle that countries have authority over actions that take place within their borders. And by attaching to geographic proxies, such as deposit taking, stock exchanges, and the investing public, financial regulations can potentially exert a broad geographic coverage, and touch the lion's share of transactions that occur within a country's borders, as well as those consummated abroad but deemed to have substantial effects or implications for local stakeholders.

Globalization, however, makes this kind of control a lot harder. First, in an age of global markets, people can move and shuffle transactions to places that are subject to lighter scrutiny. You don't like local disclosure requirements? Raise capital abroad. Are your local banking regulations too stringent? Relocate your operations and expand credit elsewhere – or just route troublesome transactions through foreign affiliates. Obviously, this is a bit glib because mobility is not costless. For instance, companies may have to buy back their own shares in order to remove themselves from certain forms of regulatory oversight, close down local operations that might be profitable, or move staff from one country to another (or fire them and rehire new staff elsewhere). But it's not impossible, and the costs of this kind of arbitrage are decreasing by the day as technology continues to reduce the costs of moving goods, information, and people. Indeed, not only are service providers becoming mobile, *but so are the consumers of financial services*, as everyday retail investors and savers now routinely participate in overseas financial markets from the comfort of their own homes and laptops.

The ability of regulated entities to move abroad creates pressure for officials to mollify them, which can be considered the second big regulatory challenge posed by globalization. Special interest groups – from investment banks and securities firms to lawyers and accountants – along with elected officials want to have transactions consummated in their backyard. Big finance is a big deal. In London, the financial services sector employs more than 250,000 people. In addition to this direct employment, it has been estimated that the expenditures of London's financial services employees directly supports a further 400,000 jobs in the UK economy.[3] Meanwhile, New York City has in recent years boasted approximately 200,000 jobs in the securities industry alone, and nearly half a million jobs overall in the financial services industry. These jobs generate nearly 20 percent of New York State's tax revenue, and each new job created in the financial services industry creates two jobs outside the financial services industry.[4]

When deals and investments are executed overseas, however, opportunities to tax are dramatically reduced. High net worth individuals move abroad, and take with them tax revenue that could be used for bridges, schools, and pensions. Plus as financial centers become less wealthy, they lose their influence and reputations as desired locales. As a result, governments are often prepared to customize rules in ways to attract and keep market participants (and their money) in their territories. At times, this pressure can be useful, and can spur the reevaluation of what might be ultimately costly or inefficient rules. But it can also result in an unhelpful form of "regulatory competition," dismantling even efficient regulations that promote investor protection or financial stability. In such situations, a proverbial race to the bottom can again ensue, endangering not only investors but also the health of the international financial system.

Together, regulatory arbitrage and competition create seemingly unprecedented quandaries for international economic diplomacy. On the one hand, globalization forces officials and supervisors to regulate. Supervisors have to remain on top of fast-moving financial institutions and market participants in order to stave off fraud and bank runs, among a litany of other nasty problems. On the other hand, their hands are often tied if they want to act unilaterally. Mobility generates opportunities for governments to exploit one another's decisions, good and bad. This can be helpful insofar as it forces regulators to think twice about their rules and by extension, the costs of inefficient policies. If their rules are too onerous, people might conduct their financial affairs elsewhere. But it also creates incentives to placate powerful financial interests even in the face of systemic risk. The prospect of financial institutions running for the proverbial exit doors to foreign shores can scare officials into adopting weak standards.

Notice how this dynamic compares to what we've seen in trade. In trade, bottlenecks in global, multilateral negotiations have led to increasing competition for lower tariffs, which plays itself out in minilateral clubs and alliances. Meanwhile in finance, technology has enabled regulatory competition between financial centers and their supervisors. But the risks and rewards of competition in both sectors are not the same. Regulatory competition in trade generates what at least at the global level is widely regarded as net welfare benefits. For the most part, lower-cost providers of goods reduce costs for consumers. Jostling among financial authorities, by contrast, might generate better rules, but it can also facilitate fraud and even introduce massive financial instability. Moreover, just one weak link – like poor banking supervision in the United States, Spain, or Cyprus – can potentially undermine the entire global economy if its bad decisions spill over to the balance sheets of foreign financial institutions. This returns us to one of the point we saw at the outset of this chapter – that financial regulation requires broader forms of participation and cooperation than trade, even though there may be real incentives for countries to undercut one another for quick gains.

HOW STATES DON'T COOPERATE

Financial globalization thus makes broad-based, international engagement necessary since capital and mobile market participants can increasingly escape any one country's supervision. Countries need to cooperate in ways that both ensure efficiency and prevent the most important countries and jurisdictions from "defecting" to hazardous, low quality rules that can upend the global economy.

And indeed, financial authorities have responded to the challenge by creating an array of international forums and organizations aimed at promulgating cross-border standards, best practices, and prudential guidelines. Institution-building of this sort shouldn't be entirely surprising given the important role institutions can play as focal points for problem solving, a point we highlighted at the outset of this book. Global finance, perhaps more than all other sectors of the international economy, is constantly reinventing itself, with new products and distribution systems coming online every day. As a result, managing it requires continuous attention rather than one-shot solutions. Corralling ad hoc alliances to deal with regulatory problems as they arise is a similarly inefficient approach. Instead, institutions are required to help develop habits of cooperation and allow sustained attention to be brought to bear on financial regulation.

But before getting to just how it all works out in practice, let's start with what countries *don't* do to regulate international markets.

First, governments don't indulge in the classical model of public diplomacy that relies on "formal" international organizations to make cross-border rules. Besides occasionally being incorporated in a country in order to carry out its operations and own real estate for doing business, the institutions through which agreements are forged are for the most part highly informal. They don't usually tout any distinctly or widely recognizable international legal identity. Moreover, their organizational features are often ill defined. Procedural rules relating to how an organization should make international rules and standards or how voting should occur are, if they exist at all, for the most part ad hoc and posted nonchalantly to websites. Consensus decision making often dictates policy.

This is a big change from what has been the standard practice in foreign affairs. Traditionally, states interact with one another through organizations, such as the United Nations, World Bank, and IMF, that are themselves the product of formal treaties or articles of agreement between participating governments. In these organizations, countries delegate highly negotiated responsibilities and powers to an international body to pursue and to carry out specific duties. As such, international organizations are recognized under international law as international actors and enjoy their own independent legal personality that is distinct from their members.[5] They also tend to be highly structured, often with plenary bodies, an executive, and a professional staff of international civil servants.[6] Majority voting may also be common.

Another important departure from other traditional areas of international economic affairs is that in addition to eschewing fancy international organizations, countries don't memorialize agreements with one another as formal treaties or international obligations. Instead, virtually all of their agreements are *informal or explicitly nonbinding*. This is a big deal in part because international treaties have long occupied a special place in global economic affairs, and public international law more generally.[7] Part of their popularity lies in their overt democratic trappings: unlike customary law, where people effectively have to deduce the existence of international rules from the consistent practice of states, treaties often require approval by national legislatures. As a result, treaties are not only able to express commitments in more precise terms than customary international law, but they are also imbued with legitimacy insofar as they imply the "consent of the governed."[8] They are also explicit, and express in overt terms the preferences and commitments of parties.

Just as important, treaties seem naturally situated to tackle tough distributional challenges, as in trade, where some parties may seem to "win" more than others (or unexpectedly end up "losing") once the benefits from cooperation are carved up.[9] For one, treaties are universally recognized as formal international obligations. Thus failure to comply violates international law. Furthermore, treaties require significant levels of governmental participation, and often necessitate ratification processes involving both heads of state and legislatures. Thus, they not infrequently articulate promises made by multiple levels of government, which are then expected to be reciprocated by the relevant signatories to the agreements.

This is all-important because the legal and political significance of treaties can give them considerable disciplinary power. States may face considerable reputational costs if they ultimately fail to honor their treaty obligations. By failing, say, to afford some foreign goods MFN treatment after promising to do so in a trade agreement, governments send a signal that they can't always be trusted. They thus not only risk other governments rescinding their preferential treatment in turn, but if their backtracking is bad enough they can also gain reputations that hamper future prospects for cooperation with others. All else being equal, they will find it harder to secure agreements in the future.

Treaties can also help discipline behavior insofar as they tend to enable the creation of mechanisms that make non-compliance unattractive.[10] Because treaties require deep political commitments and often years of lengthy negotiations, participants often want to make sure signatories live up to their commitments. As a result, treaties are not only substantive; they can (and often do) create or enable the creation of institutional structures that penalize parties for breaking rules. Mechanisms can be introduced to better monitor parties and thus make it easier to identify and punish cheaters. Forums can be created to solve disputes between members as to the terms of the accord. And enforcement mechanisms can be devised to add to the "bite" or costs of noncompliance, such as measures permitting retaliation from aggrieved parties. In doing so, treaties can help establish new areas of supranational law.

As proof of this magic institution-building quality, people usually point to the WTO. As we saw earlier, the GATT evolved, through successive rounds of treaty negotiations, to include deeper substantive commitments aimed at tackling trade barriers and reducing the disparate treatment of imported goods. This evolutionary process culminated with the creation of the WTO in 1995, a true international organization with a distinct legal personality and an almost universal membership of nearly 150 countries. As well as enjoying the authority to interpret laws, it is equipped with more efficient and formalized disciplinary mechanisms than the GATT, where countries could block decisions and hamper compliance with member commitments. Perhaps most importantly, through its dispute panels, the WTO can authorize states harmed by rule violations to retaliate by suspending equivalent concessions otherwise enjoyed by the violating state. The WTO even sports an Appellate Body to oversee the work of the dispute panels and, when necessary, review their decisions in order to ensure consistent monitoring and enforcement of member-state commitments.

You don't see any of this in international finance, which has given heartburn to plenty of lawyers and policymakers. But the system is not as bad as one might think.

THE GUISES OF SOFT FINANCIAL LAW

Getting international trade and finance lawyers in the same room can be a trying experience, in part because they don't really speak the same language. Part of this is because of the nature of their fields. Trade law almost presupposes that government is the problem, as states create seemingly insanely inefficient barriers that choke off growth. Financial regulation, by contrast, sees government as a necessary partner in preventing crises and protecting investors in a world of intermittent market failure. But where they really talk past each other is when they inevitably start to talk about "international law." Trade lawyers, for their part, brag about the finely developed WTO and point to the "hard law" evoked by formal treaty commitments. International financial regulation, by contrast makes no pretense about being "real" international law – to the consternation of the international trade community.[11] Instead, they point rather freely to the fact that their accords are decidedly informal "soft law" commitments that are meant to direct the behavior of national financial authorities and supervisors. Then the trade lawyers frown, and the debate ensues about whether this is the right way to conduct international economic affairs.

Before jumping headfirst into the debate, it's useful to touch on just what we mean by soft law. Because of its informality and soft-law underpinnings, international financial regulation can assume several different guises that may not necessarily strike the average person as very legalistic. Nevertheless, its various permutations can still have wide reaching implications for the regulation of markets.

Overall, we can carve up the universe of international financial agreements into three basic categories. First, international financial law often takes the form of best practices, or rules of thumb, that promote sound regulatory supervision. Many times, best practices concern discrete issue areas, such as the amount of reserves banks should hold, or the kinds of disclosures companies should make to investors. They may be transmitted by coalitions of regional bodies consisting of public officials, as well as by private legislatures blessed by national authorities. However, in other instances, best practices have a broader scope, and outline in a general sense the things governments must do to bolster their financial systems, like enhancing crisis management and improving corporate governance. Particularly important in this regard are standards comprising "core principles" of regulation promulgated by each of the major international standard-setting bodies – the International

Organization of Securities Commissions (IOSCO) (for securities regulation), the Basel Committee on Banking Supervision (for banking), and the International Association of Insurance Supervisors (for insurance), as well as other standard setters. Instead of necessarily focusing on one specific topic, they provide an overview of what qualities or institutional features are necessary for sound supervisory and prudential oversight in a particular sector.

Best practices are also articulated through codes of conduct that function as primarily normative pronouncements concerning the ideal conduct not so much of regulatory officials, but of private parties. Codes of conduct promulgated by IOSCO prohibit, for example, certain forms of self-dealing among securities analysts, and, in other instances, work to remove conflicts of interest that often inhabit the operations of investment banks and credit ratings agencies. Although codes of conduct are aimed at private actors, and even more importantly, are not mandatory from a legal standpoint, they, similar to best practices, are guidelines with which national regulators overseeing their own domestic firms and institutions frequently comply. As such, they are of interest to both the private and public sector.

Although not necessarily the highest regulatory standards for all countries – in part because most states differ radically with regard to the market and regulatory challenges they face – best practices are generally described as comprising the minimum standards necessary for a healthy or "good" financial regulatory system. They thus exert a significant normative valence by dictating correct behavior. To the extent that a country falls short and fails to live up to best practices, there are grounds to suspect that its approach may be underdeveloped. Best practices also serve an instructive purpose insofar as they provide off-the-rack rules of good behavior, while still being broad and informal enough to provide flexibility in how they are implemented. Standards can thus be tailored to meet local needs and circumstances. A country searching for a better regulatory framework does not need to start from scratch. Instead, it can both learn from and expound on international best practices and guidelines that reflect broad, cross-border consensus.

Although rarely acknowledged as such, the data collected, assessed, and ultimately utilized by national regulators to craft policy serve as a second important form of international financial law. Reports create an official record of fact. At times, these records merely recount data; at others, they record official opinions and institutional perspectives as to financial data and their implications for the broader global economy. In either case, reports help establish a basis for policymaking, and often generate normative undercurrents that help define the appropriateness of different regulatory responses. They also, by extension, generate authority for policy responses. As a result, they have a distinctive role in the establishment of the international financial system. In the wake of the 2008 financial crisis, for example, a range of reports from international organizations offered retrospective analyses that identified causes of financial market disruptions or, conversely, attempted to identify future challenges. Meanwhile, other reports have centered on problems in existing regulatory approaches.

Reports also impact governance by helping to establish tacit commitments by national authorities to pursue certain policies. Where, for example, reports identify problems in existing regulatory approaches, sponsors of the document are at least implicitly sanctioning future efforts to devise solutions to help solve the problems discussed in the account. In this way, reports can serve as expressions of the limited consensus among regulators regarding the causes of emerging challenges even where agreement as to the responses may be lacking. Moreover, where reports identify certain regulatory practices as "bad" or inefficient, sponsors of the report are at least tacitly committing not to adopt such practices. In this way, reports take on covenant-like qualities insofar as signatories have wide discretion as to future actions, but are at least expected by one another (and often outsiders) not to engage in behavior contrary to or conflicting with the values or norms expressed in the reports. They are, for this reason, highly debated and negotiated instruments.

Finally, many international financial agreements spell out the procedural means by which greater information sharing and enforcement cooperation can be achieved. Information-sharing agreements, usually promulgated through Memoranda of Understanding (or MOUs), address at both regional and global levels the reality that many financial institutions are engaged in financial activities all across the world. As global actors, it is often difficult from a regulatory perspective to gain adequate information that might be relevant to assessing the risk exposures of banks or the possibility of transnational fraud or money laundering. Consequently, authorities of both banking and securities markets routinely enter into information-sharing agreements whereby national authorities commit to better coordination with one another in order to enhance their prudential oversight and monitoring at home.

Enforcement agreements, by contrast, spell out the terms by which different countries agree to provide one other with assistance in enforcing their domestic rules and obligations abroad.

ORIGINS OF THE SOFT-LAW SYSTEM

The international regulatory system has developed in fits and starts, giving rise to a fragmented architecture of financial oversight and supervision. That being said, most experts see the origins of the modern soft-law system of financial regulation springing from the failure of the Herstatt Bank in Cologne, Germany, in 1974. Just before its collapse, Herstatt was the thirty-fifth largest bank in Germany, with total assets of DM 2.07 billion at the time, and was active in the foreign exchange market.[12] But in September 1973, Herstatt's foreign exchange business suffered losses four times the amount of its capital because of an unanticipated appreciation of the U.S. dollar.[13] When the German banking authority discovered the loss during a routine audit, it withdrew Herstatt's banking license and ordered it into liquidation. This announcement then sent global markets into turmoil because prior to the announcement of Herstatt's closure, several of its counterparties in the United States had irrevocably paid deutsche marks through the German payment system expecting a return payment of U.S. dollars in the future. However, once the German authority's decision was announced, Herstatt's New York correspondent bank (as well as others) suspended Herstatt's account. The mess would end up roiling international markets, and spur calls for greater international coordination.

The Herstatt crisis was a jarring lesson for financial regulators in developed countries on the potential risks of global banking markets and the value of enhanced coordination. The crisis would coincide with a similar fiasco in the United States – the failure of the Franklin National Bank of New York in May 1974, which was at the time one of the twenty largest in the country. Like Herstatt, its failure would wreak havoc not only in the United States, but also on global Eurocurrency markets, exacerbating in effect the shock of the Herstatt collapse.[14] Regulators had no choice but to emerge from their previously insulated domestic jurisdictions and acknowledge the need for international regulatory cooperation. By the end of the year, central bank governors of what was the "Group of Ten" leading industrialized countries established a committee to address the pressing need for new and better rules for the global banking market. Housed at the Bank for International Settlements in

Basel, Switzerland, the Standing Committee on Banking Regulations and Supervisory Practices (now called the Basel Committee) took on the task of coordinating and harmonizing the prudential regulations of its member governments.[15]

At the same time, cooperative initiatives were gearing up in other sectors as well. The same forces that drove the internationalization of banking also drove forward the internationalization of securities and derivatives markets. Bretton Woods' collapse, along with financial and technological innovation, made markets more interconnected than they had ever been before.[16] This development in turn spurred a range of institutions to start thinking on a more global scale about how markets were structured. Accountants and auditors created their own cross-border guilds to better harmonize rules relating to how financial statements were prepared for investors. Meanwhile, securities regulators from North and South America established the Inter-American Association of Securities Commission to coordinate the supervision of stock markets and issuers of stocks and bonds, which was then relaunched as the International Organization of Securities Commissions (IOSCO) in 1986.[17]

Indeed, a range of acronym-laden clubs would pop up during the 1980s and 1990s – from the International Association of Insurance Supervisors (or "IAIS" for, not surprisingly, insurance) to the Financial Action Task Force (or "FATF" for money laundering) – as the pressure to collaborate on shared issues grew. Globalization not only brought markets together, but those who regulated them as well.

But these initial efforts were less ambitious than they appeared. The primary objective for most regulatory bodies was information sharing. Authorities were hoping, for the most part, just to figure out what their colleagues were doing in their respective jurisdictions, and to identify common points of regulatory interest. Conflicts in approaches across jurisdictions were also sought out and identified, although often for purposes of enhancing efficiency and trade and not so much for combatting regulatory arbitrage.

The big exception to this trend was the 1988 Basel Accord (or "Basel I" given its subsequent updates in the following two decades), a product of the Basel Committee. In one of the first concerted forms of international administrative rulemaking, banking regulators sought to create stringent, cross-border capital standards for multinational financial institutions. The effort was, at least initially, the product of UK and U.S. cooperation sparked by a spate of bank crises linked in part to poorly supervised lending to financial institutions scattered across Latin America.[18] To prevent their banks from making overly risky international bets, regulators in both jurisdictions initiated efforts to more tightly supervise their domestic banks and ensure that they were prudently managed. One of the central features of the reforms were tougher capital requirements for financial institutions. The idea was that the riskier a loan, the more money a bank should hold in reserve in case the loan ended up turning sour. That way, taxpayers wouldn't have to bail them out if their loans went bad.

Efforts to toughen global rules were, however, put at risk by Japanese banks that were moving overseas and eating into the market share of American and British financial institutions. Tougher domestic regulations had the prospect of making Japanese banks more attractive than international rivals, because with lighter rules – and less stringent capital charges on their loans – Japanese institutions could potentially earn higher profits. Fewer capital requirements meant that Japanese banks would be subject to fewer reserve requirements. This in turn meant they could lend out more money to borrowers, and thus increase their returns. Japanese banks could also offer their client depositors and borrowers more attractive rates given their lower regulatory requirements.

With such benefits at play, Japanese regulators balked at the prospect of following the UK-U.S. regulatory push, since it would diminish what had in effect become a competitive advantage for their banks. At the same time, American and British regulators feared letting Japanese banks go unregulated given the impact it could have on their own domestic banks. So after several frustrating rounds of negotiations with Japan in 1987, U.S. and UK regulators resorted to hardball negotiation tactics. The two countries decided to strike their own bilateral deal on capital standards, and then worked to multilateralize it by proposing it as a model for global capital standards at the Basel Committee. Then, as the final coup de grâce, the Bank of England and the Federal Reserve threatened Japanese banks with exclusion from Western markets if they didn't sign on to the agreement.[19] In the face of mounting pressure, and consensus on the need for stronger rules for banks, Japan eventually relented, handing the United Kingdom and the Federal Reserve one of their most famous victories in financial regulation.

The Basel I capital accord was – and still is – viewed as one of the marquis achievements in financial statecraft. It was, however, rather unique for its times, and nothing would come close to its significance for nearly a decade. The capital accord was born of a brief historical moment – when there was widespread interest in regulatory oversight and heightened concerns over what appeared to be an inexorable invasion of Japanese firms and companies abroad. For the most part, however, financial market regulation was still considered a largely domestic matter. So, all in all, regulators indulged in relatively few other big, prescriptive rulemaking maneuvers.

WHEN IN ASIA, DO AS THE IMF

The most significant steps toward broader international standard making would instead wait until 1997 and the outbreak of the Asian financial crisis. This is in some ways surprising because weak financial regulation was only one of several causes of the crisis, and not necessarily the most obvious. Still, weak financial regulation was an issue. Starting in the early 1990s, countries across the region opened the door to international markets – and capital – as part of broader reforms geared at modernizing their financial system. Moves to liberalize the cross-border flow of money, and increase domestic banks' access to international capital, were not, however, accompanied by better regulation of financial intermediaries. As foreign investors poured money into newly opened economies, cavalier domestic banks loaded up on speculative real estate investments without keeping enough cash in hand in the event that their bets went wrong. When bets in Thailand took a bad turn, speculators became concerned with the health of other countries in the region, and Malaysia and Indonesia's currencies cratered, tagged as being guilty by regional association. Lending froze across Southeast Asia, prompting multibillion-dollar IMF bailouts.

National regulatory agencies, along with international regulatory authorities like IOSCO and the Basel Committee, launched new initiatives to work toward preventing crises of the same sort from happening again in the future. First, a new institution, the Financial Stability Forum, was created with the purpose of identifying internationally accepted standards, which if adopted by countries, could help prevent financial crises. And second, a new program called the Standards and Codes Initiative was launched to develop and promote high quality rules of the road for international financial activities. The idea was to give what had been low-priority and often ad hoc best practices and regulatory guidance a new prescriptive edge.

To bolster the reforms, the Bretton Woods institutions were brought into the regulatory foray. Up to that point, the role of the IMF and World Bank in matters of financial market regulation was highly limited. As we saw earlier in the book, only the IMF was actively involved in market supervision. Article IV of the IMF's Articles of Agreement required that each member collaborate with the Fund and other members via surveillance to assure financial stability (or more precisely, "orderly exchange arrangements and to promote a stable system of exchange rates"). This meant the IMF would periodically assess and explore issues such as foreign direct investment, government spending and transparency, and exchange rate controls in the interest of economic management.

The new push toward codifying best practices would, however, move these surveillance activities squarely into the world of financial market regulation. Under the new reforms, the old Article IV examinations would be broadened to include inspections of members' financial market supervision and oversight. Second, a new financial sector assessment program (FSAP) would evaluate how the rules operated "on the ground" in countries at the domestic level. Intended to be more muscular, intrusive, and trenchant, the FSAP program would call on experts from the IMF and World Bank to parachute into countries such as Thailand or South Korea to examine for themselves the extent to which national regulators complied with internationally-agreed upon best practices. The results of the inspections would then be shared with the country under examination to help that country's policymakers identify the "strengths, vulnerabilities, and risks" of their financial systems and design appropriate policy responses.

There was also supposed to be some coercion behind the new system. Most important, the codes and standards being assessed under the FSAP were routinely incorporated into IMF and World Bank aid programs. In theory, this meant that if you wanted a World Bank loan for a power plant, then funding could be tied, however subtly or explicitly, to satisfying some of IOSCO's core principles for sound securities systems. Or if a government needed IMF assistance for a balance-of-payments crisis, it might have to comply with the Basel Committee's best practices or capital standards. In this way, standard-setting bodies became more than just advocates of good principles of government. Instead, they were elevated to sources of real regulatory authority.

The creation of a formalized surveillance system under the FSAP program thus represented a revolution of sorts. For the first time, prescriptive standards would be deployed to shore up weaknesses in financial systems. And just as important, countries experiencing economic and financial difficulties would face considerable pressure to adopt them.

But it was still far from a perfect arrangement. One of the biggest problems was that it was a largely voluntary model of global governance. Many countries didn't have to subject themselves to FSAP surveillance. Instead, only countries receiving aid from the IMF and World Bank were required to undertake assessments and apply international best practices. The rich world of donor countries largely escaped such annoyances. The double standard seemed self-explanatory at the time. For many experts, financial crises were problems of the developing world, and were of limited relevance for the West. Emerging markets like Mexico, Russia, and Southeast Asia periodically experienced crises, but countries like France, the United States, and Canada didn't. Instead, they were called to the rescue to bailout the troublemakers. So industrialized countries never believed it necessary to subject their own systems to the scrutiny of IMF bureaucrats. And few did.

FSAPs also suffered from what one could describe as an information problem. Although World Bank or IMF experts might camp out in countries for one to two weeks to interview officials about their regulatory systems and to examine the laws on the books of the countries being assessed, the data ultimately mined and used was of questionable quality. First, the raw data used for analysis was in many instances self-reported. The idea was in part efficiency-oriented, and geared toward getting information quickly from the party with the best access to it – the country whose regulatory system was being evaluated. But for the most part, it was to enhance the collaborative nature of the exercise, and make the process a little less intrusive. The problem, of course, was that the information could be compromised or manipulated. In the worst-case scenario, countries could misrepresent their systems. Or, less ominously, countries could simply lack the resources to carry out a meaningful assessment and analysis, in which case any information supplied might not accurately depict the level or nature of compliance with international regulatory standards.

Finally, even if you could ensure that the information received was reliable, there was no guarantee that the country undertaking an assessment would allow you to pass it on to others. Instead, information gained from the key IMF and World Bank surveillance mechanisms – observance reports, financial sector assessments, and surveys conducted by national regulators – could only be published or disseminated to other authorities at the consent of the assessed country. It has thus remained at a country's discretion whether to allow information regarding its compliance with international best standards to be shared with other domestic regulators or market participants. Having a choice meant that there was what statisticians would call an "adverse selection" problem. In short, countries that performed best would be the most inclined to tell the world about it, and those that did poorly would just quash any disclosure as to the strengths (or weaknesses) of their domestic financial systems.

A VERTICALLY INTEGRATED SYSTEM EMERGES

The 2008 crisis would humble Western policymakers and give new direction to the international surveillance system. Throughout the 2000s, the U.S. Federal Reserve Bank's ultra-low interest rates, along with large inflows of foreign capital seeking better yields in U.S. capital markets, had increased speculation in U.S. real estate in unprecedented ways. Lending to subprime borrowers – the riskiest category of borrowers that did not qualify for traditional loans – boomed. Through products like adjustable rate mortgages, borrowers enjoyed easy access to loans they couldn't afford, with many simply believing that they would be able to refinance their debt in the future when payments increased or became due. And lenders agreed, believing that the long-standing trend of appreciating housing prices would continue indefinitely and eventually allow even borrowers with questionable credit to increase their wealth seamlessly. Similar kinds of loans were used in other sectors, including credit card and auto loans, driving consumer debt skyward.

Fueling the lending spree was the popular technique of loan securitization. In essence, banks and other financial institutions that extended loans were not required to keep the debt on their books. The loans could be bundled, packaged, and sold off to investors. An important consequence of the "originate to distribute" model of banking was that lenders no longer had to concern themselves with the ultimate ability of borrowers to repay loans. Risks could be transferred from the originators of loans to the end purchasers of the securities, freeing up capital for a new round of origination and lending. Meanwhile, purchasers of the securities believed that securitization enabled greater portfolio diversification, reducing any concentration of risk. If enough subprime mortgages could be packaged together from different parts of the country, and different kinds of exposures generated from them, one could diversify holdings such that a substantial quantity of subprime mortgages

could enjoy AAA-rated prices, provided the correlation between mortgage defaults was low.

Eventually, investment banks, hedge funds, and other minimally regulated entities entered the financial real estate market as speculators.
Demand for mortgage-backed securities increased, and bonds tied to
the real estate market became more complex and exotic. Pooled investments were sliced into different tranches based on perceived levels of
risk in instruments called collateralized debt obligations (CDOs). Then
investors routinely entered into bilateral contracts, called credit default
swaps (CDSs) to minimize exposure on their investments. In those
contracts, one party (the protection buyer) would be entitled from the
other party (the protection seller) to the par value of the bond on which
the contract was made, should the third-party borrower default on its
payments. Eventually, even "synthetic" CDOs were created, based on
a portfolio of CDSs and other instruments, where two or more counterparties entered into payment obligations with respect to the underlying
referenced securities. The only problem was that the risk associated
with these kinds of deals received minimum scrutiny. Companies that
were packaging the deals off-loaded the risks to ill-informed investors.
And credit rating agencies, which were paid by the issuers of the securities, had little incentive to practice robust levels of due diligence.

With few checks, speculation involving such derivatives instruments
and complex securities took off because they seemed to be relatively
sure bets. Plus bets were increasingly easy to make. With the advent of
synthetic instruments, for example, traders no longer needed even to
originate new mortgage loans in order to wager as to their performance.
They could simply make an infinite number of bets on the bonds that
already existed, assuming investors were available on the other side
of the bet. Not surprisingly, both the number and value of financial
instruments tied to the housing market exploded – just as the real estate
market itself benefited from low interest rates and cheap financing.

In 2006 and 2007, however, interest rates began to rise, and housing prices started to drop, making refinancing more difficult. As house
values fell below outstanding balances on home mortgages, many hom-
eowners who had lost their jobs during the recession were forced to
default on their payments. When the housing bubble popped in 2008,
financial institutions reported major losses because of their borrowing against, and exposure to, subprime mortgage-backed securities
investments.

The firms that were first affected by the downturn were those directly involved in home construction finance and mortgage lending, such as the U.S. mortgage giant Countrywide Financial. More than one hundred mortgage lenders went bankrupt during 2007 and 2008 as the U.S. real estate market crashed. The crisis then spread as it became apparent that major banking and financial institutions all over the world also held large exposures of "toxic" assets tied to U.S. real estate. Huge swaths of the U.S. financial system failed, were bailed out through government-sponsored acquisitions, or were taken over by the government. The affected institutions included commercial banks such as Washington Mutual and Wachovia, investment banks such as Lehman Brothers, and brokerages such as Bear Stearns and Merrill Lynch. Government-sponsored entities such as Fannie Mae and Freddie Mac, as well as the insurance giant AIG (American International Group), were crippled. Across the globe, similar financial-market turmoil erupted as a result of bailouts required for Germany's Landesbanken, Belgium's Fortis and Dexia banks, the United Kingdom's Northern Rock, and many others exposed either directly or indirectly to the U.S. mortgage finance industry.

The crisis highlighted a series of gaps that pervaded not only national regulatory regimes, but also the greater corpus of international financial law. International regulatory forums like the Basel Committee and IOSCO had devoted very little time to thinking about securitization and mortgage-related securities, derivatives, shadow banking, or "too big to fail" institutions that increasingly dominated the financial systems of advanced industrial countries. Part of the problem was ideological – major industrialized countries viewed many newfangled financial innovations as mitigating risk instead of enhancing it. Plus up to that point, major countries had never themselves caused crises, but were instead the first responders when poorer countries found themselves in a financial bind.

As the international regulatory community realized that no one, not even the United States, was immune to the dangers of financial meltdowns, a new system for global coordination was devised along with an ambitious agenda for regulatory reform. In the most significant institutional step, the G-20 was named the world's premier economic forum, essentially displacing the G-7. Additionally, the Financial Stability *Forum* (FSF) was renamed the Financial Stability *Board* (FSB). This board was elevated to a kind of technocratic counterpart to the G-20

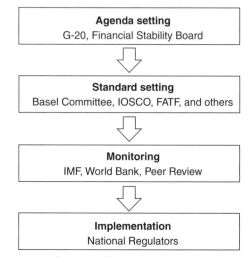

FIGURE 3. The vertically integrated regulatory process.

to aid in coordinating standard-setting activities of different regulatory agencies and to ensure that complex, interdisciplinary topics didn't fall through the cracks of different organizations' mandates.

Together, the two institutions would more aggressively direct standard-setting processes and work streams, as well as coordinate between what had been rather disparate and disconnected standard-setting bodies. In this way, what was a somewhat disjointed system was vertically integrated under G-20/FSB leadership, and took direction from it. Meanwhile, the Basel Committee, IOSCO, and other forums for accountants, auditors, and insurance regulators, would write new rules for banks under a new-generation "Basel III" Accord, as well as articulate a slew of new standards for reregulating the financial industry writ large. Yet as before, these rules would not be memorialized as treaties, but as informal best practices, observations, reports, and information-sharing exercises between regulators.

Finally, to support the newly integrated system of rulemaking, surveillance was ramped up. The IMF and the FSB required FSAPs as part of their members' obligations, and would even require to varying degrees publication of their results. Additionally, the FSB launched a series of "thematic" and "country" peer reviews to take stock of existing practices in particular policy areas and focus on the progress made by individual FSB members' jurisdictions in implementing FSAP regulatory and supervisory recommendations. Similarly, the Basel Committee, IOSCO, and other standard setters refined and revamped their own in-house surveillance systems to better track and identify implementation of best practices by their members.

THE PROBLEM OF MAKING COMMITMENTS STICK

Soft law has a number of features that make it an extremely attractive instrument of international coordination. Perhaps most important is that it can be done quickly and efficiently. In contrast to treaty making, which often entails months – if not years – of negotiation between heads of state or their representatives, soft law provides a decisively easier means of agreement making because it does not require extensive participation by heads of state or lengthy ratification procedures. Instead, agreements can be entered into between administrative agencies and technocrats with relatively little political involvement. Parties can also, because of the flexibility afforded by soft law, amend accords relatively easily, with few procedural hurdles. Because they're not real obligations under international law, parties retain the flexibility to avoid unpleasant surprises if the consequences of pursuing a particular course of action turn out to be less than beneficial.

But in order for soft law to effectively facilitate cooperation among regulatory agencies, all parties concerned need some assurance that everyone will perform their obligations in a reasonable and comprehensive manner. Indeed, for this reason, some political leaders, academics, and journalists tend to prefer more formalized agreements with enforcement mechanisms.[20] Yet soft law is, by its nature, informal. And as such, it doesn't display the overt sanctioning and coercion that one might see where, for example, a country ignores some of its trade commitments or where an embargo is imposed on a despotic ruler. This rankles many people who want a robust financial system. For these critics, the same features that make soft law attractive also make it problematic. Rules are only as useful as they are observed. Where rules can be regularly flouted by governments, or when parties don't follow through with their commitments to obey agreed upon rules, "law" becomes a lot less "legal." And a financial system without rules can look pretty scary – and dangerous.

Advocates of cross-border financial regulation have not spent a ton of time considering the degree to which the absence of formality impacts financial stability. And it shouldn't be surprising. After all, the driving force behind international financial regulation is the realization that regulatory lapses in one jurisdiction – going back to Hirsheifer's example of Anarchia – can have spillovers that can imperil the prosperity and growth in the others. Global cooperation is a bulwark against such lapses. Banks and depositors can be assured that foreign financial institutions have met capital adequacy requirements and manage risks properly; meanwhile, investors participating in foreign markets can be assured that the foreign firms in which they are investing are making adequate and accurate disclosures. International financial regulation is, along these lines, a win-win. There is no need to police compliance, so legalization is of little relevance.

The problem with this assumption is that it overlooks the difficult trade-offs and distributive problems that can stymie lasting coordination.[21] Adopting common, cross-border standards can be a tough business. Because of history, culture, and custom, countries have vastly different starting points for the kinds of regulations they have in place and what they would prefer. Effective compliance with some standards could require more adjustments than complying with others. Countries with already stringent rules on their books will find the adoption of a strict international standard to be less costly than would a country with weak standards in place. In the country with the weaker standards, a range of adjustments may have to take place: the domestic regulatory architecture may have to be revised, shifting the balance of power between administrators and politicians. Or switching could require scarce resources to be allocated to enforcement activities where they might otherwise be put into other government functions, such as education or social welfare. Or, even more likely, local firms might have to bear higher compliance costs, such as hiring lawyers, auditors, and accountants to help guide them to the new, stricter standard. In the process, the adoption of new rules could undermine a country's ability to attract certain kinds of capital and financial transactions.

Plus if you think reaching an agreement can be hard, imagine how hard it is to maintain one without some kind of enforcement mechanism. From a bird's-eye view, international regulatory policymaking is pretty straightforward: politicos come up with agendas, regulators work through technocratic forums to set standards, and then after coming up with an agreement, they implement it at home. The way things get done, however, is rarely so easy. International standard setting and implementation constitute a deeply dynamic process. New information may arise that can cause countries to backtrack or ignore earlier commitments. A state may, for example, recognize an opportunity to attract new business or transactions to its borders by offering less onerous disclosure requirements. Or implementing a particular standard may turn out to be more costly (economically or politically) than authorities that committed to the standard originally expected. Resources may have to be diverted to regulatory activities that are more valued by legislators or the general population, or the volume of financial transactions taking place in a country may unexpectedly suffer after entering into a particular international regime that imposes certain kinds of limitations on securities firms or banking institutions. To avoid these costs, they may choose not to fully implement or operationalize the relevant best practices.

A system of international financial regulation thus requires some kind of disciplinary mechanism in order to make it effective. Without discipline – some way of ensuring that countries internalize at least some of the costs of reneging – the international system can descend into chaos as countries indulge themselves in all kinds of opportunistic behavior. After all, leaders have long held, as Machiavelli did in the sixteenth century, that a "prudent ruler cannot keep his word, nor should he, where such fidelity would damage him."[22] And there would be plenty of ways for the (im)prudent financial supervisor to backtrack and break his (or her) word. For instance, he could cherry-pick certain aspects of international agreements without embracing them comprehensively. So if a particular global agreement contains fifteen best practices, a ruler could choose to comply with only those that promote his own competitive position or financial market strength. Or he could just lie about adopting a rule by embracing it in public, and then under-enforce it at home.

So what then are the disciplines for the informal system of international financial governance? To be sure, "discipline" and "informality," at least at first blush, seem mutually exclusive. Indeed, when international lawyers talk about discipline, most usually have in mind punishment by international police or military forces, or through trade embargoes – something that can literally force an individual or state into acting a particular way or in accordance with an international obligation. International financial regulation operates differently, however. For one, you don't send in the tanks. And trade embargoes of the traditional sort have very limited applicability. Instead, other tools are relied on to generate compliance, tools that can, though do not necessarily, rely on state-run, top-down systems of coercion.

THE POWER OF REPUTATION, AND REPUTATIONAL CAPITAL

One important tool is reputation. Simply put, when a country makes a promise to do something, pressures related to its perception in the international community can arise that motivate it to follow through, even when doing so may bring few tangible benefits. Why? Because not following through on promises or obligations makes a country less trustworthy. If one government makes a promise to another government, reneges, and then needs to cooperate with that country in the future, it may have to expend more resources convincing the country that its promises are credible. Its tarnished reputation makes future cooperation and alliance building more costly.

That being said, just what reputation means in international finance is a bit tricky, because most agreements are explicitly nonbinding. As we have seen, they're not treaties of any sort, but instead communiqués, reports, MOUs, and declarations by various forums and networks of experts and policymakers. So the question is, what are the reputational consequences of not following through on such less-than-legal arrangements? Do violations of soft law hold reputational consequences?

Many international lawyers are dubious. For some, commitments can't be made in the absence of any international legal obligation. So any reputational disciplines, they surmise, must be weak. These conclusions often miss the mark, however, because they overstate the importance of legality, especially as it relates to the coerciveness or compliance pull of international financial rules. It turns out that even though international financial regulation is pretty informal, it can still express a wide variety of commitments, strong and weak. As one might suspect, in many cases, commitments may not be too serious. Cloaked in nonbinding, informal documents, soft law can be a great way to hedge bets, articulate tentative understandings, or make general observations about the global economy or emerging problems. And as such, soft commitments may just serve as way stations to more elaborate or formal regimes in the future.

But in other circumstances, even soft law can be quite serious – and hard. To understand why, it's important to emphasize that regulatory agencies like the SEC and Federal Reserve often take the pole position in hammering out international agreements relating to the supervision of financial markets. These agencies tend to be smaller and nimbler than foreign ministries; moreover, they tend to have the expertise to deal with difficult technical issues and advance complex policy proposals. But as bureaucrats, and not heads of state or elected politicians, regulators have limited powers in international affairs. They do not draft financial regulation treaties for execution by legislatures and the executive. And even if they could, for most countries the time required to negotiate a treaty and then ratify it would not keep pace with the dynamism of financial markets in which new products and services are being constantly devised and invented. Substantive formal agreements would consequently have limited practical value.

So at least in finance, soft law is often as much a necessity as it is a choice. Complex markets require technocratic competence, and financial authorities need to be able to talk with one another and express their preferences, intentions, and commitments in ways that are more flexible than treaties. Soft law meets these demands through MOUs, codes of conduct, and best practices. Even in analytical reports and studies, countries may implicitly articulate a range of commitments or beliefs as to what kind of behavior is optimal or desired.

Promises made through these kinds of devices need not be hollow. Indeed, there can be real costs if a regulator makes a commitment and then later fails to follow through on its promises. This might especially be the case where one party's backtracking causes harm or problems for another. Imagine, for example, a situation where two regulators sign an MOU in which both agree to help one another solve crimes or address violations of one another's financial laws. Technically, the terms may lack any binding effect. But if a regulator fails to live up to commitments it made to provide assistance – by, say, neglecting to provide its counterpart with access to witnesses or evidence that may be located in its home territory – its partner pays the price. It won't be able to prosecute an offense as effectively as it anticipated. Backtracking from or noncompliance with agreed-upon protocols in such circumstances can lead to reputational consequences that can cause would-be allies to rethink or reevaluate their expectations concerning the regulator's future behavior. It can also undermine their incentives to cooperate with the regulator in the future, when and if it makes similar requests for assistance.

The failure to comply with internationally agreed-upon standards can also create reputational costs for governments – and private actors. As with enforcement cooperation, a failure to adopt or implement standards can undermine a government's reputation as an honest or reliable partner. This is more than a problem for national pride. A tarnished reputation makes it more difficult for a country's officials to convince others to change behavior in ways that they would like, or to credibly commit to new standards and accords. It also impacts a country's capacity for economic statecraft as governments find it harder to promote their own policy preferences or act as opinion leaders among their peers.

Backtracking on commitments can also impact market participants in surprising ways. International financial regulation is not like other areas of international law, such as human rights or environmental law, that often rely on the goodwill of countries to comply. Instead, it is mediated at least in part through capital markets and investors. This is important because under the right circumstances, markets can provide important incentives for adhering to high quality international financial standards. How? Assuming they are properly informed, investors will reward a firm for adhering to practices that are perceived to make the firm more profitable. The converse is true, too: capital markets will, as a general matter, penalize firms that stray from behaviors that are perceived to maximize a company's returns. So to the extent to which investors believe that international regulatory standards are good – and enhance the returns of firms or the protection of their interests – they will punish firms that fail to abide by them.

Another example can help make this point clearer. Let's suppose you have two firms, A and B, which are both seeking to raise capital by selling their stocks to investors. Imagine further that firm A is operating in a jurisdiction where local officials require companies to provide very high levels of disclosure to investors, and that failure to disclose material information – such as annual financial statements, information about key officials, and the company's business strategy – can lead to serious sanctions. Firm B, meanwhile, operates in a jurisdiction that only requires very minimal levels of disclosure, and enforcement of even these standards by local officials is weak. Which would you be more inclined to invest in? I'd wager the first would be more attractive to you, all else being equal. And you'd probably command a little extra from firm B – in the form of a lower stock price – given the additional risk accompanying the poor disclosure.

One of the more interesting features of international financial law is that it can operate in this way even when countries have not necessarily committed to a particular regulatory regime. Just because a country hasn't committed to an international banking standard doesn't mean that it has no practical relevance to its local banks. Indeed, market participants frequently perceive adherence to major international standards as a mark of good regulatory practice. Academics have long suggested that in order to lower their costs of capital some firms seek to become subject to the laws and supervision of major financial centers (and especially the United States) so that they can signal to investors throughout the world that they abide by strong disclosure and corporate governance practices. Similar market disciplines can inform behavior in other areas as well. Banks, for example, and even some insurance companies, often seek to adopt the Basel Committee's capital standards to signal that they are solvent and well capitalized, as well as to signal to investors that they meet the most stringent regulatory oversight. Moreover, where firms ignore or do not comply with well-regarded international standards, investment analysts will at times attempt to evaluate the risk embodied by the compliance gap – even where firms are still abiding by (less rigorous) national hard-law obligations. Of course, this doesn't mean that investors always agree with the law. Indeed, what precisely constitutes efficient rules or standards is often debatable, even among investors. But international standards can matter, regardless of a government's commitment.

TATTLETALE DIPLOMACY

Alongside reputational and market disciplines, particularly egregious instances of noncompliance with international standards can trigger sanctions by and from international organizations and financial institutions. We've already seen how this operates with IMF and World Bank conditionality, where financial assistance itself can depend in part on adherence to strong international standards. But standard-setting bodies can create their own pressures, too. Most obviously, they can set up rules of good standing. Important countries can create clubs with high membership standards. If you don't live up to the rules, you can't join the club, or if you're already a member, you may risk expulsion. Either way, you don't get to enjoy the club's benefits, and you risk losing voice and prominence in the international community.

Still, these are potentially drastic remedies. If you exclude members, you risk alienating them and finding yourself unable to call on them to cooperate. And that itself can be a source of systemic risk. So, not surprisingly, regulators have resorted to other institutional means of pushing countries into compliance. By far the most important is to "name and shame" stragglers who either refuse to adopt, or grossly delay adopting, best practices. Instead of relying on regulators to build reputations, and waiting on market participants to make their own judgments about the value of particular regulations, countries have decided to speed up the process by not only disclosing compliance to the public, but also combining it with some form of official opprobrium by the institution.

Perhaps the most famous form of name and shame in finance is that practiced by the Financial Action Task Force (FATF). Throughout the 1980s, regulators noticed a spike in cross-border drug trafficking and money laundering. Conscious of what up to that point had been a largely national means of bank and judicial oversight, efforts were ramped up to improve international cooperation in what was an escalating war on drugs. In 1988, the Basel Committee released its Statement of Principles on Money Laundering, urging banks to put into practice better procedures for combating money laundering and cooperating with regulators; and in the same year the UN Vienna Convention Against Illicit Traffic in Narcotic Drugs and Psychotropic Substances was drafted and signed, obligating parties to criminalize and extradite money laundering and to cooperate on international enforcement. Yet despite these measures, by 1990 only six countries had adopted strict money-laundering statutes requiring banks to improve information gathering associated with organized crime and to share that information with authorities.

Progress was slow because not all countries had an interest in promoting tighter anti–money-laundering policies – especially so-called offshore financial centers that attracted capital to their shores by offering secrecy and lax regulatory oversight. For them, tougher regulations could ruin their economy. With few other competitive advantages, countries concluded that the forced feeding of stricter international best practices held the prospect of making them significantly less attractive destinations for clients (including legally questionable enterprises) seeking discretion and ease of doing business. As a result, these countries were strongly inclined not to cooperate in anti–money-laundering efforts, and some actively resisted them.

To respond to this challenge, the G-7 announced the launch of the FATF at a summit in 1989 and called on it to take more concentrated and aggressive action in the sector. In 1990, the FATF issued a report, referred to as the Forty Recommendations, which outlined steps to be taken to combat money laundering. Over the next decade, additional standards were devised to identify countries that were failing to adopt international standards and not cooperating with the international community in the fight against illegal financing. The resulting "blacklist" – a term that quickly gained currency to describe the FATF's list of identified countries – would then eventually be made public and shared with domestic financial institutions. It was even used as the basis for possible capital market sanctions against firms based in weak regulatory jurisdictions.

Blacklisting evolved in part from an approach taken with Turkey in 1996. There, the FATF saw one of its own members refuse to pass legislation criminalizing money laundering or adhere to the group's primary legislation, the Forty Recommendations. After nearly five years of relatively subtle negotiation aimed at getting the country to reverse course, the organization opted for a more aggressive approach and issued a press release that, among other things, instructed banks and other financial institutions to scrutinize capital market transactions with Turkish businesses and individuals. In response to the public rebuke, the country instituted new money-laundering regulations just months later.

The idea behind name and shame is simple. By identifying noncompliance and also making public a country's intent not to cooperate, the technique heightens the potential reputational consequences of nonobservance of particular standards. Purposeful nonobservance, when it occurs, is a sign of the (implicitly nefarious) regulatory preferences of a particular country. Regulators in the identified jurisdiction are thus publicly ostracized and isolated from the members of the organization publishing the list. Additionally, by doing such shaming publicly, regulators are able to potentially sharpen the market consequences of noncompliance. Market actors, in short, can take cues from the emphatic expressions of disapproval from regulators, for instance, that a particular country presents special risks or dangers to the stability of the financial system.

Since starting up, the FATF program has published several name and shame lists. The most extensive list came out in June 2000, when fifteen countries were identified as uncooperative in the fight against money laundering. Another high-profile list, with eight additional countries, was published the following year. In all, more than a half dozen annual reviews of Non-cooperative Countries and Territories (NCCT) have been conducted (not always resulting in a new list), and the exercise has largely been hailed as effective. Noted political scientist Dan Drezner has reported that of the fifteen countries identified, four acquiesced completely to the FATF, passed all of the anti–money-laundering laws, and staffed the requisite agencies to implement them; another seven made significant concessions; and three passed laws that responded sufficiently to the forum's demands to avoid more significant sanctions.

Since then, the FATF's naming and shaming, as well as the prospect of reputational consequences, has been used to exert pressure on a wide array of countries – even the Vatican.

THE DREAM OF AN INTERNATIONAL FINANCIAL COURT

Transparent governments are, to be sure, usually the most accountable ones. When market participants get to observe the decisions made by foreign governments, they are better positioned to price the risks and rewards of cross-border investments. Transparency also helps with diplomacy. It makes it harder for governments to backtrack on commitments to adhere to international best practices. Where backtracking can be identified, international forums and bodies promulgating standards are better equipped to impose membership penalties and even sanctions on bad actors. Consequently, soft law can, under the right circumstances, have its hard edges: the mere prospect of reputational costs, higher costs of capital for firms, and exclusion from important standard-setting forums can all push financial authorities to raise standards. Indeed, the simple availability of transparency mechanisms can incentivize firms to voluntarily adopt or comply with international best practices, even when their home regulators may not formally require them to do so.

Discipline of this sort is not without its precedents, as students of legal history and philosophy will notice. In some ways, it approximates in an international setting the famous penological design known as the "panopticon," an eighteenth-century prison model made famous by the English utilitarian philosopher Jeremy Bentham, and later by Michel Foucault.[23] In this kind of prison, the guards on duty were hidden from the inmates, and as a result prisoners never knew exactly when they were being watched. This created an enormous amount of discipline among prisoners, since the very prospect of surveillance made them behave as if they were. Inmates were always conscious of their visibility, creating "the automatic functioning of power."[24] Without knowing when they were being observed, inmates were forced to obey the rules of the prison and not attempt escape, even where in fact no guard was watching.

In considerably less dramatic fashion, regulators, too, find themselves increasingly subject to the gaze of the many – including other regulators, international standard-setting bodies, the Bretton Woods institutions, and even private market participants. Whether acting alone or in interdisciplinary cross-border networks, these institutions extract and reveal information about a country's financial behavior through both formal (institutional) and informal (market) processes. And as with the panopticon, the new international regulatory system is designed, at least in part, to generate consciousness of surveillance. Governments know that they are occasionally subject to observance, and face the threat of higher costs of capital, a damaged reputation, and lost standing in the international regulatory community. Thus even modest soft-law instruments can, at least under the right circumstances, affect the behavior of the governments, and by extension, the operation of the global financial system.

For policymakers, the crucial question is whether the existing institutional backdrop provides sufficient incentives for international regulators and firms to hew to international best practices. In this regard perhaps the biggest challenge has been the absence of a formal dispute resolution mechanism. Unlike many – but not all – areas of more formal international economic law, there is no means of systematically solving cross-border regulatory disputes once they arise. Instead, as we have seen, problem solving relies on a combination of shaming, market discipline, and institutional threats, and ad hoc negotiations between regulatory agencies and other financial authorities.

This creates considerable uncertainty in international financial law. Unlike the WTO, where special panels resolve disputes between members and in the process fill in gaps and clarify ambiguities arising under treaties, there is no universally acknowledged forum for countries seeking to bring grievances publicly against one another. Instead, the World Bank and IMF occasionally conduct compliance assessments of (often cash strapped) governments. And even here, there are informational deficiencies, and neither institution holds a monopoly on surveillance activities. Instead, as we've discussed, standard-setting organizations are increasingly conducting their own independent peer reviews of their members' compliance with best practices, creating multiple, overlapping systems of surveillance.

In theory, a dispute resolution regime would clear the disaggregated clutter from today's rulemaking. At its strongest, it would provide a focal point for handling disagreements between financial authorities on regulatory policies that have been outlined with only a broad brush and without specificity at the international level.[25] It also introduces the possibility of a more highly institutionalized enforcement regime. In international trade and investment, dispute panels enjoy a variety of tools to directly sanction members who fail to live up to their decisions. No such mechanisms exist in international financial regulation, however. When regulators decide not to adopt, implement, or enforce best practices, the disciplines they face are often indirect. Markets and political wrangling operate in lieu of third-party rule-based analysis, although with unpredictable and at times suboptimal outcomes. The creation of an international body with the power to rule on regulatory behavior and compel certain actions through the imposition of sanctions of some sort is thus a seductive prospect for any reformer of the international regulatory system.

Whether or not an international financial court would be at all possible is, however, another matter altogether. After all, getting an international court or panel of experts up and running – with the power to rule on the regulatory conduct of sovereign states – is no easy feat. Just setting one up requires a range of difficult steps. Institutionally, you would have to think through a range of basic but important questions. Where will disputes be resolved? Who will decide, and on the basis of what rules? How will panels rule on soft law? What will be the legal effect of their rulings? And how will they be enforced?

Then, once you have a game plan, you have to try to sell it to other countries, a task easier said than done. Nobody likes creating international courts and dispute panels. Courts by definition limit the flexibility of governments to ignore standards. They monitor compliance with international standards, and when governments don't comply they point it out for all to see and potentially order penalties of some sort to be imposed as well.

Furthermore, there is also no guarantee that courts will always, or even usually, get their decisions right. International financial rules and principles are often very broad. This speaks in part to the difficulty of creating one set of rules for countries with very different financial and legal systems. Every once in a while, you have to pitch principles at a 10,000-foot level in order to speak to the heterogeneity in existing approaches and to get consensus among very different regulators. Furthermore, rules are pitched broadly to provide policymakers with the discretion and flexibility to tailor those best practices to local market participants and to existing circumstances, such as the amount of risk built up in a country's financial system and where in the economic cycle a country finds itself. In times of economic distress, for example, more permissive rules may be smart policy for cash-strapped banks and firms, whereas in times of high growth, stricter standards may be more appropriate to prevent undue risk taking. Finding a regime that can accommodate the cyclicality of economics and regulation – and that can still apply rules across countries at different stages of development – seems for most experts quixotic, at best. And rolling the dice on a panel of experts to make wise decisions relating to such circumstances seems too risky for most political leaders. A full-throttled delegation of the kind we see in trade thus remains highly unlikely.

SUNSHINE RULES

With so many practical difficulties, it's probably not surprising that regulators have focused on improving those tools that they already have at their disposal in order to combat systemic risk. And in this regard, bolstering existing surveillance capacities has been a priority.

Perhaps one of the worst kept secrets prior to the financial crisis was that monitoring compliance with international standards was far from robust. We've seen that prior to 2008, responsibility for monitoring international best standards was primarily the responsibility of the IMF and World Bank. In addition, the data provided to international institutions was often voluntary and self-reported by national authorities. Since 2008, however, things have changed a good deal. Members of the G-20, FSB, and IMF have all committed in various ways to undertake FSAP assessments. Moreover, individual standard-setting bodies – from the FATF to IOSCO and the FSB – have also launched or bolstered their own in-house monitoring activities and peer review systems for their own members.

Just ramping up surveillance won't be a silver bullet for all of the financial system's regulatory ills, however. Smart choices have to be made about what kinds of standards should be observed. Right now, the codes and standards forming the basis of international financial regulation are strewn across nearly a dozen publications, each with potentially dozens of different, more granular standards that, depending on their nature, can be supplemented by various methodologies and prescriptive guidance. The Basel Committee, for example, publishes an annual report, a quarterly report, and various committee publications, of which the Basel Accord is just one. And peppering the pages of the Basel Accord are complex formulas for measuring the capital and risk of banks. With so many standards, an extraordinary amount of resources has to be devoted to enhancing transparency in order to make the system effective. And surveillance beyond governments can still be rather poor, especially with regard to the stress-testing of financial firms themselves.

So there is still plenty of work to do if regulators really want to optimize the minilateral system of financial market regulation. A good place to start is to direct surveillance to where it's most needed. Regulators should emphasize those rules and standards that will contribute most to financial stability. Then, once standards are prioritized, surveillance should involve more than just looking at the statutes on the books of countries and determining how they relate to potentially complex international best practices. Instead, monitors should become thoroughly familiar with the financial and regulatory systems of the countries they are inspecting, a task that in most cases will require more than weeklong visits by foreign regulators parachuting into countries for talks with local regulators. Relevant information from financial institutions must be culled and then assessed in order to determine to what extent rules on the books have been translated into action on the ground.

Transparency also means making information useful and useable. FSAPs, similar to many in-house peer reviews conducted by standard-setting bodies themselves, are all too often a dismal read, even when judged against other financial reports. For the most part, information is disseminated in vague financial sector proclamations or in detailed, technocratic reports of limited relevance to people beyond the international regulatory community. I've suggested before in other writings that perhaps the better approach would be to model assessments after investment prospectuses. In every annual assessment, an executive summary, for example, could be included, along with a general rating or scale of country compliance with especially important standards. Then, in addition to the executive summary, an in-depth explanation could be provided to explain the process of data gathering and the regulatory measures taken by the government in question. Toward the end of the report, national regulators should be given the opportunity to contest the score that they earned or the merits of the international standard at issue, or to explain their reasons for not fully implementing that particular standard. And a summary of these reports could be required to be contained in the prospectuses of financial firms when selling their securities.[26]

Ultimately, these kinds of reforms could be integrated into an enhanced peer review process that begins to resemble more traditional forms of dispute resolution. In the not-too-distant future, a system could be developed at the Basel Committee or IOSCO whereby national regulatory authorities concerned with the behavior of others could petition international standard-setting bodies to assess and rule on that behavior. Armed with beefed-up surveillance reports, a nonbinding but public analysis could be undertaken by peers or a designated group of independent experts. In this way, a more rationalized surveillance system could add bite to compliance and leverage the participation of both the international regulatory system and market participants. Baby steps such as these could also help advance the cause of a more prescriptive and formal dispute resolution regime. Monitoring would be more than just observance; it would also demand prescriptive judgments about what kind of conduct comports with international best standards and the expectations of the international regulatory community. And to the extent to which these kinds of judgments could be systematized and proven to be effective – and regulators made more comfortable with the prospect of their actions being judged by others – dispute resolution could gradually become more widely acceptable, even in the ever-evolving world of international financial regulation.

4

Hedging Bets in the Monetary System

As important as trade and finance are for the global economy, neither is possible without some system of exchanging money for goods produced and services rendered. We have seen in earlier chapters that gold and silver, cast into coins of varying weights and sizes, played major roles as money for more than a millennium. Today, however, the international system is dominated by government-backed national currencies – with dollar notes, yen, euros, and pesos populating global markets. Unlike earlier forms of commodity money, which had some intrinsic value, these "fiat" currencies derive their purchasing power exclusively from the fact that they are declared legal tender in the country that backs them – and that people accept them. Nonetheless, they play an indispensable role in defining the value of goods and services, recording and invoicing commercial transactions, and facilitating business across borders – even though they are often fragile instruments of trade, and susceptible to bouts of strength and crushing decline.

Despite the importance of a sound and stable global monetary system, coordinating economic policies and their impact in a world of different national currencies is difficult. Countries use monetary tools – which include interest rate policy, central bank purchases of government debt, and various interventions in local and international capital markets – for plenty of things, including combating unemployment, rescuing financial institutions, and ensuring price stability. Thus placing limits on their ability to use these tools impacts their ability to manage their own domestic economies, and is not undertaken lightly, even in the name of international cooperation and potentially the greater good. There are circumstances in which coordinating international monetary policy can be in a nation's best interest, but others in which a selfish approach might produce better economic outcomes from a strictly internal point of view.

International monetary policy – and the quest for international monetary stability – consequently turns out to be a complicated dance of national interests. And in this dance, market forces play an important role. Like other assets, the value of most major currencies is driven by basic market forces of supply and demand that play themselves out in international markets. If investors want to own a particular national currency – perhaps because the country backing it is a major exporter and people want to purchase its goods – that currency will appreciate. Conversely, if people do not want to own or hold a particular currency due to a diminished or limited utility in international commerce, it will depreciate. Currency values would then reflect the interplay of movements in such demand factors against changes in the supply of each currency.

Yet few things affect the supply and demand for a currency more than the policies of the government that issues it. On the supply side of the ledger, a central bank can effectively create money by lowering interest rates and beefing up lending, or less conventionally, by buying the bad debt of struggling financial institutions. The cash lent out then turns up again in part in the banking system and supports further lending. Similarly, when a central bank decides to purchases bad debt from troubled banks, it not only injects money directly into financial institutions, but it also encourages lending. And when the supply of a currency increases, all else being equal, the currency's value will depreciate.

Policy decisions likewise have considerable ramifications on demand for a particular currency. All things being equal, if a government commits to low inflationary policies and small deficits, and creates only a limited amount of new money, its currency will likely remain a safe store of value and find itself in demand for transactions. People know that if they purchase the currency, it will retain its worth and maybe even appreciate. So they will purchase the currency on the open market – or buy government bonds offering future returns in the country's national currency. Meanwhile, a government's decision to create money aggressively or purchase toxic securities off the books of banks in order to stave off bank defaults could undermine investors' confidence in the currency's market value.[1]

Currency crises arise when the forces of supply and demand reel out of kilter, leading to expectations of inflation and causing investors to swiftly liquidate their holdings of a particular currency. These expectations can, and often are, self-fulfilling. A widespread belief that a country will run large deficits and thus be at risk of high inflation can decrease demand for the national currency even before a country takes out its first loan. Even if supply is unchanged, the lowered demand will translate into inflation.

Investor panic can be sparked in many ways, from banking crises to political dysfunction, though it is traditionally associated with chronic balance-of-payments deficits. In simple terms, a country is like any other person who has to make his own way in life. You have to make money to spend money. One way a country earns revenue for its essential imports and even some domestic services is through exports – selling goods in foreign markets. If it is not exporting enough and not acquiring foreign currency through the sale of assets to foreigners, a nation must borrow money to finance purchases of foreign goods and pay for welfare services. But this is sustainable only for a while. Over time, debt and interest payments mount, and creditors may increasingly suspect that the government will not be able to repay its debt. When this happens, investors will not wait for the government to default – instead, many will pull out their money, and dump the bonds and foreign currency they own, causing the currency's value to collapse on the foreign exchange market. Borrowing costs then spike.

The classical response to currency crises involves debtor countries adjusting their economic structure and changing the way they do business. Customarily, this involves doing things that reduce borrowing and make the country more competitive as an exporter. The first thing to go is usually government spending on welfare, education and perhaps defense. Dramatic changes are also common in the private sector. Firms fire employees, or make them work longer for less, to drive down costs. And monetary authorities will occasionally allow for a controlled depreciation of their country's currency in order to reduce the price of its exports – and conversely increase the cost of foreign imports relative to domestically produced goods. So all in all, everyday life becomes harder. People have to work harder and longer, and sometimes for less money, just as the state pulls back social services and spending in the name of austerity.

The old Bretton Woods system provided a fail-safe of sorts for countries facing adjustment – a Rumpelstiltskin's spinning wheel for the global financial system. An international monetary law, memorialized in the IMF's Articles of Agreement, established global rules aimed at preventing balance-of-payments deficits and outlined a narrow range within which currencies were permitted to trade. Each country would establish a par-value for its currency, either in terms of gold or the U.S. dollar, which was the only currency convertible to gold. And if a country eventually faced a monetary crisis, either the United States or the IMF could provide emergency assistance for the country, or even back the country's debt with dollar-instruments. The struggling country could then use the assistance to ease into adjustment and enjoy a little breathing room when responding to crises and undertaking tough governmental reform.

Over the last four decades, however, this system has been subject to increasing bouts of stress. As we saw in earlier chapters, when America adopted a floating rate system, international monetary law was largely reduced to little more than a formality, with few rules of the road or sources of discipline for guiding the monetary or fiscal policies of nations. Plus many of today's largest financial crises require assistance and interventions beyond the IMF's available resources, a point exemplified in the recent Eurozone crisis. Indeed, the very balance of economic power is in transition, with the United States now a chronic debtor nation.

Nevertheless, there is an unprecedented amount of monetary statecraft underway. But instead of clear and predictable rules concerning currency valuations administered by the IMF, today's international monetary system is being driven by at times ad hoc, transactional deals and arrangements focused on coordinating the provision of liquidity for trade purposes and for times of crisis. These arrangements can be both political and technocratic – with various officials and even elected officials committing to currency unions, currency swaps and other complex financial relationships. By embracing new financial technologies, not only are governments slowly diversifying their sources of monetary reserves, but they are also creating a slew of new financial instruments and arrangements, all in an effort to hedge against excessive U.S.-dollar exposures or unexpected volatility in their own local currency markets. In the process, central banks and monetary authorities have at times come to resemble hedge funds and broker-dealers just as much as they do typical government bureaucracies.

AMERICA'S ADJUSTMENT CHALLENGE – AND THE WORLD'S

The fact that currency crises arise at all is in many ways a product of dramatic changes in the international monetary system over the last several decades. We've already seen in earlier chapters that the cornerstone of the 1940s postwar economic order was a new, decidedly international monetary system to replace the gold standard that had disintegrated in the 1930s. The rules of the new game were memorialized in the IMF's Articles of Agreement.[2] IMF members committed to fixed values for their currency in gold or U.S. dollars, and promised to intervene in foreign exchange markets by buying or selling their own currency near par value to maintain the fixed rates. All the while, countries would maintain the convertibility of their currency for trade-related transactions, in order to help revive and relaunch the international trading system.[3]

Some shock absorbers were allowed. Both Keynes and White, the architects of the Bretton Woods system, were skeptical of untrammeled capital flows, and thought that unbounded mobile capital could undermine a country's ability to undertake structural adjustment. The sheer size of the world's capital flows dwarfed the IMF's resources, meaning that widespread changes in investor sentiment could strip a country of its reserves and wealth in ways that could not be checked or significantly mitigated by even multilateral cooperation. Consequently, capital controls were permitted.[4] That said, the Bretton Woods system operated loosely enough that a country could still run out of the foreign currency reserves needed to maintain its par value if it became uncompetitive relative to others and if it remained so over time. If it did not export enough, a government could, sooner or later, run out of the funds necessary to intervene and protect its currency and pay its foreign denominated debt.

This didn't stop, however, the very lynchpin of the global monetary system, the United States, from eventually running persistent deficits. The great system of economic governance devised by Keynes and White included no mechanism for ensuring that the U.S. would behave in a way consistent with maintaining adequate gold stocks.[5] America was under no formal obligation to maintain trade surpluses per se, and with unmatched reserves and the world's leading military, prudent fiscal or monetary policies were not always the highest priority for leaders focused on the military and ideological threat posed by the Soviet Union. Nevertheless, the country's preeminence would fade in relative if not absolute terms. And after spending vast resources reconstructing Europe, funding the Korean, Vietnam and Cold Wars, and dramatically expanding its social welfare system, even the United States, the world's leading economy, had to abandon gold convertibility by the 1970s.

Yet abandoning the gold standard was not viewed as necessarily embracing a future of perpetually reckless fiscal and monetary policies. Even in the twilight of the old gold standard there was considerable monetary flexibility for the United States, the world's biggest economy. Since the U.S. dollar was the leading currency and had been a virtual proxy for gold, the United States could borrow well beyond its means without experiencing the painful adjustment the gold standard had long implied. Instead, the primary limitation on its ability to run deficits was the willingness of foreign central banks to hold U.S. dollars without redeeming them for gold. If foreign banks just held the dollars, and never traded them in for gold, the country's gold stocks would remain full. And indeed, for years export-oriented countries like Germany refrained from redeeming gold from the U.S. treasury, even when they realized that there were insufficient gold reserves to meet all of America's outstanding obligations. The United States was a first-tier trading partner, and an important purchaser of foreign exports – plus it subsidized its allies' security and protection through its own massive defense expenditures and international deployments.

Switching to a floating system thus held the allure of a new, market-based system guiding monetary relations, whereby the leading currencies would be stacked up and measured against one another as investments. Market forces would provide the appropriate constraints for countries' domestic policies insofar as external funding would dry up in the face of extended, unsustainable profligacy. Optimists hoped that leaders would be forced to make prudent macroeconomic decisions and adjust domestic economic policies in the face of headwinds in order to maintain the confidence of foreign creditors.

In practice, however, markets have not always worked so efficiently. Even after the United States abandoned the gold standard, the dollar remained a highly sought-after asset. Central banks around the world continued to flock to U.S.-denominated investments, and by 1977 nearly 80 percent of all international reserves were denominated in dollars.[6] Only Iran altered the composition of its reserves.[7] Indeed, though depreciating in the wake of Nixon's announcement, the dollar rebounded throughout the early to mid-1980s – despite current account deficits and a major recession – and a coordinated effort with major trading partners (the so-called Plaza Accord) was required to *reduce*, not increase, the value of the dollar.

At first glance, the greenback's durability in the post–Bretton Woods period is surprising. In some ways, the movement away from gold comprised a move towards the market and (financial) market discipline. But markets are about supply and demand, and the "supply" of credible alternatives to the dollar was low. The United States was the world's top exporter and boasted the largest financial markets.[8] And like Britain in the 1800s, U.S. capital markets continued to serve as a financial intermediary for the rest of the world, channeling savings toward productive investments in Europe, Asia, and beyond. Thus even after de-linking from the gold standard, the U.S. remained the fulcrum point for the global economy.[9] Equally important, no other currency was backed by an economy as large as America's. And no other country could boast similarly mature or stable political institutions. With no rivals offering this combination of benefits, the dollar continued to serve as an unrivaled medium of exchange and unit of account for much of the postwar period.

Moreover, these advantages helped preserve U.S. dollar dominance even as America's balance sheet began to erode from debt and deficits. Because most exporters settled their transactions in dollars given the sheer size of the U.S. consumer and financial markets, they had an incentive to use dollar-based pricing for the goods they sold, and for the stock and bonds they issued. It also made sense to save dollars earned for future international transactions, whether with U.S. companies or other foreign counterparts.[10] The utility of the dollar meanwhile provided a powerful incentive for financial institutions to continue to hold and maintain high dollar cash reserves, even in a world of gradually declining U.S. power.[11] Switching to another currency was costly; it made little sense to opt out of the dollar system until other banks and firms made attempts to diversify their currency uses. A first mover *dis*advantage stymied change.

An analogy, albeit a bit off topic, can make this point a lot clearer. One way to think about this is to consider "friends and family plans" of cell phone providers. In short, many popular packages for cell phone users in the United States allow subscribers to call any friends and family who are members of their designated network at any time, without having to pay for the minutes. This incentivizes people to contact the most important people in their lives and to make sure they use the same company.

But notice what happens when family and friends choose the same company. Once they opt in, the network itself has value regardless of the actual value provided by the phone company. If, for example, another company comes up with better phone reception, and even offers its own friends and family plan, it is not necessarily a given that any individual members in the network will switch to a new cell provider. Why? Because if they move, and others do not, they will lose their network benefit and will have to incur the costs of their friends and family who operate in the other network. Of course, if other members join, the costs decline as a new network displaces the other. But the costs for first movers will be highest, and people will prefer to sit and wait for others to switch first in order to lower the costs of operating in the new system.

Now the obvious question: Why don't they all switch at the same time, then? Well, in the abstract that is obviously an option. But coordinating a joint, simultaneous move in the real world requires a lot of work. You would have to call all the members in the plan to coordinate the switch. That, unfortunately, takes time, may require convincing Grandma and Grandpa of the merits of the move, and then making sure that the move is done in an organized fashion. So people tend to stay where they are and play in the same telephonic sandbox.

Currencies work the same way. The dollar became a major currency as a product of America's enormous post-war gold holdings. Indeed, it was precisely because of its massive holdings that the IMF would come to rely on the dollar as a gold substitute. Once the dollar was firmly entrenched as the premier international money, however, it became a lot harder for countries to move to another currency, irrespective of U.S. gold holdings. Just having agreed on the dollar as a medium of exchange created network benefits unrelated to the actual size of the U.S. economy since governments and companies knew that dollars could be used freely pretty much anywhere. As a result, people have been reluctant to relinquish the dollar, even as the economy on which it is based has declined relative to global GDP.

Indeed, if anything, the incentives to hoard U.S. dollars only increased in the 1990s, and especially in the wake of the Asian financial crisis. Early in the decade, investors flocked to Southeast Asian countries to fund local development projects. When it became clear, however, that many of the investments were not going to be successful enough to repay the loans, the region experienced a collapse in short-term investment. Fewer people wanted to invest there, and funding dried up. This created a financial panic. Local currencies like the Thai Baht plummeted in value, generating enormous difficulties for countries and companies that had borrowed U.S. dollars on global capital markets. With weaker currencies, U.S.-dollar denominated debt suddenly became much more expensive. Adding to the problem, central banks had insufficient reserves to loan dollars to cash-strapped local companies.

In the absence of sufficient resources at their disposal, Thailand, South Korea, and others were forced to go to the IMF for assistance, and in exchange for aid were subjected to rigid reductions in government expenditures that in the view of many experts unduly lowered their growth rates. As they recovered from the crisis, most governments pledged to never again have to go to the IMF. So to protect themselves against the prospect of another crisis, they began to amass enormous foreign-exchange reserves – with the U.S. dollar being the currency of choice.[12] Additionally, other notable powers like China discovered that purchasing dollars – or at least U.S. dollar denominated debt – could propel their own exports if coupled with smart financial engineering (a topic we will explore later in this chapter).[13]

The resulting savings glut by major exporting countries has created a series of perverse economic dynamics that have both perplexed and disturbed commentators. Strong capital inflows, generally in the form of credit from eager lenders, have kept U.S. interest rates low, even as the country continues to amass historical levels of debt. Meanwhile, low interest rates over the last two decades have made everyday Americans disinclined to set aside savings, and have even encouraged more consumption, with only the 2008 financial crisis serving to put a big dent in foolhardy spending habits.

No one really knows how much longer such "macroeconomic imbalances" can or will last. In theory, the accumulation of dollar reserves is attractive only when there is no question about the dollar's value. And in the postwar years, there was indeed little doubt as U.S. savings and surpluses were channelled to a world starved for dollars. Now, however, the United States is one of the world's biggest borrowers – and emerging markets act as the biggest lenders. Since 1999, America's capital inflows (for the most part due to borrowing) have been equivalent to more than 1 percent of global GDP, and rose to a record 1.7 percent of GDP in the mid 2000s.[14] And in 2013, U.S. debt sat at over 75 percent of the country's GDP, nearly twice the 39 percent average experienced over the past four decades – and the 36 percent seen as late as 2007.

Then again, some relatively more optimistic economists argue that the tide may once again be turning in America's favor. As natural gas exploration and refinement advances, America is fast becoming an energy exporter and as such will be better positioned to reduce its trade deficit and current account in the coming years. In addition, the amount of debt relative to the size of the economy is declining as growth slowly picks up, and as a controversial sequester on government spending has restrained expenditures. Yet even here, these factors may portend only short-term deficit relief for the United States. The government's budget office has predicted that net outlays for entitlements in 2023 will total more than the *total* federal spending in 2012. With baby-boomers aging and entering retirement, mandatory spending on healthcare and social security will skyrocket, and likely at a time when interest rates will rise.[15] As a result, the long-term trend continues to raise modest concerns about the country's fiscal solvency and its very willingness to service the obligations it has incurred – a once unthinkable scenario that has become less so in the wake of successive budget battles in the U.S. Congress and not-infrequent talk of government default.

THE EURO'S TROJAN HORSE

How then do you break the pull of history, economics, and tradition to diversify the international monetary system – besides, of course, counting on a possible dollar crash? Perhaps nobody has grappled more with the issue than the economist Barry Eichengreen. He has noted that at least for Europe, the solution has been, as with trade, a turn to regionalism. Ever since the Latin Monetary Union (LMU), monetary cooperation has long been an aspiration of many of the continent's leaders and peoples. And the age of U.S. hegemony has in many ways only heightened interest in a deeper economic union. For all of the benefits of U.S. leadership, politicians and regulators of virtually every country on the continent have at one point or another grumbled about the "exorbitant privilege" enjoyed by the United States to essentially spend dollars without much concern for the impact on the demand for its currency. And Europe, a huge purchaser of U.S. debt, was often one of the biggest enablers.

But no country could do anything about it, at least not individually. France, the backer of the original LMU, had always sought greater monetary influence, though it did not have the economy to support such ambitions. Its financial markets were small, and overshadowed by not only the United States, but also those in then–West Germany and the United Kingdom.[16] Germany, for its part, enjoyed both the economic size and strength to internationalize its currency, though it had never sought to institute policies that would undermine U.S. economic hegemony. Close cooperation with the United States was necessary in the Cold War; plus, it was unwilling to provide the kind of global liquidity and debt-obligations that the United States was willing to provide.[17] A change in attitude would only come after the fall of the Soviet Union. The Cold War was won. Plus Germany needed French assent to reunify East and West Germany, and France's permission was arguably conditioned on German support for a common currency.

The eventual agreement for monetary union, the now-famous Treaty of Maastricht, was secured in 1992. In the accord, a series of benchmarks were established for transitioning to a new common currency. Among the most important, the eleven soon-to-be Eurozone members would abolish restrictions on the movement of capital within the bloc, and establish what would later in 1999 comprise "irrevocably fixed exchange rates" referencing the euro. The idea was that the relative value of the national currencies could be determined by a vote of the European Council based on exchange rates reflected in international markets. Once that value was determined, the euro could operate as an accounting unit, and ultimately be printed and exchanged for the old national currencies. Switching was thus a cost imposed by treaty on Eurozone members – and not the market. From an operational standpoint, the plan worked well: three years after its introduction as an accounting and invoicing instrument, bills were printed and introduced in 2002, with widespread circulation soon thereafter.

The Treaty of Maastricht would also, critically, establish a series of new institutions to support the common currency. None was more important than a new European Central Bank (ECB). Like national banks before it, the ECB would be responsible for member countries' monetary policy. It would also operate independently of the European Commission, the European Union's executive, and, as a condition to German support, its ability to finance government budget deficits would be limited.[18]

But the Treaty of Maastricht was unlike many arrangements one might have imagined to hold a continent of varying economies together. The institutions grounding the EU were, for one, extremely weak. In contrast to most countries, where governments control both monetary and fiscal policy, the European Union lacked powers to dictate fiscal policy to member states. Although some countries may have been prepared to surrender monetary policy tools like the power to set interest rates at the regional level, no one was ready to relinquish all control over their economies. Politicians and regulators alike wanted to preserve levers with which to pursue their own growth and market stability objectives. Doing otherwise would be a wholesale forfeiture of sovereignty, and with it, many believed, statehood itself. Consequently, the euro could boast the dubious distinction of being the only modern currency that was not backed by a fully-fledged state. No central bureaucracy controlled the macroeconomic policies of members, or just how and in which way euros created by the ECB would be spent or used by governments.

Instead, a Stability and Growth Pact was adopted the same day the euro was established. Under the agreement, countries agreed to rules that restricted fiscal deficits to 3 percent of their GDP and public debt to 60 percent of GDP. Any country that ignored the rules would be subject to sanctions that could amount to several points of countries' GDP. But in practice, the agreement still required considerable consensus by members, and big countries themselves quickly began to flout the rules – beginning with Germany in 2004. In the absence of leadership by the strong, the rules were effectively interpreted away, leaving few effective checks on spending. Eurozone member states were consequently left to borrow from one another and from international capital markets with scarce constraints imposed at the federal level by the European Union.

The relative absence of discipline would have serious consequences when Greece joined the euro in 2001. Early on, the country turned to Goldman Sachs to help it enter the Eurozone by masking the extent of its deficits through creative (and by some accounts, fraudulent) financial engineering and sleight of hand. Then later, even as the extent of Greece's borrowing slowly became known, its bad habits were in some ways sustained and even encouraged thanks to the currency union in which it participated.

How so? By the time Greece's problems began to deepen, Germany had returned to fiscal sobriety. This meant that even if Greece spent wildly beyond its means, its profligacy could be counteracted by Germany's tendency to save, at least from a monetary perspective. Greeks could thus participate in a monetary system that artificially inflated its currency – driving its spending habits onwards. And Germany could continue to enjoy a weaker currency than would be

the case if it were still relying on its old money, the deutsche mark –
allowing it to export goods at artificially lower prices. All the while,
international banking regulations, including early iterations of the
Basel Accord, effectively proclaimed U.S. and European government
bonds to be risk-free assets, with little distinction between different
countries.[19] So private investors loaded up on sovereign debt, feuling
spending even further since more money – and cheap financing –
seemed limitless.

Complicating the absence of discipline was the additional problem
that the EU also lacked the ability to respond to financial crises once
they arose. For instance, in the absence of any fiscal solidarity among
member states, the European Union was unable to pool resources to be
used if weaker members experienced balance-of-payments crises. This
made the EU very different from, say, the United States, where more
affluent states regularly subsidize federal activities in less affluent states,
and where states pool resources to respond to both common and individual crises. Furthermore, unlike the U.S. Federal Reserve Bank, whose
mission is "to promote effectively the goals of maximum employment,
stable prices and moderate long-term interest rates," the ECB's mandate
was intentionally devised to be much more limited. It has been tasked
with maintaining, above all else, price stability, and could only consider
a secondary objective like employment when its primary mission was
not being impaired. This mandate has been interpreted by the ECB to
mean that inflation should not be more than 2 percent – restraining the
extent to which authorities thought they could sell bonds or intervene
in markets to assist cash-strapped debtors.[20]

With few official checks to borrowing, the private market would
ultimately provide the first and last source of fiscal discipline, a lesson learned by Greece the hard way. Even before joining the euro,
Greece suffered from persistent trade and budget deficits. Joining the
euro did nothing to reverse the trend. Public sector wages rose nearly
50 percent in the early 2000s, and massive loans were taken out to
finance the Olympics in 2004, with neither representing any measure
of the fiscal prudence many economists had viewed as necessary for
the country's long-term economic success. Exports had been slow for
years and the country relied on tourism to meet balance-of-payments
challenges. When the global economy started to slow in the wake of
the 2008 financial crisis, investors started to get nervous about the
Greek government's ultimate capacity to service the debts it had accu-
mulated. Nervousness then turned to panic as it became equally clear

that no country, including mighty Germany, indicated any willingness to open its purse and help the struggling Greek economy survive. The politics of assistance were simply horrible for the German government: the one thing people hate more than bailing out their bankers is bailing out someone else's bankers, whether in pursuit of financial stability or not.

Inaction was not really an option, however. Some kind of outside assistance was necessary. The politics in Greece made any quick restructuring of the economy impossible. In addition, the response most governments would take – namely devaluing their national currencies in order to increase exports and regain competitiveness – wasn't possible since Greece was a member of the euro. Greece didn't have any old drachmas to debase. So without assistance from someone, the country would likely default on its debt payments and probably leave the Eurozone.

How bad this would have been for the Eurozone at the time is hard to overstate. First, any loans extended to Greek companies and financial institutions in euros or dollars would not likely be repaid in euros, but instead be repaid by whatever new, debased currency the Greek government decided to adopt. Similarly, deposits by banks and individuals would be redenominated in a new, weaker currency overnight. So if you were a French bank that had extended loans to a Greek company, you might get only half your money back. Or if you were a major German financial institution that had deposits with a Greek bank, you could find those deposits – potentially hundreds of millions of euros – worth only a fraction of what you thought, gone overnight.

Even worse, the prospects of a Greek default suddenly made the possibility of other indebted countries making similar decisions much more realistic. Investors cast a suspicious eye towards other Mediterranean countries like Spain and Italy, who in their judgment posed similar risks. Borrowing costs and interest rates throughout Southern Europe began to rise. Even hedge funds began to make big bets against (or "short") the euro in global markets, all in anticipation of an eventual dissolution of the Eurozone.

THE MECHANICS OF EARLY EUROZONE BAILOUTS

With nerves fraying, the ECB stepped on to the scene as a first responder. It realized that the best way to speak to a growing crisis was to make clear that a Greek default was unlikely. That way, people's fears about it and other countries' debt woes would be reduced. But instead of picking up Greece's tab, the ECB offered indirect assistance, and made funds available to banks that could then be used to purchase Greek government debt – and thus finance the Greek government circuitously. This was extremely attractive for banks, since they could charge Greece three or four percent interest for any loans, while borrowing from the ECB at only one percent.

Still, as would often be the case for the next two years, emergency action by the ECB helped to calm jittery markets, but it didn't solve the underlying Eurozone problems. Greece was still heavily indebted. And with the country's economy struggling, it had become increasingly obvious that some kind of bigger bazooka would be needed to fight off default, especially as bond rates in it and other countries like Spain and Italy began to rise. Yet agreeing on a policy response still proved excruciatingly difficult for Europe's leaders. Politicians in creditor countries from Germany to Slovakia did not want to be seen bailing out what many believed were their profligate southern neighbors.

Collective bailouts were also unappealing. The idea of Eurozone countries banding together to issue joint bonds backed by all member states was panned by Germany, the continent's leading economy, because in its view, such an approach could encourage free-riding and even strategic defaults by debtor countries. In other words, if chronically indebted countries knew that other countries were on the hook for their bills, the thinking went, debtors could choose, after receiving financing, to default on repayments and force other countries to cover the losses. Or they could use the prospect of default to renegotiate repayment terms with the countries that effectively co-signed their loans, or with other international creditors. So no blank checks or generous payouts were on the table.

Until, that is, the very future of the Eurozone was once again cast in doubt. By early May, alarm bells had returned to fever pitch among bond traders and analysts of euro area sovereign debt markets, and EU heads of states convened an extraordinary meeting of the Economic and Financial Affairs Council to address the problem. At the end of the summit, leaders emerged from their deliberations to announce two unprecedented bailout facilities. The first device, the European Financial Stability Mechanism (EFSM), would provide up to 60 billion euros of support, which would be on terms and conditions similar to those typically imposed by the IMF since assistance from the organization would accompany EFSM support. Meanwhile, the second fund, the European Financial Stability Facility (EFSF), established an independent firm – what looks a lot like what lawyers would describe as a "special purpose vehicle" – to tap international capital markets and facilitate lending for the crisis-ridden southern periphery. The EFSF would issue debt, and the proceeds from its borrowing could then be lent on to financially strapped governments or financial institutions.

The genius behind both rescue mechanisms is that they were structured in ways to minimize, to the degree possible, the political costs of the bailout. Most of the innovation was in terms of how the deals were made credible without directly exposing creditors to borrowers. Instead of pledging tangible cash, the EFSM ultimately used the EU budget as collateral. The much larger and more important EFSF, meanwhile, was backed by individual commitment guarantees from Eurozone member states, rich and poor alike. In this way, countries were only responsible up to the amount they committed to up front. Creditors had no recourse beyond country pledges. Under this system, even cash-strapped borrowers were required to make guarantees – including Greece, which was on the hook for over 12 billion euros. Yet at the same time, rich creditor countries dominated the voting and corporate governance of the bailout entities, and consensus would be required for virtually all lending decisions. Thus if indebted countries waivered on undertaking tough reforms – which were negotiated to varying degrees alongside the IMF – creditors could deny debtors additional assistance.

Neither mechanism had, however, a clear legal basis in the EU treaties, and corners were cut to get the two facilities off the ground. Article 125 of the Treaty of the Functioning of the European Union, which lays out the EU's operational architecture, unambiguously proclaimed that the federal EU government would *not* assume the liabilities of member states. By doing so, it provided the proverbial red-light prohibition against bailouts. Therefore, EU officials had to find an alternative legal basis for putting up the money. Ultimately, EU lawyers had to settle on Art. 122.2 of the treaty, which provides for financial assistance to members states where members face "natural disasters or exceptional circumstances beyond its control," as a basis for the EU's actions. Yet this argument was far from satisfactory, even for proponents of a bailout, since the crisis was, by most accounts, well within the "control of Greece" – and though a disaster for the nation, it was far from a "natural disaster."[21]

With the less-than-stellar legal basis for the treaty, both measures were, like earlier ECB measures, cast as temporary relief efforts, and Germany in particular emphasized the need for an eventual treaty amendment should a more permanent facility become necessary. This was not a popular suggestion. Ratifying EU treaties had become an increasingly harrowing affair, and in some instances even required national referendums. Nevertheless, as the crisis gained momentum, Germany's position would prevail as the EU council pushed through a two-line treaty amendment that would formally permit a permanent bailout facility.[22] EU heads of state also eventually approved a separate treaty establishing the European Stability Mechanism (or ESM), a permanent, stand-alone mechanism to ultimately replace earlier, temporary programs.

The diplomatic breakthroughs were cheered by the market and, for the most part, politicians on both sides of the Atlantic. For the first time, a durable mechanism was in place, enshrined by law, to provide funds for addressing the economic crisis. That said, no one believed the crisis was over. Indeed, even the most optimistic technocrats understood that a final solution to the Eurozone crisis was still a long way off. Two problems persisted. First, even after all of the legal gymnastics, the ESM still wasn't big and bad enough to stave off mass panic if Greece stumbled out of the euro. Indeed, many experts had estimated that the total costs of financing a bailout could reach €2.4 trillion – well beyond the management capacity of the ESM, or for that matter, any single country, including Germany.[23] So there were still plenty of jittery investors concerned about the fallout that would ensue should Greece or any other country leave the Eurozone.

Then there was the massive political problem presented by how the bailouts were structured. Critically, the ESM, like its predecessor funds, wasn't authorized to spend money immediately or proactively, but instead just made resources available if certain conditions were met. In practice, this meant that money would be made available, but only when the donors felt that credit should be extended. Sovereign creditors would have to agree to disburse the money, and their agreement would depend on recipients making tough policy reforms. And therein lay the problem. For its part, Germany, the largest and most important lender, has demanded more structural reforms for aid than some countries ever imagined. And the package of austerity reforms pushed by Germany has been consistently rebuffed by Greeks. Indeed, the country's technocratic government, praised by the international community for initiating the process of adjustment, was effectively removed *from* office after less than a year *in* office.

THE ECB GOES FOR BROKE – AND THE EUROZONE FOLLOWS

Doubts persisted, dragging down European markets, the euro, and the global economy. And so, on September 6, 2012, the ECB again took matters into its own hands to restore confidence. But this time the bank tried a new approach to calm nerves. From his Frankfurt headquarters, the ECB's head, Mario Draghi, unveiled a new "Outright Monetary Transactions" (OMT) program under which the bank would buy an unlimited amount of short- to medium-term sovereign bonds in the secondary market. In exchange for buying the bonds – and essentially providing debt-strapped countries with liquidity by lowering the interest rates on the debt they sold to private market participants – the ECB would require adherence to the same strict conditions demanded by the EFSF and ESM.

By vowing to deploy its vast resources in this way, the ECB solved at least one of the two big problems associated with the ESM. As we saw above, the ESM's firepower was viewed as too small to bailout the Eurozone, and there were all kinds of political questions as to whether its resources would actually be used. The OMT, by contrast, presented no such problems. The ECB could open its purse strings and participate in capital markets alongside other securities firms and hedge funds as both a market participant and an independent monetary authority. This highly unconventional monetary program reflected Draghi's view that "severe distortions" throughout the European sovereign debt market – caused by "unfounded" fears of a euro collapse – necessitated unprecedented steps by the central bank.

So like a knight in shining armor, the ECB rode to the rescue of teetering Eurozone governments, and committed to potentially unlimited sovereign bond purchases on secondary markets. By promising to do, in the words of the ECB chief, "whatever it takes" to address the crisis, the ECB was able to stare down speculators otherwise bent on betting against the euro. With Draghi bashing down yields, fewer people were willing to bet on default, and the cost of borrowing quickly fell.[24]

The OMT Saves the Day?

- The ECB purchases short term (1 to 3 years) government debt in secondary markets
- Strict conditionality based on EFSF/ESM programs is required
- The ECB's price stability mandate determines extent of intervention

That said, even with the OMT, another dragon had yet to be slain. The cruel fact remained that some countries in the Eurozone were more competitive than others, and as such ran chronic surpluses, just as others were uncompetitive and tended to run deficits. And insofar as both kinds of countries shared a common currency, debasement, the typical remedy for kick-starting growth, still wasn't possible. Indeed, even as the euro weakened in the wake of the ECB's sovereign debt interventions and declarations, the initial benefits of a cheaper regional currency were skewed. With few world-class exports, Spain, Greece, and Italy saw few of the initial benefits of a weaker currency one might expect. Instead, Germany reaped the most benefits of a declining currency, and the country saw its exports surge as its cars and other manufacturing goods became less expensive on the global market.[25] The data highlighted the fact that without changes in the competitiveness of Eurozone periphery countries, the ECB's technocratic assistance isn't enough to solve the euro's ills. Weak countries would have to become more competitive, or some kind of transfer mechanism would be required whereby stronger countries support weaker ones.

Even early on, commentators and policymakers recognized the problem, and a wide range of institutional reforms have been launched to rebalance the region's economic growth. One of the most important is the idea of a fiscal union. According to proposals that are still very much on the drawing board, responsibility for key policies like tax, spending, and welfare could be transferred from national authorities to the federal EU government. In doing so, macroeconomic imbalances could be cured by ensuring fiscal solidarity among members. Strong countries could devote resources to weaker ones to help keep them afloat, much like what happens in the United States, as richer regions contribute to assisting their weaker neighbors through taxes. Meanwhile, the EU's power over the budgets of Eurozone governments would be increased. Big spenders like Spain and Greece would be forced to reign in their deficits, just as stingy ones like Germany might be encouraged – or required – to open their fiscal purse strings and spread the wealth, so to speak, through greater spending by their citizens.

How exactly to operationalize such reforms has become a considerable point of contention, however. Finance ministers and national legislatures routinely debate the appropriate powers of a federal fiscal authority and the extent to which any assistance – whether via the ESM or a shared fiscal authority – should be given. Plus periphery countries are quickly tiring of EU-imposed austerity measures.

All the while, the project of fiscal solidarity has increasingly taken a back seat to more immediate questions relating to regional financial regulation. Crises in Spain and Cyprus, as well as the vulnerability of German and French banks to the Greek financial sector, have underscored the fact that institutional reforms for the euro won't mean much if the continent's financial sector is under constant duress. Banks fund governments, and vice versa, and the failure of a member state's banking system could well bankrupt it and other countries' banks, and in the process endanger the euro. With this in mind, EU officials have approved a new Banking Union to lend greater oversight over large financial institutions that could create cross-border shocks if they ran into economic difficulties. The elements of such cooperation would include a "single supervisory mechanism" for overseeing big banks, a single rulebook that banks would be required to comply with, and a Eurozone-wide deposit insurer and "single resolution mechanism" for unwinding big banks that fail.

The single supervisory mechanism, for its part, would add to the ECB's already considerable responsibilities tasks related to the preservation of the financial stability of all euro-area banks, though national supervisors would continue to play an important role in day-to-day oversight and implementation of ECB decisions. As the fulcrum point of the supervisory system, the ECB would be charged with ensuring compliance with minimum capital requirements as well as taking appropriate action where risks like real estate bubbles were identified that could undermine the stability of the European financial system. Meanwhile, another agency, the European Banking Authority, would be tasked with developing a Single Supervisory Handbook to preserve the integrity of the single market and ensure coherence in banking supervision for all 28 EU countries. Finally, a new single resolution mechanism would assume responsibility for the resolution of the Eurozone's 6,000 banks, just as an insurance scheme would protect the bank deposits of the region's savers.

Yet a banking union, like a fiscal union, is still very much "under construction." As of this writing, the Commission and member states have outlined steps to implement a single resolution mechanism for the Banking Union, which would only apply to Eurozone banks, and would be incrementally set up over the next decade. But that proposal must be approved by the European Parliament before it can become effective. Furthermore, as with the debate over early bailout mechanisms, German authorities, including the country's influential finance minister, Wolfgang Schäuble, have argued that any move to take away decision-making authority from national authorities and to give it to Brussels would breach EU treaties. Thus a new treaty or treaty reforms will likely have to be hammered out.

How a deposit guarantee system would operate is also unclear. On the one hand, European finance ministers agreed in December 2013 that banks should contribute to national insurance schemes that could be drawn on to refund depositors where banks collapse. However, the amount of money that would be available under such schemes is suspected to be insufficient if a new crisis erupts in the near future, especially since the funds are to be paid in only gradually. Instead, sovereign governments will potentially remain the principal backstops for assistance for more than a decade, and the ESM may be necessary as a supplemental source of funding. This is particularly troubling, as commentators including the Wall Street Journal's Tom Fairless have noted, since the entire idea of a Eurozone deposit scheme is to shore up confidence and certainty where national governments are unable to do the job themselves. There thus remains considerable debate as to just how to provide the critical funding for protecting the Eurozone financial system.

Europe's Minilateral Integration Program

EU Mechanism	Purpose
EFSF/ESM	Bail out governments and banks
OMT	Restore the transmission of monetary policy by reducing rates on government bonds
Banking Union	Create a common supervisor, deposit insurer, and resolution mechanism for Eurozone banks
Fiscal Union	Create a common central authority to manage euro area government finances

Europe thus continues to walk a tightrope. On the one hand, the common currency appears at least off of death-watch with the promise of ECB intervention if things go sour for debt-strapped governments. And with that kind of backstop, few Wall Street analysts are still getting up each morning wondering if the euro has disintegrated overnight. But if Eurozone members can't eventually agree on how to treat the economic drivers of the crisis, or on the institutional reforms necessary to prevent or address new ones, the prospect of an exit by periphery countries could well loom once again. And if that happens, we could be faced with the same doomsday scenarios that precipitated Draghi's actions and the EU bailouts: in the absence of political consensus, investors could preemptively yank their money from periphery banks or taper off lending to a struggling Mediterranean government out of a belief that they won't get their money back.[26] Fear could then create a self-fulfilling prophesy and force a cash-strapped country to in fact default on its debt and even abandon the Eurozone.

Under such circumstances, the departure of just one country could put the entire common currency in jeopardy. It would show that the very basis and founding assumptions of the Eurozone were illusory. When it was created, the euro was supposed to be a final decision on the part of member governments as to the issue of their monetary sovereignty. Indeed, the currency was a proverbial "roach motel" for currencies – it was assumed that countries could check in, but after joining they couldn't check out. This presumption would be turned on its head, however, if a country was permitted to leave. As Martin Wolf, the prominent *Financial Times* journalist perceptively noted, the Eurozone "either is an irrevocable currency union or it is not. If countries in difficulty leave, it is not. It is then [only] an exceptionally rigid fixed-currency system."[27] And its utility as a store of value and instrument of commerce would be greatly compromised.

These risks have left the euro far from what one would expect of a normal, dependable world currency. On the one hand, it is the regional powerhouse – and the euro dominates invoicing and commercial and financial transactions in many of the world's most developed economies. But at the same time, its very future remains, if not in doubt, then at least clouded, just as the very tenability of the Eurozone project remains an open question. Not surprisingly, the likelihood of the euro eclipsing the dollar as the world's dominant currency remains for most experts extremely low in the short to medium term, even with America's periodic economic travails.

ASIA'S CURRENCY CLEARINGHOUSE

Europeans aren't the only ones to consider regional approaches to monetary cooperation and stability, or to use creative financial engineering to promote cooperation. Countries throughout Asia have also sought closer monetary relations. But efforts in the region have not centered on a common currency or on political unification – although attempts to sketch out an Asian Monetary Unit have passed across the chalkboards of more than a few academics dreaming of a common currency. Instead, leaders have employed much more modest tools to coordinate monetary policy.

The most important instrument has been the currency swap. In a swap transaction between central banks, an agreement is reached to exchange (or make available) one currency for another – and to reverse the transaction at a date in the future.[28] In this way, swaps can provide lifelines to countries facing financial crises. So, by way of example, if the United States and Costa Rica entered into a swap agreement, and if Costa Rica suddenly faced a balance-of-payments crisis and investors began to dump pesos, Costa Rica could draw on the swap lines to secure higher quality currency from abroad and move U.S. dollars to its own domestic treasury. In one fell swoop it could improve its capital structure. Or it could use the currency to meet international debt payments, especially if its loans are in a foreign currency (like dollars) and its own domestic currency has depreciated.

Swap agreements hold a variety of important advantages over the kind of unitary monetary cooperation that we saw driving the later stages of European regionalism. For one, they can act as both pre- and post-crisis coordinating mechanisms. The mere availability of swap lines can potentially calm the nerves of otherwise nervous investors who might want to dump their holdings of a country's debt. And when a crisis breaks out, a country under duress can activate existing swap lines to bolster its reserves and financial firepower. All the while, they do not require the same formalities that the European Stability Mechanism, banking union, and fiscal union required. Instead, they are entered into between central banks, and do not explicitly create any binding international legal obligation. As such, they are a species of what can be considered soft law.

As a result, swaps between central banks have always been popular. In the 1920s, for example, the Federal Reserve had a swap agreement with the Bank of England to help provide gold as the sterling limped back on to the gold standard. And in the 1960s, as U.S. deficits mounted, the Fed created a network of swaps to help protect it from speculative attacks, just as it would later use swaps to deliver the greenback to dollar-starved trading partners in the wake of the 2008 financial crisis.[29]

Perhaps nowhere, however, have swaps arrangements been as institutionalized among so many different kinds of countries as in the Chiang Mai Initiative. Strict demands by the IMF and World Bank on governments during the Asian Financial Crisis soured countries' taste for traditional multilateral sources of funding and assistance. In order to begin weaning themselves from such dependence, the ASEAN +3 group of countries agreed to more interventionist policies in foreign exchange markets and reserves accumulation, and collectively pushed the IMF to adopt policies better suited to the kinds of crises the region was likely to face. Additionally, and perhaps equally important, they created a series of bilateral swap agreements that could be activated for countries in the region when needed. Termed the Chiang Mai Initiative (CMI), the idea was to provide an extra firewall for countries facing a balance-of-payments crisis and diminish dependence on the IMF. Later in 2010, members built on the program by multilateralizing the agreement and transforming what was an ad hoc network of accords and agreements into one formal, $120 billion accord, the Chiang Mai Initiative Multilateralization (CMIM). Critically, the referenced obligations under the accord are U.S. dollars.

The CMIM is viewed in many respects as a highly flexible instrument. No country commits funds under the mechanism. Instead, it operates as a self-managed system in which reserves are not physically collected and pooled in a common fund but are instead held by national central banks and earmarked for CMIM purposes. Thus the contributions to the CMIM do not involve an outright transfer of the committed amount, but instead take the form of a commitment letter, whereby the relevant monetary authority issues a promissory note for a value equivalent to their committed contribution. Furthermore, decisions to extend credit would turn on votes by two-thirds of the voting shares in the facility, giving major donors virtual veto rights.

This kind of flexibility was and still is prized among the CMIM participants. Informal cooperation has always been a defining feature of Asian regional cooperation, in part because of the area's staggering economic diversity. Countries not only have wildly different economic cycles, but also occupy very different stages of development. Japan and China may have world class GDP numbers, but their per capita income numbers are worlds apart, with Japan's average person earning over ten times that of her Chinese counterpart. Monetary coordination can consequently be difficult since they and other countries may have very different macroeconomic objectives – with richer countries perhaps emphasizing stability in their stewardship of their economy, and others opting for growth. Not to mention the fact that there are plenty of longstanding historical and cultural animosities – even between major trading partners, and the prospect of a potentially military confrontation between neighbors lingers to this day. As a result, countries are most comfortable cooperating in ways that do not require ceding core aspects of economic sovereignty, and which maintain policy independence and flexibility. And the CMIM accommodates such priorities to the letter.

That said, the CMIM comprises an instance of financial engineering that is quite likely too flexible for its own good. It is a highly secretive arrangement between regional central banks, and not all of the terms have been shared with the public. But from what has been revealed, the degree of comfort the agreement would provide in a time of crisis is questionable. Ultimately, the success of the program depends on wealthier (or at least more stable) countries exchanging liquid or in-demand currencies for unwanted ones. Yet given the limited geographic scope of participating countries, it is entirely possible that more than one member may need assistance at one time, and in the process overwhelm the fund's $240 billion resources. Moreover, under the terms of the agreement, donors enjoy effective veto rights to "just say no" to assistance if it so suits them. Indeed, because regional intervention requires a two-thirds majority of voting shares in the CMIM, and thus multiple stakeholders are needed for the facility to be activated, the discretionary nature of lending decisions will turn on not only legal but also political considerations – and above all, the preferences of Japan and China, the primary backers and biggest contributors to the program.

Additionally, even if a country is somehow outvoted on the activation of a swap, there is still no guarantee that it would actually deliver on its commitment to provide foreign exchange assistance. We've already seen that under the CMIM no money changes hands among signatories; the program does not employ a pool of collective funds where centralized decision makers determine payouts. Countries merely promise to participate in the program and keep cash in special accounts at national central banks. Furthermore, pledges to help one another are not cloaked in any formal international obligation. They are not memorialized by treaty, but instead are legally ambiguous and decidedly informal commitments between banks. There are also, to my knowledge, few if any means of resolving disputes under the accord if countries disagree on how to act responsibly. Like most soft-law instruments, the swap program does not reference any particular court or international body for adjudicating disagreements. In this way the CMIM distinguishes itself from the ESM, where disputes can ultimately be resolved by the European Court of Justice. Moreover, unlike many species of international financial regulation, there are no natural market disciplines, leading to persistent doubts as to how reliable the experiment really is. Indeed, perhaps for this reason, no country has yet sought assistance under the program, leaving it an as yet untested safety net.

The ultimate impact and usefulness of the CMIM thus remain hotly debated. The CMIM clearly lacks the institutional pillars we have seen in other areas of international economic affairs. It is informal, albeit seemingly contractual; it is secretive, though some key provisions have been described for the public; and it does not involve an immediate commitment to act, but instead activates responses by members once a series of procedural and political steps are fulfilled. All the while, the CMIM, like the CMI, continues to rely on the U.S. dollar – not a member country currency – and additionally remains linked to the IMF's policy prerogatives: a country is only able to access 30 percent of its emergency link of credit without seeking IMF approval. Afterwards, the prospective borrower has to enter into negotiations with the IMF, which as we have seen can consist of stringent austerity measures. The CMIM is consequently less independent and less attractive than many backers originally envisioned, especially given the aspirations many countries had of freeing themselves of IMF supervision.

THE RISE OF THE REDBACK

Deeper monetary regionalization is still moving apace in Asia, however. But the driver of tighter coordination is not a collection of loosely affiliated Southeast Asian countries. Instead, it's been China, the regional hegemon and up-and-coming world power.

For over a decade, China has been the world's dominant exporter to the United States and is now widely acknowledged as having (at least) the second largest economy, having displaced Japan in 2010. So perhaps not surprisingly, it is increasingly known as the country you call first when you want to make anything work in Asia, or for that matter, on the global stage. As the limitations of the CMIM became more apparent, for example, finance ministers from across the region sought China's moral and financial support for the project. And indeed, China – for the most part unwilling to pay the political price for refusing to cooperate with its regional neighbors – has obliged, both by vocalizing support for the new CMIM and by ramping up its existing bilateral swap programs with trading partners to complement regional efforts. But notably, the commitments made in many of its swaps are not the provision of U.S. dollars as liquidity support, but instead the Chinese national currency, the RMB.

For many people, the increasing role of the RMB – or as some have described it, the rise of the "redback" – is just a natural extension of its growing prominence in the international economic system.[30] Indeed, the sheer gravity of China's prowess could enable it to become, as the economist Arvind Subramanian has surmised, "the premier reserve currency by the end of this decade, or early next decade."[31] The logic certainly seems inexorable: Central banks stuff their coffers with foreign reserves for two reasons – namely to pay off foreign creditors and to purchase exports. According to this logic, the RMB should seem pretty attractive. China is by virtually all measures becoming a critical source of credit and investment. Plus it is arguably the world's top trading nation. By contrast, the United States is facing historic postwar debt levels, and runs chronic trade deficits with key trading partners, most importantly China. Not surprisingly, at least when measured against other major currencies, the dollar has lost a quarter of its value since first going off the gold standard, and in the last forty years, four-fifths of its purchasing power when measured against the cost of a basket of consumer goods.[32]

Nevertheless, a key tenet of China's domestic development policy has for decades been to keep its currency inconvertible – meaning that the government has traditionally prohibited foreigners from exchanging it for another currency, and the RMB's use has been restricted to trade purposes. Foreign companies have thus been prohibited from issuing or selling RMB-denominated stocks and bonds, that is, at least until recently. Furthermore, the value of the RMB has been pegged to the dollar and strict capital controls have been in place to minimize any appreciation of the currency.[33]

China's embrace of tight monetary control is surprising in some regards because most commentators assume that countries want to internationalize their currency. Internationalization, after all, allows a country's domestic firms to avoid foreign exchange risks as well as the costs of converting currencies, since deals are done in its local currency. But history has shown internationalization to not always be popular, especially for rising world powers. Three reasons seem to indicate why. First, internationalizing a currency inherently increases its value. It becomes not only a means of exchange for domestic citizens, but also an instrument of value for foreigners. Thus foreigners, like domestic parties, will seek to own it. Heightened demand will increase the value of the currency, and by extension make a country's exports more expensive vis-à-vis others. Consequently, the United States largely shirked from asserting the dollar as an international currency in the 1910s and 20s, just as Germany and Japan sought to prevent greater use of the Deutschmark and yen in the 1970s and 80s.[34]

A country's decision to loosen its grip on its currency and internationalize it can also make borrowing more expensive for its domestic firms. When capital is trapped in a country, a government can tinker with local regulations in ways that divert resources to preferred firms or economic activities. For example, by capping interest rates on bank deposits, a government can ensure that capital remains cheap for special interests or sectors of the economy. This "financial repression" ties savers to low returns on their bank deposits, but also reduces the cost of capital for favored firms and industries that take out loans from banks.[35] Internationalizing a currency undermines these kinds of policy tools, and by extension government control of the economy, giving savers a wider number of options. Savers don't have to keep their money in a bank that is offering threadbare returns on deposits. Instead, they can invest elsewhere, and even abroad, if doing so would offer better returns. On the flip side, however, capital becomes more expensive for domestic firms since local banks may have less capital to lend.

Finally, the internationalization of a country's currency can unwittingly unleash all kinds of financial chaos. Internationalization enables the free flow of money across borders, which in turn can make possible large, volatile swings in the movement of capital in and out of the country. As a result, it is necessary that domestic banks be extremely well regulated before the gates are opened to foreign money. In the absence of supervision, banks tend to put all their money into one or two sectors – and usually real estate – causing an unsustainable bubble in asset prices that can burst in ways that bring down the domestic financial system. Additionally, you need deep, diverse and liquid bond markets denominated in the currency for absorbing (and withstanding) capital inflows and outflows. If a country doesn't have one or both of

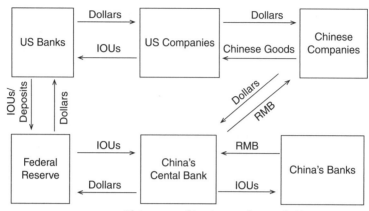

FIGURE 4. Chinese sterilization made simple(r).

these bulwarks, it's probably not in its long-term interests to lift capital controls and float its currency. In such cases, there are usually considerable lags in time between a nation's emergence as a first-rank power and the internationalization of its currency. Even the U.S. dollar did not become the dominant currency until 1945, nearly 70 years after displacing the UK as the world's largest economy.[36]

With this in mind, China, too, has often resisted internationalization, and chosen instead to embrace financial repression and the trade advantages proffered by its cheap currency peg to the dollar. When a company like General Electric purchases a Chinese factory, or a retailer like Wal-Mart buys Chinese-made goods, they exchange U.S. dollars for RMB. These purchases create an overall surplus in the balance of payments in the country. Under normal circumstances, in the absence of governmental intervention, these surpluses would increase the money supply and cause higher prices. However, instead of letting the free market operate, China's central bank intervenes almost daily to buy those dollars with RMB, and then removes those same RMB by selling bonds and raising reserve requirements – in effect forcing banks to cough up their excess foreign currency. The dollar proceeds are then used to purchase foreign exchange reserves, usually U.S. Treasuries. This intervention keeps prices from rising, and in the process helps protect China's trade surplus with the world, and especially the United States.

It is in many ways an effective, but not entirely novel approach. Other countries have embraced the strategy when experiencing their own rise to global prominence – including the United States. From 1921–1929, when most of the world relied on gold as the primary form of reserve money, the nation's gold stock grew by about 50 percent, reflecting its trade surplus and America's competitive position in the global economy.[37] Eventually, however, the Federal Reserve became concerned that the rise in reserves would begin to stoke inflation. So in 1923, the central bank started to sterilize the incoming money, and in response, wholesale prices fell steadily throughout the remainder of the decade.

Sterilization rarely comes without costs, however – and the costs usually fall on other countries. In the case of 1920's America, many of the most serious consequences of sterilization fell on major trading partners, especially those who were trying to maintain or rejoin the gold standard.[38] Given its persistent trade surplus, the United States should have seen an increase in its gold supply, causing domestic prices to climb, making its exports more expensive, and eventually restoring the global trade balance.[39] Sterilization short-circuited this adjustment mechanism, so there was no increase in the prices of U.S. goods and exports. Instead, less competitive countries were forced into a period of self-imposed deflation and were ill-positioned to compete with the American export juggernaut. Meanwhile, Britain, the waning superpower, instituted a slew of new tariffs that contributed to the collapse of the gold-standard system and, according to some experts, exacerbated the Great Depression.[40]

As with U.S. policies decades earlier, Chinese sterilization tactics have also had at times unfortunate consequences for the country's trading partners. But sterilization has also posed real challenges for China. By keeping the RMB cheap, sterilization tends to encourage over-expansion of the export sector, while inflation, or at least any adjustment of the exchange rate to reflect the country's competitiveness, is delayed.[41] At the same time, Chinese banks are driven to purchase bonds from China's central bank instead of lending to consumers, which likely drives their interest rates higher.[42] All the while, and perhaps most important, resources are piled into assets that may not necessarily generate positive returns. In short, dollar assets – indeed even U.S. Treasury bonds – are no longer risk-free. The near-death experiences of U.S. financial institutions in 2008 – from Citibank to government-backed Fannie and Freddie Mae – along with incessant political dramas over the U.S. budget and debt ceiling, have exposed unprecedented economic and political risk associated with U.S. investments. There is, in short, a *possibility* that the United States may not be able (or willing) to pay its debt – or that it may do so with dollars that will be worth a lot less in the future than they are now. The unthinkable just a decade ago is now *thinkable*, even if unlikely.

HOW CHINA EXPORTS THE RENMINBI

In 2008, the risks of dollar hegemony prompted then Chinese president Hu Jintao, on a visit to London, to call for a "new international financial order that is fair, just, inclusive, and orderly."[43] With the world still reeling from the fallout of the massive U.S. bank failures, he proclaimed confidently that the global financial system needed to reduce its reliance on the currency. Immediately, a torrent of news and media speculation erupted as to just how such a system could and should arise. Part of the speculation related to the fact that there are, as we will continue to see in this chapter, many ways of potentially democratizing the international monetary system. So people were curious to know just what the country had in mind. Yet for long-time China observers, the country's strategy had been in the works for nearly a decade – and it was clear that the country would seek to step up internationalizing its *own* currency and raising the profile and the popularity of the RMB in international commerce and global financial transactions.

Internationalizing a currency is not, however, something that officials do overnight. It is instead a process, and involves steadily increasing the availability of a currency and the ways it can be used. As a result, economists largely recognize various degrees of "internationalization." A minimum level of internationalization involves whether a currency is popular as a unit of account and as a means of exchanging value between merchants, including those who themselves may have no ties to the country that issues the currency. So as a simple example, if the RMB met this threshold of internationalization, a seller of watches in Brazil would be tempted to list the price of her watches in RMB, and a purchaser in Russia would be able to use Chinese currency to purchase the watches if both parties so agreed. An even greater level of internationalization would go a step further, and allow financial firms to sell stocks and bonds in the country's currency, both at home and abroad. Expanding the use of currency for financial transactions diversifies the use of the currency, and bolsters a country's capacity to absorb capital inflows and outflows. Finally, a highly internationalized currency would be transferable to such a degree that foreign companies, financial institutions, governments and individuals would be able to hold the country's currency, as well as financial instruments denominated in it, in amounts that they deem useful and prudent.[44] So along these lines, the RMB could operate alongside the dollar as, among other things, a dominant reserve currency for firms and central banks.

A full-blown internationalization of the RMB would have a dramatic impact on the global monetary system. By increasing the RMB's prominence as a unit of account, medium of exchange, and store of value, China could reduce its dependency on the dollar – and in the process increase the RMB's own market share of international transactions. In doing so, China's exposure to dollar depreciation could be minimized, and Chinese firms could enjoy the privileges of seigniorage we outlined earlier.

And internationalization *is* undeniably moving apace. In many regards, the increasing prominence of the RMB is a natural outgrowth of the country's rapidly growing economy and expanding middle class. HSBC, the international bank, has noted that China's cross border trade with neighbors has risen consistently over the last twenty years, favoring the RMB for trade settlement. Because more countries traded with China than anyone else, save perhaps Japan, it was only natural that its currency came to dominate many regional transactions. At the same time, "rising income levels are sending increasingly more Mainland tourists abroad, armed with their overseas RMB-denominated shopping budgets."[45] Consequently, nearly 60 percent of the cash in local circulation in Mongolia is in RMB, just as the RMB is accepted in shops and restaurants in South Korea. Meanwhile, in Vietnam the RMB can be exchanged via unofficial banking, which has been at the least tacitly supported by the government.[46]

Yet even for China, internationalization requires a set of enormous policy adjustments. Most important, it entails freeing the flow of RMB in and out of the country, and around the world. We've already seen that such liberalization can come at a price with regard to currency appreciation, the cost of capital, and financial market volatility. But it's also worth highlighting that it also comes at a cost to macroeconomic autonomy. For decades, economists have shown that where countries embrace the free movement of capital, they can't enjoy both exchange rate stability and monetary sovereignty.[47] You can enjoy two of the three – an independent monetary policy, a fixed exchange rate, and free capital flows – *but not all three*. China's developmental path up to this point has included monetary sovereignty and a fixed exchange rate – but no free movement of capital. Internationalization implies, however, that something has to give.

China, for its part, has pursued a measured (and partial) combination of the three macroeconomic policy postures. It has opted for managed, as opposed to total, exchange rate flexibility, and coupled this approach with a reduction in monetary independence and gradual global integration. In this way, the three dimensions of the "trilemma" configurations – monetary independence, exchange rate stability, and financial openness – are themselves characterized by varying degrees of compromise.[48]

One of the first important official steps toward internationalization was taken in 2002, when China introduced a program allowing licensed foreign investors to buy RMB-denominated "A" shares in China's mainland stock exchanges (in Shanghai and Shenzhen). Prior to the program, stock exchanges on China's mainland had been closed to foreign investors due to capital controls that restricted the movement of assets in and out of China.[49] But by permitting a limited number of firms to move their capital in and out of the country, over 30 billion U.S. dollars of investments have been made since 2002.[50] Later in 2007, a second Qualified Domestic Institutional Investor scheme was introduced that permitted Chinese institutional investors to invest in foreign markets.

Loosening capital controls were then coupled with a series of policy changes in the 2000s aimed at increasing the allure of the RMB. In 2005, China dramatically weakened its peg to the dollar, catalyzing a steady appreciation of the currency. As its value rose by nearly 20 percent, the RMB became an attractive asset for currency speculators, even after the RMB was re-pegged following the crisis.[51] Then in 2007, a new offshore RMB bond market was launched – commonly referred to as the "dim sum" market – which evolved such as to support issuances by multinational corporations, including McDonald's in 2010.

Efforts have also been stepped up to enhance the RMB's attractiveness as an instrument of invoice and accounting. In 2009, the People's Bank of China initiated a pilot program that allowed mainland-designated enterprises and their international trading counterparties to use RMB to settle trade payments outside of China. The program was extended a year later to allow corporations anywhere in the world to use the RMB as a trade-settlement currency when doing business with approved companies in specified provinces and municipalities in China. Through these reforms, virtually any financial institution or company can open up an RMB-denominated bank account in Hong Kong, just as financial institutions in the city are largely free to create RMB-denominated investment products.[52] Restrictions on the type of corporations that can be granted RMB loans have also been lifted, paving the way to greater provisions of RMB-denominated credit. Taken as a whole, "[the new rules are] a big step in promoting the international use of the renminbi."[53] Firms around the globe have opportunities to better manage their RMB payments and receipts, which increases working capital efficiency and mitigates costs and other risk associated with currency exchange rates.[54]

Finally, China has turned to new tools of financial diplomacy to export the RMB for commercial purposes. Here again, the currency swap has proven indispensable. As we saw at the outset of this chapter, a currency can be quite desirable if the country issuing it is a major exporter of goods, since people need money to buy the goods. In the case of China, the world's leading trading nation, this means that its economy creates a natural demand for its currency. To feed that demand in the wake of the crisis – which had been bottled up by convertibility restrictions – the People's Bank of China initiated a new program promoting a range of swap agreements with other central banks to effectively provide the world with additional liquidity.

In some ways, the swaps mirrored past U.S. practice, and allowed countries to rely on the RMB as a store of value and a hedge against any depreciation of their own currency. If a country was hit with a speculative attack, it could draw on the RMB to bolster its balance sheet. But there was also the distinct objective of internationalizing the RMB. Under the terms of most agreements, a bank participating in a swap accord could use it to provide local companies with the RMB needed to make purchases from China. This has radically changed the very nature of swaps from stability-enhancing devices to trade- and RMB-promotion vehicles.[55] The agreements not only created, as the economist Nasser Saidi has noted, the potential for more commerce with China, but also set the stage for the establishment of a "Redback" zone in Asia and elsewhere.[56]

For most commentators, China's ever-expanding spate of financial and macroeconomic reforms portends the establishment of the RMB as a leading international currency. How quickly, however, is hotly debated. Indeed, from virtually any perspective, it's clear that the RMB isn't quite there yet. Despite liberalization, China still imposes its currency peg. Investment capital can flow more freely in and out of the country than before, but it is still highly regulated. Plus the data aren't always kind with regard to the RMB's prevalence. RMB-denominated bonds were a drop in the bucket of all outstanding international securities in 2011. The dollar accounts for nearly 85 percent of global turnover in international markets, followed by the euro at about 40 percent; the RMB, by contrast, barely reached 1 percent in 2011. Similarly, the RMB barely registers as a global reserve currency, even though the country's economy is the second largest in the world.[57]

But again, the world is changing. Slowly but surely – and yet faster than many people realize – the RMB is becoming globally available even as restrictions on convertibility remain in place. Transactions settled in RMB have increased 13 fold over the last couple years, just as deposits in the currency jumped tenfold since the country began to more actively pursue internationalization.[58] And Arvind Subramanian and Martin Kessler have suggested that the RMB has become the dominant reference currency in East Asia.[59] More currencies now co-move with the RMB than with the dollar or the euro. According to the economists, the currencies of South Korea, Indonesia, Malaysia, the Philippines, Taiwan, Singapore and Thailand all more closely track the RMB than the dollar. The dollar only dominates in Hong Kong, Vietnam and Mongolia. And equally important, the RMB's influence is growing even beyond Asia as the RMB is the dominant reference currency for Chile, India, Israel, South Africa and Turkey. Consequently, Subramanian and Kessler estimate that even without broader monetary and financial reforms, the RMB could become a global reference currency by the mid-2030s.

Whether China will stomach more reforms in the short term that would accelerate even further the RMB's rise as an actual reserve currency is, however, far from clear. After years of unprecedented growth, the country's economy is beginning to slow, and its banks are financially strapped due to a glut of shaky loans tied to bad infrastructure projects. More reforms would add to the pain. China would have to enlarge its bond market, making the RMB and RMB-denominated debt more easily tradable and thus more attractive for investors seeking liquid markets in which to trade. And this would go against the business model of China Inc. – particularly the cheap capital made possible by capital controls that have enabled the funneling of the country's savings to companies and industries favored by the government.

As we've discussed, people in China currently have no choice but to stuff their savings in local banks, which are then on-lent to companies favored by the state, since governmental restrictions block foreign investment options offering better returns. Liberalizing economic policy would, however, ramp up competition among banks for the savings of Chinese workers and retail investors alike – inevitably driving up the cost of capital, just as the value of the currency would rise as foreign speculators gain access to the newly freed currency. Chinese goods would consequently become more expensive to export, and likely less competitive. And Chinese companies might not get the same cheap financing that they enjoyed in the past. So whether or not China will continue along the road of fast-paced monetary reform remains anyone's guess.

ANOTHER BASKET CASE

Uncertainty in China only complicates what has already become a complicated world of competing yet interconnected national monetary policies. In the wake of successive financial crises, a half decade of controversial monetary policies in the United States and Europe helped cheap dollars and euro-denominated debt flood the world's capital markets alongside a rising amount of Chinese RMB. And even traditional deficit stalwarts like Japan turned to expansive monetary policy as a means of pulling themselves out of their economic doldrums. Now, as economies in the West begin to normalize, efforts to reverse such policies are generating equal concern as the prospect of higher effective interest rates in the United States (and thus better relative returns for foreign investors) has helped to catalyse large outflows of capital from some emerging markets.

With so much monetary disunity, calls for a new international currency have gained traction. But instead of looking to a new national currency to assume the role of the U.S. dollar, some officials have called for the creation of an international central bank that could issue its own global currency for use in international economic affairs, and in the process provide greater stability for the international monetary system.[60]

This kind of device is attractive because it would cure in one swoop the problems of exorbitant privilege and persistent macroeconomic imbalances that seem to be plaguing the global financial system. It could provide a source of liquidity as economies restructure. Furthermore, a new, truly *international* currency could operate in ways untethered to the dictates of any one national economy, and thus all countries would face the same source of economic discipline.

But as a policy prescription, a supranational currency faces a steep uphill battle. Of the many questions surrounding such an institution, besides whether or not it would work, is whether any powerful country or monetary authority would ever support this kind of initiative. This is an especially pertinent question for the United States, and to a lesser

extent the European Union, which both enjoy modern-day privileges
of seigniorage. Few countries in their position would be willing to give
up the advantages of lower borrowing and transaction costs, just for the
global welfare benefits accorded to more sure-footed macroeconomic
stability. Indeed, by definition, an international bank's monetary policies would never be good for all countries all the time; as with countries within the Eurozone, there would be winners and losers with any
particular policy decision, and just who should benefit or not would
be a contentious, if not irreconcilable, problem.[61] Delegating monetary
decisionmaking to an institution whose actions would not always be in
their interest would be a hard pill for U.S. and EU leaders to swallow,
to say the least.

Another open question is whether or not any supranational currency
would even be effective at resolving the macroeconomic imbalances
that have undermined the health of the global economy. In many ways,
an international bank could have the same problems of credibility and
liquidity that the United States currently faces with the dollar. It would
have to guarantee that there is enough liquidity in the system while at
the same time ensure that its currency won't chronically depreciate,
either against other currencies or even commodities like gold. This is a
difficult, and potentially impossible "catch 22" that could, over time, end
up swinging global monetary policy in the direction of either extreme
profligacy, with lots of the new currency being printed by the bank, or
worldwide austerity.

Given the considerable political and economic questions revolving
around an international currency, prospects for a multilateral system
have focused on more incremental steps. The most popular argument
is that the current bookkeeping system for international monetary
affairs – the Special Drawing Right (SDR) – should be revamped in
ways such that it could be positioned to increasingly function as an
alternative reserve currency, and over time lend greater stability to the
global economy.

SDRs are effectively credit accounts at the IMF that countries can
draw on when they need financial assistance. The idea would be to
empower the IMF to convert SDRs into higher utility instruments
that could be used to directly back public and private loans, and thus
offer even more liquidity to countries experiencing a balance-of-payments crisis. And then one day, over time, they could even be used
for the everyday payment of foreign goods and services. By expanding
the function of SDRs, the thinking goes, SDRs could begin to lessen

the stranglehold of dollars as the primary international reserve currency as well as reduce the exorbitant privilege accorded to the United States.[62] In principle, the global economy could then begin a process of healthy macroeconomic rebalancing, and do so in ways that would build directly on the existing international regulatory architecture. Proponents reason that we obviously have an IMF, which acts as a lender of last resort. Plus SDRs already make up a small proportion of central banks' reserves. We just need to change SDRs into something that could operate more effectively as a store of value and, at least one day, as a means of transacting.

That said, the practical challenges surrounding such reforms are enormous. For the SDR to really come to rival the dollar (or for that matter, the euro or other major currencies), its liquidity would have to be ramped up. And for this to happen, not only would one need more SDR allocations, but sovereigns would also have to step up issuing debt denominated in SDRs. Meanwhile, a private market for SDRs (or SDR claims) would be needed. Banks would ideally diversify their credit operations and make loans referencing SDRs, and borrowers would repay in kind. Even exporters would have to have the ability to convert SDR claims into national currencies via large banks or, more likely, exchanges. Consequently, one would need to develop an infrastructure to support all this financial activity. As Eichengreen notes, "someone would have to create liquid markets in SDR forwards or futures, on which firms and investors could hedge against the risk of changes in the value of local currencies against SDRs."[63] This would be costly, given the relative absence of SDR market participants, and first movers would incur the most costs related to SDR-denominated transactions. A catalyst of some sort – an international treaty, perhaps, as with the creation of the euro, or perhaps coordinated subsidies by central banks – would almost certainly be required.

This leads to the final complication: national governments, like private institutions, would have to be encouraged to adopt full-throttle the SDR as part of their reserve portfolio. But this is perhaps an even higher hurdle than getting banks to switch. SDRs aren't just synthetic reserves; they are also the basis for voting at the IMF. Countries that provide the most funds for SDRs get the most voting power. So to the extent to which more SDRs are created, new kinds of institutional arrangements might have to be made that could well impact IMF leadership and governance. Countries would also have to decide on just what basket of currencies should constitute the new reserve currency. For the last fifty years, the dollar, along with major European currencies (currently the euro) and the yen, have dominated its value. But if countries really want to adopt a credible alternative to the dollar, changes would have to be made to reflect the growth of emerging markets. A revamped SDR would thus have to be devised, one that would rely to a greater extent on a broader range of currencies like the Brazilian real and the RMB.[64] These are, however, hard steps to take where various structural arrangements permit developing and developed countries to periodically – if unsustainably – tap cheap exports or cheap financing. Getting a broad-based agreement in the absence of widespread economic and political incentives thus remains elusive. The SDR won't be the new gold standard any time soon.

A NEW INTERNATIONAL MONETARY SYSTEM, SORT OF

So what are we to make of today's international monetary relations? At a minimum, the unilateral, minilateral, and even multilateral maneuvers by governments underscore what is an unprecedented amount of monetary diplomacy. But this diplomacy looks very different from what people have generally thought of as policy coordination. It's not formal, global, or for that matter even a forward-looking set of rules coordinating the values of the world's major currencies. Instead, increasingly experimental and transactional modes of international cooperation dominate monetary relations. Freed from the golden handcuffs of commodity money, countries are undertaking breathtakingly ambitious new forms of cooperation that center on the provision of liquidity for both trade and macroeconomic emergencies. In doing so, they're cooperating in ways scarcely imaginable a generation ago – from a multistate European currency union to regional and bilateral swap agreements based on not only the dollar, but also the RMB. Even the BRICS countries (Brazil, Russia, India, China and South Africa) are considering their own international version of the CMIM to help provide assistance in times of financial turbulence, with China the leading donor.

The rise of RMB swaps in particular – both as supplements to the Chiang Mai Initiative and as facilitators of bilateral trade – highlights the increasing prominence not only of China, but also financial engineering more generally in today's monetary affairs. On the one hand, swaps lines backed by in-demand currencies can offer a measure of financial security for a country that can draw on them when needed. As in the private sector, swap lines can help bolster investors' confidence in a country's economy, and provide evidence of a country's ability to meet any possible short-term liquidity challenges. Consequently, they can alleviate the pressure many countries now feel to stuff their balance sheet with U.S. T-bills and even serve as a useful hedge against possible declines in the dollar.[65] At the same time, RMB swaps can (and are) being used as a means of facilitating trade with China, and by extension, boosting the circulation of the Chinese currency. Swaps can be drawn on not only for macroeconomic liquidity, but also for trade liquidity when companies need RMB to purchase goods from China. In this way, the RMB swaps are helping to export the RMB both regionally and internationally, and are rapidly elevating its importance in the global economy.

Yet even with the increased prominence of the RMB, the transition to a truly multipolar monetary system where the RMB and euro rival the dollar's prominence won't happen overnight. The euro's immediate future is hazy and hard to predict, to say the least. Meanwhile, the Chinese government's own commitment to liberalizing the RMB is unclear. And even if officials dove into internationalization head first, sufficient incentives would have to arise to set in motion meaningful transition away from using the dollar into motion. But the dollar's incumbency status can undermine incentives even under the best of circumstances – since, by definition, its very popularity makes the dollar valuable, regardless of its inherent value. So even in today's dysfunctional currency system, a country or financial institution's embrace of the RMB or any other dollar alternative would require that they pay an illiquidity premium; then they would have to work hard to incentivize others to join them by creating an infrastructure capable of absorbing the large capital inflows and outflows one would expect of a global currency. Nevertheless, the sheer size of the Chinese economy suggests that there is movement, and an accelerating use of the RMB as a reference currency, as trade with the Asian giant reshapes the contours of the global economic balance of power.

But multipolarity, even once it arrives full-tilt, will not magically make a truly multilateral monetary system spring to life. Ever since the collapse of the gold standard in the 1970s, monetary sovereignty has been widely viewed as a key ingredient of national economic sovereignty – and as a tool for meeting domestic policy priorities. And in an age of economic stagnation, elected leaders and the technocrats they appoint are more focused on local growth and employment than the dangers their decisions may pose to external or international financial stability. This makes the likelihood of a broad-based, multilateral monetary accord of the kind seen in the 1940s highly unlikely. Economies of all shapes and sizes would have to be committed to undertaking deep structural changes in order to synch monetary policy with one another. Deficit countries would have to make deep adjustments like cutting wages and social welfare programs in order to boost exports. Surplus countries would have to refocus their growth on increasing domestic demand and purchasing foreign goods and services.[66] New rules of the road would have to be devised to foster macroeconomic discipline and provide for international liquidity management.[67] It's hard enough to accomplish in the Eurozone, and globally – where democracies are more prevalent and heterogeneous than ever before – it's probably impossible.

With prospects of such a revolution in macroeconomic coordination unlikely, international monetary rules have followed the minilateral script spelled out in the previous chapters – and popped up as often-modest commitments adopted in discrete regional or bilateral alliances. The progress should not be underestimated, however. As in the other domains of international economic affairs, even small and incremental steps can, over time, have a big impact. The CMIM may prove to be a stepping stone for an eventual Asian Monetary Unit along the lines of the euro, or serve as a basis for an Asian Monetary Fund capable of challenging IMF hegemony. The euro, too, even with its tarnished reputation, will continue to provide a potential threat to dollar hegemony – if not in the short run, then at least in the mid- to long term assuming political integration proves successful. And the RMB is virtually guaranteed to assume a role as a regional and perhaps even international rival to the dollar in the next decade, and in the process multiply the venues and means by which countries park their savings and transact. The big question, of course, is whether these developments will add more discipline to the international monetary system – or whether they will catalyze greater fragmentation and instability in ways we have yet to begin to predict.

5

Managing Minilateralism

We've seen throughout this book that minilateralism can arise in different guises and forms, each with the objective of lubricating interstate economic relations in a world of more diffuse power. But because it provides a means to an end – and is not an end in and of itself – minilateralism can't (or at least shouldn't) be understood as inherently good or bad. Instead, it represents an expanded toolset of options for countries navigating a world of increasingly heterogeneous economic interests and preferences.

So it's important to keep in mind that minilateralism provides no one magic bullet for solving all problems in international economic relations. The challenges facing the global economy are big *and* diverse. Not every problem can be tackled the same way, with the same partners, or with the same commitments or market-related instruments. Instead, to be effective, minilateralism inherently requires what Harvard professor Joseph Nye and humanitarian Suzanne Nossel have separately described as "smart" power – the ability to customize policy responses in ways that most effectively speak to the challenge or opportunity at hand.[1] Unlike Nye and Nossel's conceptions of smart power, however, which tend to involve simultaneous uses of military, economic, and cultural power, minilateral statecraft is a matter of deploying governmental and market-based instruments in the service of financial stability and growth. Nonetheless, both smart minilateralism and smart foreign policy require government policymakers to ask the same basic set of strategic questions. First, they have to determine their own preferred policy objectives. Next, they have to identify what tools are possibly available to achieve their objectives, and the likelihood of success with each. Finally, officials have to ask whether their actions will be viewed by other relevant actors and stakeholders as legitimate uses of power.

In the following pages we will see that the first two inquiries are sequentially related, with means flowing from ends. The third inquiry about legitimacy, by contrast, informs both. A government's objectives and tools for achieving them are most likely to be effective when other countries, citizens, and market participants view them as legitimate. To the extent that they are not, financial diplomacy will be put under considerable duress. This can be a real problem for minilateralism since its effectiveness often resides, at least in part, in avoiding the trappings of multilateral statecraft like universal membership and formal legal rules. Consequently, a smart minilateralist tackles the problem of legitimacy head on by maximizing opportunities to embed financial diplomacy in processes that are explainable as democratic or at least widely accepted as such. Otherwise, democratic deficits can themselves serve as a source of systemic risk, regardless of whether people act with the best of intentions.

THE STRATEGY IMPERATIVE

One of this book's takeaways is that today's financial statecraft is a response to a new, multipolar global economy. In a world of more equally distributed economic power, nations have often found multilateral coordination harder, not easier, even as technology has improved communication and the movement of goods and capital. As a result, a new toolset has been developed to help navigate a world of disparate interests and objectives.

But using these tools wisely requires asking and answering a tough set of questions that were not routinely considered in the postwar era. In the 1940s, clear routes and forums for problem solving were institutionalized by the IMF, World Bank, GATT, and later the WTO. These institutions espoused a particular mission, backed by the hegemonic power of the United States. In addition, a stable set of legal instruments were used to forward economic diplomacy.

Today's statecraft is comparatively more complicated – and freewheeling. National authorities have to determine their preferred policy objectives in a world with more, not fewer, diplomatic focal points, and in a world where power is more diffuse. Then they have to figure out which tactic, or combination of tactics, best helps them achieve their objectives. Minilateral trade agreements, for example, might help you get consensus on tariff schemes, and circumvent hold up problems where one country threatens to veto global agendas. But a treaty won't necessarily fix problems that are constantly evolving and require continuous updating and renegotiation. And even if parties strike a minilateral trade deal, it might be undermined as other regimes in international monetary law unravel, or if it clashes with other minilateral or multilateral commercial pacts.

Managing minilateralism thus requires, as a first step, understanding complex issue areas and policy goals, and making tough choices between them, which isn't always easy. Indeed, countries have long debated the proper objectives of financial diplomacy. For some, it's a question of economic stability. According to this view, financial diplomacy should be geared above all else toward preserving the health of the global economy. Playing it safe is thus paramount in order to prevent a major stock market crash or bank failure. Authorities should focus on policies like high capital requirements to shore up cross-border financial institutions, implement prudent trade restrictions to prevent large-scale local dislocations brought on by free trade, and, like Keynes and White, bless sound emergency policies like governmental restrictions on convertibility in times of economic crisis, in order to prevent currency crashes that can destabilize financial markets and economies.

For others, however, financial diplomacy should be oriented foremost toward promoting economic growth, not just staying in place. From this perspective, market volatility and even unemployment are necessary predicates to even greater prosperity and wealth. The objective of financial diplomacy should be to promote economic development, even when it is at times bumpy, so as not to slow it down. And this is best done when government takes a back seat to the private sector. Perhaps not surprisingly, this view tends to predominate among trade specialists, who routinely fight what they perceive to be inefficient governmental barriers to cross-border commerce. But financial authorities might be similarly disposed, particularly where their mandates not only include financial stability, but also the promotion of economic growth. Strict rules and regulations might be helpful in protecting investors and facilitating capital formation and stability. However, by prohibiting financial institutions from taking certain kinds of risks, regulations can dampen investment and the provision of credit – and in the process dramatically slow GDP growth and put local financial firms at a competitive disadvantage vis-à-vis their foreign counterparts.

Policy debates on the relative importance of financial stability and economic growth are usually carried out on a case-by-case (and

country-by-country) basis. And as part of the discussions, people naturally take into account the relative costs and benefits associated with
adopting any policy posture – whether it be free trade, financial regulation, or monetary policy – for local stakeholders. That said, the two goals
are increasingly viewed as interconnected as opposed to incompatible –
especially as lapses in supervision have erased decades of growth in rich
and poor countries alike. As a result, policy objectives – like achieving
financial stability at the lowest cost possible to growth – have become
much more nuanced over the last decade.

But even once a country can identify and articulate its goals, a second
query quickly follows, namely, what are the tools available for achieving
them? To answer this question, authorities have to not only figure out
what resources are available in a more general sense, but also, as Nye
recognizes, determine whether the availability of such resources is subject to change in different strategic situations.[2]

This book has surveyed the major tactics employed by today's financial diplomats, and we've seen how different tools have dominated various issue areas and sectors of the global economy. Numbers games,
as we have seen, have long taken a high profile in trade, allowing
parties to overcome the deadlocks of the global trade agenda with
willing parties. Soft law, meanwhile, has proven useful where parties
need to speedily conclude agreements among many parties – especially where, as in matters of market oversight, the optimality of a
particular policy is uncertain. And financial engineering is slowly
helping states hedge their bets with regard to not only the stability of
their own currency, but also with respect to the global money supply.
While these may be more modest means of cooperation than Bretton
Woods had envisioned a half century ago, each presents new possi-
bilities for how states can potentially interact with one another in a
post-American age.

Fortunately, none of these strategies are necessarily mutually exclusive, and each can to varying degrees be deployed in other areas.
Financial regulation involves not only soft law, but also numbers games
in institutions like the G-7 and G-20. Trade can employ numbers games
and under-enforce formal obligations, making them akin to soft law – a
strategy we saw with the WTO's rules on regional trading blocs. And
monetary coordination can leverage soft-law contracts among clubs of
central banks just as it does financial markets and currency controls.

Indeed, minilateral techniques can even be paired with multilateralism in ways that are mutually beneficial. Both GATT and the WTO

anticipate regionalism and free trade agreements. Soft law, meanwhile, can and does operate alongside hard-law institutions like the World Bank and IMF, which often serve as the basis for monitoring countries' commitments to global best practices for the regulation of financial markets. Even much of today's monetary engineering in Asia, including the Chiang Mai Initiative, operates in conjunction with Bretton Woods, as countries seek to diversify from their U.S.-dollar holdings and hedge their bets against volatility in their own currency markets.

That said, financial diplomacy is a game of skill. You can't rely on any one tool in the toolbox whenever you wish. Not everything works all the time, or to the same degree. And there may be policy trade-offs as well as unintended consequences across different sectors of the economy whenever particular strategies are employed. As we observed earlier, the "harder" soft law's edges become and the more enforcement you get, the less attractive it may become when parties are uncertain about the costs and benefits of cooperation. So you end up, to some extent, with the same traditional problems of hard law. Closed regional agreements, meanwhile, can undermine and even reduce incentives to cooperate at a global level, since a party may want to block others from sharing the advantages it enjoys with a particular trading partner. Similarly, financial engineering can certainly create its own potentially unfair trade advantages – and resentment from it might not only undermine the global trading system, but also catalyze new rounds of protectionism as countries seek to retaliate against perceived unfair trade practices.

Smart minilateralism, like smart power more generally, thus requires sound management and a strong grasp of the "relationship between various tools and policy options, as well as which goals and tools involve zero-sum choices over others and which involve joint gains."[3] Knowing what you want to achieve isn't enough. You also have to determine how various objectives interact with one another, and how one's choice of diplomatic tools can change or affect the very objectives one seeks to realize. The ends may ultimately determine the means, but the means can likewise affect which ends are possible, and at what cost.

MULTILATERALISM'S MALCONTENTS

Yet identifying objectives and tools is in some ways just the easy part. Of all the essential elements of smart minilateralism, legitimacy is the most difficult, at least nowadays. Legitimacy is, at its simplest, understood as the acceptance of the rulers (and their rules) by the ruled – an acceptance which usually turns on the degree to which authority wielded is based on some form of democratic consent. Any way you cut it, however, minilateralism always carries some real risk of just not appearing fair. Numbers games mean that not every concerned stakeholder will be at the table or have a say when big decisions are made. Soft law, meanwhile, entails the use of diplomatic strategies that explicitly avoid (and arguably circumvent) legislatures and the democratic process. And financial engineering can exacerbate already exorbitant privileges enjoyed by a few powerful countries.

And it's more than just a problem of fairness. Ultimately, the same problems that can make you nervous about a lack of legitimacy might make you think twice about minilateralism as a robust governance tool. For one, it may not always mesh well with multilateral forums and institutions. Regional rules can clash with international standards, even when they establish ostensibly deeper levels of integration. Soft law can undermine and even supplant hard-law practices where treaties are silent or vague as to members' commitments, and can even recast basic notions of customary international law. Multicurrency regimes create new sources of volatility and, by definition, supplant the old global (dollar) standard. Plus without strong claims to legitimacy, these inconsistencies can create serious problems for global economic relations, and can generate all kinds of questions as to which international rules are really "rules" (or for that matter, "law"), and to what extent they should be binding on participants and non-participants alike. So plenty of scholars and commentators have looked skeptically on minilateral diplomacy in all its guises.

Before tackling the problems of minilateralism, however, it is worth keeping in mind that criticisms of international economic diplomacy – minilateral and otherwise – are nothing new, and predate even today's new financial statecraft. Many people considered Bretton Woods to be as much about the Cold War as it was about efficient global markets. After all, voting rights in the GATT, IMF, and World Bank entrenched the power of the West and served to propagate U.S.-styled capitalism. As such, each institution was subject to a variety of criticisms from countries whose ideological and economic perspectives diverged from the strict market-based policy prescriptions proposed by the United States and its allies.

Among Western policy elites, however, serious critiques of the at times lofty machinations of economic statecraft were rather muted. Instead, dissatisfaction with economic multilateralism really shifted into high gear in the 1970s, though it diminished as the Vietnam War came to conclusion, and then reappeared in the 1990s, when capital and goods began to flow in historically unprecedented ways across borders.

We've already touched on the major flashpoints over the last two decades, but they bear repeating. Perhaps the most important trigger was the seemingly overnight success – and assertiveness – of the WTO. Once established, its independent dispute panels began to crank out decisions regarding member countries' compliance with international trade obligations. The problem was, many of their rulings espoused strict interpretations of the GATT and other accords, and in doing so, panel decisions had a tendency to intrude more deeply into traditional areas of state sovereignty than many of the organization's early supporters had predicted. The United States, for its part, lost a series of high profile cases at the WTO in which its domestic environmental policies and regulations were challenged. Similarly, Europe's ability to regulate alimentary issues like hormones in beef was curtailed, even though its regulations were espoused as matters of health and public safety. In the wake of the WTO's decisions, a diverse swath of stakeholders and activists were awakened to the stakes of economic globalization, and became concerned that the evolving order was prioritizing trade liberalization over other social priorities.

The second development – or really set of developments – was the imposition of sometimes painful market and government reforms by the West on developing countries experiencing balance-of-payments crises. Nowhere was this more obvious than during the Asian financial crisis. When credit markets froze in East Asia and had to seek financial assistance from international lenders, the IMF imposed a range of severe austerity requirements in return for assistance. The logic was that countries experiencing financial crises must be behaving in macroeconomically irresponsible ways, since they otherwise wouldn't be in the predicament they were in. Either governments were spending too much, borrowing too much, or taxing too little – or, more likely, were doing a combination of the three. So one of the many conditions the IMF imposed on client states was higher interest rates – or in the words of Joseph Stiglitz, "much, much higher interest rates – plus cutbacks in government spending and increases in taxes."[4] Additionally, the IMF told governments in Thailand, Korea, and elsewhere to undertake fundamental changes not only in their economic management, but also in their political, societal, and legal institutions.[5]

Though some of the reforms may have had strong policy rationales, many of the conditions seemed to be more ideological than technical. They also entailed ceding economic sovereignty in order to "do the right thing" for presumed economic growth.[6] The conditions for economic aid thus became a serious bone of contention between the West and developing countries. Although this was mildly surprising for some commentators, it shouldn't have been. After all, creditor and debtor countries rarely agree on what is necessary for growth, and their varying incentives tend to tilt their perspectives as to what is necessary for driving the economy forward. The former tend to view debtors as profligate and inefficient, whereas the latter tend to view creditors as imperialistic and insensitive to their unique economic conditions. So it's usually difficult to come to an agreement on just how to restructure debt and economic relations where, as is often the case, creditors require changes in policy, like higher interest rates or cuts in spending, that will have, at least in the short term, the effect of cutting off demand, thereby intensifying the economic distress.

Frustrations ultimately spilled out into the streets of Seattle in 1999 during the annual WTO ministerial meetings. On November 30, in the early morning, 30,000 students, environmentalists, labor organizers, and protesters organized by the Direct Action Network arrived downtown to block street access to the WTO convention building. In response to the blockade, a state of emergency was declared and after several hours of negotiations, riot police were called in to drive out the protesters with teargas. But the activists defied martial law and stayed in the streets the entire week until finally, on December 3, talks collapsed. As hundreds of activists were being arrested, developing countries, emboldened by the protesters' push for fairer trade, balked against agreements designed to further reduce tariffs and demanded steeper concessions from the rich world. A similar scene would then repeat itself in Washington just months later in April, as protesters railed against the IMF and the World Bank, both of whose policies were accused of systematically undermining the interests of the developing world. And, as in November, the world's media saturated news outlets with pictures of mass demonstrations, confrontations between activists and police, and calls for more democratic and accountable international institutions.

Almost immediately, the protests put the brakes on globalization efforts, smart and otherwise. A raft of agenda items, including a much touted Multilateral Agreement on Investment, failed, as developing and developed countries found consensus increasingly difficult to achieve. Moreover, new rounds of trade negotiations became frustratingly difficult to secure, effectively paralyzing the global trade agenda.

For the moment, nothing short of a revolution in the international economic system seemed imminent – either intergovernmental talks would falter altogether, or radical changes in global governance would have to be made to respond to the rising tide of popular dissatisfaction. But broad-based, organized criticism would quickly dissipate in the West. Attacks on the World Trade Center on September 11, 2001 wiped globalization debates from the front page of major newspapers as national security took center stage. The upstart counter-capitalist movement lost steam in a matter of days as policymakers (and their publics) focused their attention on the war on terror. Meanwhile, economic globalization started to get a face lift in developing countries as their own economies began to take off in a world with fewer borders. With sales of goods to the United States and Europe skyrocketing, it was hard to kill the goose that laid golden eggs worth over billions in annualized growth. To be sure, plenty of developing countries resented the seemingly one-sided, Western-dominated nature of international economic governance. And neoliberal reforms proposed by the rich world have been consistently blended with local, state-led measures, and even protectionism in the form of both trade barriers and currency pegs. Yet for the most part, in the 1990s and early 2000s, most countries relented with their most vocal criticisms, even where their domestic priorities departed from the policies advocated by leading powers.

FROM SEATTLE TO ATHENS (AND ROME)

One of the perennial problems with international economic diplomacy is that faith in the ability of experts to reach smart policy outcomes lasts about as long as the economy is strong. When times are good, few tend to question ends or means, and people tend to tolerate a little less democracy. But when things go bad, after shooting the politicians, bureaucrats are usually next in the line of fire.

So with the global economy taking a dive in the late 2000s, it shouldn't be too shocking that the European Union would be the epicenter of dissatisfaction with cross-border diplomacy. As we've discussed, the EU has always been a somewhat controversial international institution. Although it behaves like a state in many regards, it sidesteps sustained participation by the region's citizens. And this was, by most accounts, intentional. Indeed, the European Union's founding fathers went out of their way to avoid populism. Hewing to the sentiments of the masses was associated with the extreme right and left, fascism and communism, and there was a deliberate attempt to achieve integration through analytical, strategic planning and baby steps.

Distrust of the masses has meant, however, that the European Union commands less respect as a legitimate player in international affairs than does a typical democratically elected national government. On the surface, of course, it has many of the bells and whistles. It is a treaty-based organization in which only democratic countries participate. And through a series of agreements, which have been ratified by member states, it has expanded its scope and mandate to become one of the world's leading minilateral institutions. Yet in practice, the degree of consent actually given remains a touchy subject. Even though the EU is based on formal international accords, the agreements themselves were adopted with what arguably amounts to limited input. Most EU citizens were never asked to vote directly on, say, forming the European Union or adopting the euro as a currency. And when voters have had a say, results have been decidedly mixed. For example, attempts to create an EU "Constitution" failed when French and Dutch prime ministers buckled to domestic political pressure and had referendums on whether to accept it. Similarly, Ireland refused – at least initially – the Treaty of Lisbon, just as Denmark's first referendum on the Treaty of Maastricht was unsuccessful.

Just as problematic, interest in EU policymaking remains embarrassingly weak. In large part, it's because few voters actually understand (or want to understand) how the EU's rule making works. It's hard to blame them: in principle, an inter-governmental Council of Ministers, composed of ministers from each member state, represents the individual EU governments. Meanwhile, a European Parliament, with members elected directly and from across the EU, represents the people. Then the European Parliament elects, on the basis of a proposal made by EU heads of state at the European Council (another body distinct from the Council of Ministers), a President of the European Commission. Next, the elected President proposes to the European Parliament the other members of the European Commission, which represents the interests of the European Union as a whole. Finally, when the governing architecture is up and running, the Commission proposes policy to the Council of Ministers and the Parliament in a multilayered process that can have varying degrees of applicability to member states. Confused yet? I haven't even gotten to the EU-level agencies, which can craft technical standards with Commission approval. The important thing to see, however, is just how complex the EU can be. Indeed, the organization's byzantine bureaucracy makes it almost impossible for even experts to understand. So the average Joe, or Jacques, has been largely unable to connect EU policy to his daily life, much less hold relevant policy-makers accountable for their decisions.

People still tolerated the EU as long as it stayed away from core matters of national self-determination like taxing policy, spending, and education. After all, nobody was really clamoring to talk about capital ratios and disclosure for securities firms. Better to leave it to the experts. The Greek crisis, however, has changed the level of deference, as well as people's perceptions of the EU and its role in their daily lives. With countries debating structural adjustments that will change the face of the EU's southern periphery, the importance of many seemingly distant technical matters has become more apparent, as have the consequences of bad policymaking. All the while, the benefits of EU membership, or least participation in the euro, have become less obvious. So quite naturally, EU politicos, citizens, and courts have started to take a closer look at the actual goals of the organization, as well as the means by which it sets about doing its business.

That said, growing popular dissatisfaction hasn't stopped the EU from successfully embedding itself even deeper in what most would acknowledge to be the sovereign affairs of member states. If anything, officials have doubled down on the institution's technocratic moorings, and the institution's influence has expanded into members' spheres of economic self-determination. The result has been that the EU has assumed a new political – and even market – valence in ways its founders would have scarcely imagined at its founding.

Take for example Greece and Italy, where both countries came to be led (briefly) by EU alumni in the wake of the Eurozone crisis. Both stories followed similar plots insofar as missteps by elected incumbents sparked economic crises that would in turn catalyze changes in governmental leadership. In Greece, George Papandreou, the country's prime minister, lost the Greek parliament's confidence after demanding a national referendum on a bailout package that he himself had just negotiated hours earlier with the EU and countries that held Greek bonds. After Papandreou's clumsy and ill-advised pronouncement, spreads on Greek debt spiked, putting the country into renewed turmoil. After a series of inter-party negotiations, Lucas Papademos was ushered into power. Papademos, a straight-laced economist and former official at the European Central Bank, was viewed as a logical choice to help calm the markets, so elections were scrapped. Meanwhile, in Italy the term of Prime Minister Silvio Berlusconi came to an ignominious conclusion when spreads on Italian bonds spiked after his promises to pursue austerity were insufficient to calm markets. A playboy and entertainment mogul tarred by sex scandals and various governmental investigations, Berlusconi had little credibility with the markets. So he stepped aside and was replaced by the senior technocrat and former European Commissioner Mario Monti.[7] And Monti, like Papademos, promised that he would not run in future elections.

Embedded in the two appointments was the belief that technocrats, and especially former EU officials, could make better commitments on behalf of their countries to pursue policies preferred by – and expected from – international creditors. The new power brokers were, in short, extraordinary signaling devices for markets increasingly cautious about lending to cash-strapped Mediterranean governments. Less swayed by politics, and not seeking reelection, technocrats could take the political heat to articulate and implement the painful reforms required to relaunch their respective economies. Bloated labor markets could be overhauled, government services restructured, and "internal" devaluations imposed, all of which would force wages lower in debtor countries.

In practice, it hasn't been nearly so simple. After just a year of implementing austerity measures, Greeks voted out the major parties that put Papademos in power. In their place, fringe parties came to the fore, throwing Greece's very membership in the EU in doubt. Similar, though less extreme politics have also hampered governmental reforms in Italy. To his credit, Monti fared better, and introduced considerable structural reforms while restoring Italy's economic reputation. Nevertheless, fighting within Monti's own cabinet and political pressures from interest groups forced him to water down key legislation originally intended to open up service industries, which then led to speculation as to who would ultimately replace him once he left office. Labor reforms slowed, and piecemeal compromises were achieved in somewhat sporadic sectors, from taxi licenses to legal services. Only once Monti had reversed himself and thrown his hat in the ring to run for Prime Minister as a democratically elected official did prospects for reform actually improve – but even then only temporarily. It showed that if he won, the reforms would have a longer shelf life and thus be more effective. But offering to run was no substitute for actually winning, and his candidacy ultimately proved a catastrophe. First round Italian elections held in 2013 were an embarrassment for the veteran official, as he lost to former Prime Minister Berlusconi as well as Beppe Grillo, a stand-up comic and policy lightweight.

WHY OTHERWISE SMART MINILATERALISM FAILS

Minilateralism operates, at least in part, on the proposition that ends-oriented policymaking is acceptable so long as outcomes are consistent with peoples' policy desires.[8] The ends, not the means, it is hoped, matter most to stakeholders. But in reality, people tend to place just as much emphasis on process as substance, especially when decisions touch on issues with big, obvious consequences for society. They want to know that they have been consulted and that their opinions matter.

This can be a challenge for technocrats because they tend to be results oriented, so they tend to overlook the importance of consent by the governed. But they shouldn't. There are, after all, a number of less-than-savory aspects of technocracy. For one, the decision makers are rarely elected officials. Instead, they're usually appointed to whatever positions they hold, or they're civil servants acting within the confines of a governmental civil service. In either case, they're not really accountable to the public. On top of that, they don't receive much everyday oversight. What they do is highly complex, making any real-time monitoring of their actions difficult, and they exercise their authority with considerable discretion since they act on at times non-public information relating to economies and markets that are themselves in constant flux. With such autonomy and power (and not to mention civil servant job security), technocrats are often viewed with distrust, and at times, hostility. People tend to only see what technocrats do once things go wrong, and in the absence of having a direct say over them, the public tends to have little patience for their mistakes and errors.

Still, economic governance does, by its very nature, require decision makers to tackle problems that are highly complex, rapidly changing, and in need of detached, professional attention.[9] As such, economic supervision generally requires a high level of expertise that is best cordoned off from everyday politics. Which is why wonk governance is so popular and pervasive. By relying on bureaucrats instead of politicians, technocracy offers the promise of not only neutral, but also reason-based policymaking. Experts who understand the complexity of the financial economy can make decisions of import for the plumbing of the financial system while not being beholden to special interests. They can tackle emerging problems decisively while taking the time to think through solutions that are objective and best for the long-term interests of stakeholders, market participants, and the larger society. In so doing, bureaucracies can create a normative – but objectively backed – consensus conducive to sound economic management.[10]

An easy way to think about technocracy's advantages is to imagine an alternative universe where all central bankers are elected officials. Central banks, among other responsibilities, determine monetary policy. By lowering interest rates, central bankers can give a boost to GDP, though if they lower rates too much, or for too long, they can create asset bubbles like the one that caused the subprime crisis in the United States in 2007. In other words, people would just use the low interest rates to borrow money to bid on property, inflating its cost in ways that do not reflect its real value. Loose monetary policies also effectively punish longer-term creditors, and make other countries and lenders reluctant to lend since the prospect of continuous or high inflation would cause the value of their loan to depreciate over time. But if people could vote for central bankers, they would probably demand expansive monetary policies anyway. Voters tend to emphasize their own short-term interests over future creditors and borrowers. Plus low-cost loans could help pump up domestic GDP and (short-term) employment. And as elected officials seeking to keep or get a job, central bankers would likely comply, and in the process undermine the economies they are otherwise sworn to protect.

Still, paternalistic arguments like these strike many as downright annoying. Moreover, they can come across as somewhat disingenuous. For most people, financial oversight seems just as political an arena of policymaking as any other area of governance. Sure, people are appointed – but they're appointed by politicians. As such, the most important decision makers are almost invariably of the same party of appointing officials, and tend to share their ideological and political commitments. Also, we can't ignore that the little guys, the wonks at their cubicles, have political instincts. Even seemingly mundane regulatory decisions are based, at least in part, on judgments that are not entirely fact-driven. Numbers may not lie, but they still have to be interpreted. And in the process of interpretation, analysts must weigh varying concerns, such as comparing the cost of a certain regulation for firms, against the benefits of reducing a perceived risky activity.

Nevertheless, even given the political and ideological features of their decisions, technocrats circumvent traditional democratic processes all the time – and especially at the international level. When, for example, the G-20 introduces a new regulatory agenda for the world's financial authorities, there is no requirement that national legislatures be consulted. Similarly, when the Basel Committee introduces new global rules for capital, national legislatures are not formally consulted; no affirmative votes or tallies by politicians are taken before new international regulations are promulgated. Instead, international administrative agencies take the lead in crafting standards and rarely need a supermajority of legislators to bless their decisions.

For some critics, you ultimately end up with what, at the extremes, can be described as the "tyranny of the nerd." Wonks may help in identifying and executing ends and means, but less so than one might think, and often at real costs to democracy. Out of touch, unaccountable, and arrogant, technocrats may know more, critics argue, but what they know isn't necessarily deployed in ways that promote the desires and interests of affected stakeholders or society. Instead, bureaucrats can function, in Weberian terms, as a "steel-hard cage" depriving people of their autonomy and freedom to choose.

There are, of course, replies to each of these criticisms. As critics themselves acknowledge, although technocrats may not always be elected, the most senior ones are selected by people who are. And because they are selected by politicians, the selection process has accountability features, with politicians' bad decisions potentially subjecting them to diminished electoral prospects in the future. Additionally, the fact that most administrative agencies are funded by taxpayers means that they are subject to annual budget and appropriations processes that keep plenty of administrative agencies on a relatively tight leash. To the extent to which their rulemaking or decisions are unpopular, or simply bad, technocrats may not be reappointed, or they may find their activities defunded by politicians.

There are also a number of administrative checks. In some countries, regulatory agencies are required to publish reports that document or explain the basis of their regulatory decision making. Furthermore, when really important decisions are under consideration, "notice-and-comment" procedures are activated whereby technocrats are required to inform the public of the policies they are considering. Stakeholders are then given (an) opportunity to provide their views on proposed reforms, and offer alternative suggestions or support. All the while, if politicians want to roll back the power of technocratic agencies, besides defunding them, they can just change their mandate or write them out of existence altogether.

These administrative hurdles can seem pretty mundane at first glance, but they serve a vital, democracy-enhancing function. By requiring regulatory agencies and the technocrats who run them to publish information about their activities, principals – both legislatures and the people who elect them – are in a better position to monitor the actions of agencies and their effectiveness. The ability to evaluate the factual record used to make regulatory decisions also allows the public to scrutinize the wisdom and reasonableness of regulatory decisions and to help identify the circumstances that give rise to poor regulatory decisions. Meanwhile, notice-and-comment requirements – which put regulators in touch with the concerns and perceptions of outsiders, including the general public – help overcome tunnel vision, ideological blinders, and the potential impact of social and professional connections by broadening the scope of information that regulators receive.

Collectively, these mechanisms provide means by which either consent or accountability can be enhanced. So even with technocrats in charge, minilateralism does not necessarily signal the demise of the world's democracies or a long slide into autocratic global governance. At its best, you still get the participation of a range of old-school actors who are active in more traditional areas of international law like heads of state and legislators who occasionally bless diplomatic efforts. But day-to-day coordination is for the most part managed by economic experts. And even *their* power does not spring from a vacuum: instead, they leverage their authority through administrative processes that are blessed by democratically elected officials, and which occasionally allow for scrutiny by the public.

BROADENING THE GEOPOLITICAL BASE

The fact that minilateralism sports some of the trappings of democracy doesn't mean that today's technocracy is perfect, however. There are still some major shortcomings: minilateralism, as a strategy of financial statecraft, is often pretty exclusive, and it's not always representative of truly "global" interests. Additionally, minilateralism routinely avoids the traditional treaty-ratification procedures associated with "real" international law, and often relies on low-level, and at times informal, economic and monetary arrangements for dealing with some of the most serious problems facing the world's financial system.

In many regards, this is the beauty of minilateralism: you can go small, deviating from the traditional, and often inflexible, economic multilateralism that has governed the global economy over the last half century – and nonetheless achieve, at least potentially, big policy outcomes. But minilateralism creates concerns, especially where decisions are made (and cooperation arises) without the full consent of those affected, and thus, in academic parlance, without proper "input legitimacy." In such circumstances, there are real dangers for economic diplomacy. Without a legitimate basis of authority, rules or decisions won't necessarily be viewed as valid or lawful. Indeed, even if you can reach agreement on important policy areas, among well-respected officials and leaders, minilateral rules may still be ignored, or perhaps even worse, deeply resented.

Numbers games present especially difficult input legitimacy problems since they are based, by definition, on avoiding broad multilateral bargaining processes. Exclusivity is very much the embraced modus operandi of coordination. As such, this brand of minilateralism abandons, in explicit ways, any pretense of global community or shared interests. Nevertheless, the decisions of even a small club or alliance of countries can have an enormous impact on the global economy – and affect nonparticipants in the process.

Yet it's worth noting that exclusivity can be a deceptive and malleable feature of coordination, and there are plenty of things technocrats can do to broaden the base of input – and even consent – while still constraining the amount of haggling that can make negotiation costly. Perhaps the most direct strategy is to increase the number of chairs sitting around the table where vital economic issues are discussed, but without necessarily going global. This was the tack taken by the European Union as it expanded at various points to its current twenty-eight members. Though originally created to solve the problem of Germany after World War II, it also came to serve as an indispensable vehicle for the reintegration of Eastern Europe into the European community after the end of the Cold War. To generate the incentives for switching from the central planning models of growth adopted under the aegis of the Soviet Union, the prospect of EU membership was used to induce a more full-throttle adoption of capitalism in the 1990s, and to nudge states towards fully democratic political systems. Dictating from afar, the logic went, would never be as useful as offering countries a seat at the EU table.

Even still, the best example of broadening the base is found in today's premier international economic body, the G-20. Before the crisis, the G-7 was the focal point for international cooperation – a group of countries including the United States, leading European powers, and Japan. But with the onset of the crisis, the G-20, an expanded group of eleven additional states and the EU, would dominate global policymaking. And for the first time, at least one representative from every major continent would participate along with the original G-7, including the leading emerging markets of Brazil, Russia, India, China, and South Africa (as noted before, the "BRICS").

By increasing its membership, the G-20 was able to strengthen both its geopolitical effectiveness and claims to legitimacy. The earlier G-7 configuration was useful when the United States, Germany, France, Italy, and Japan dominated the global economy. But in a world where the BRICS alone account for 56 percent of growth, and some are among the world's major creditor countries, solving the global economy's problems requires a larger tent.[11] As we've seen in the previous chapters, one can't solve the problem of global macroeconomic imbalances without China. Trade has to involve the participation of not only developed, but also developing countries. Financial regulations have to address banking rules in Southeast Asia just as much as they do U.S. policy. So to achieve big policy goals, you have to bring in the big (or at least relevant) powers. And here the G-20 succeeds in spades. Even if the G-20 does not truly represent the world – more than 172 countries, after all, are not represented – it does a good job of at least reflecting economic reality. Combined, the G-20 countries sport 90 percent of the world's GDP and they can collectively render decisive decisions on monetary, financial-market, and economic policy, assuming, of course, they can come to agreement on what steps to take.

This last caveat is particularly important given how different many of the members of the G-20 actually are from one another. Unlike in the past, where members all hailed from largely homogeneous economic philosophies, and even cultures, the G-20 consists of countries at vastly different stages of development. Although China's GDP, for example, is the second largest in the world, the median income is only 11 percent of that of the U.S.[12] Similarly, although South Africa is the largest economy in Africa, its economic output and growth is dwarfed by the other leading emerging markets like Brazil and China.[13] As such, the

G-20's members are likely to have very different agendas, and to place varying degrees of emphasis on tradeoffs. Development, rather than financial stability, could well dominate some decisions on issues like banking regulations, which tend to disadvantage companies and institutions in riskier parts of the world; similarly, topics like debt forgiveness for poorer countries or AIDS funding could take precedence over discrete policy initiatives like executive compensation or the oversight of hedge funds.

For this reason, broadening the geopolitical base is often accompanied by other institutional innovations to accommodate the twin objectives of enhanced participation and effective decision making. Most commonly, international bodies divvy up their membership into privileged decision makers who can make or decide policy, and a broader membership that plays an advisory role. Typically, you tend to think of this kind of strategy as associated with the United Nations, where the Security Council makes the tough decisions regarding military conflicts and breaches of the peace and the General Assembly provides advisory guidance on those decisions and their implementation. But you also see it in the world of international economic diplomacy. For example, in IOSCO, the leading body of securities regulators, a tight-knit policy core called the Technical Committee generates policy on issues relating to securities firms and credit rating agencies, and other committees provide largely advisory guidance. Then, in a limited number of circumstances, the entire membership can vote on global best practices to be promulgated across the world. Similar kinds of structures exist in bodies for international insurance regulators and even accounting bodies. Even the EU eventually deviated from traditional "one country – one vote" ideals by balancing its growing membership with weighted voting powers for each country based on the members' home populations.

Ultimately, choices made by participants in international organizations reflect, among other things, the reality that gains in input legitimacy can be outweighed by losses in the quality of output, and vice versa. That is, when input legitimacy is advanced beyond a certain threshold, an organization's output may suffer due to delays, conflicts, strategizing, and a plethora of heterogeneous interests. Meanwhile, if input legitimacy is weakened or overly diluted, an organization's legislative output may increase, but it may have less acceptability and persuasiveness for the outside world. From this perspective, the challenge of international regulatory governance is thus to identify which countries are most needed (and worthy) to get a seat at a table with a very finite number of chairs.

OF BALLOT-BOXES AND GLOBAL MARKETS

The problem of exclusivity need not only concern the absence of countries around a table. It can also involve the degree to which people themselves get to more directly participate in decision making, especially when there's a big issue at stake that touches on the everyday lives of citizens in very tangible ways.

This begs the question of how to maximize the legitimacy of technocratic decision making. Probably the most direct approach is to allow stakeholders themselves to vote on technocratic policy proposals. We see this, for example, in the United States with issues like Wisconsin's gubernatorial recall or California's perennial election referendums. It also arises from time to time in the European Union. Some members, like Ireland, require that significant changes in EU governance be approved directly by their publics; at other times, politicians are pressured into bringing policy initiatives before local legislatures or to have referendums of some sort or another. The idea is that by giving voters a direct say in legislation, treaties effectively receive double legitimacy – both through the heads of state who helped negotiate treaties and the citizens themselves.

Ballot-box legitimacy can be risky, however. At its extremes, it "transforms the electorate into part-time legislators."[14] Ostensibly, this is the best form of democracy – a modern-day Jeffersonian ideal of democracy in the hands of the people. Yet voters are not usually as informed as parliamentarians and legislators, much less technocrats. And this can in itself generate enormous policy uncertainty and risk. For example, when in 2013 David Cameron called for a referendum on the United Kingdom's membership in the European Union, it was more about renegotiating the island nation's relationship with the rest of the continent – and threatening Germany and France with outright withdrawal – than it was about establishing or bolstering the organization's domestic legitimacy. But in playing the membership card, he created enormous concern about the future of not only the euro, but the European Union as well, since the issue was poised to be debated less on analytical grounds than on political and rhetorical ones. By cutting out the middle men, so to speak – the legislatures and regulators – and bringing the complex matter of membership directly to voters, Cameron opened up the prospect of potentially more emotional and capricious decision making on an issue that most assumed had been settled decades earlier.

All of this can create enormous drags on economic growth, especially where issues have significant financial implications. Consider once again the Eurozone crisis. In June 2012, the world waited with bated breath as Greece held parliamentary elections that would effectively determine whether or not the country would stay in the common currency. Markets rose and fell with each unofficial poll leading up to the June election, wreaking havoc not only on Greek but also European and world stock exchanges. Investors, like politicians, understood that a vote for the anti-euro party could spark panic in global markets and possibly catalyze the departure of other periphery states throughout the Mediterranean. And they also knew that despite the stakes, the local debate wouldn't be dominated by just pie charts and econometrics. More than a couple of other politicians from the extreme-left to the ultra-right were instead stoking fears of a resurgent German imperium, and the danger of a new, modern-day invasion of the country by economic, as opposed to military means.

And that was a relatively happy instance of ballot-box governance, at least from the standpoint of the EU technocrats and creditors. After all, the conservative New Democracy party squeaked by its rivals, ensuring Greece would remain in the Eurozone for at least the short-term. But to be sure, things haven't always worked as well when technocrats take their case to the public. Just consider the ill-fated EU Constitution, mentioned briefly at the outset of this chapter. In 2004, a treaty had been negotiated that would have replaced all prior European treaties with a single text. It would have also streamlined decision making at the federal level by replacing unanimity with qualified majority voting among member states. The idea was simple enough: make the EU a more effective and efficient organization, and prevent the ability of any one country to hold up or block policy initiatives that had been largely agreed upon.

Yet it was this virtue that also condemned the treaty. The European Union had always worked (or lumbered along) through consensus-like rulemaking, and the prospect of narrow majorities of neighbors dictating sensitive areas of economic policy was rejected. Across Europe, opposition parties called for referendums on the matter, arguing that governments should defer to the will of the people in the face of such important decisions. Meanwhile, governments were at pains to explain how the treaty worked, given the complexity of some of the treaty's voting provisions, and were outmaneuvered in the fight for public support. In the end, referendums would indeed be had, with several countries, including France and the Netherlands, rejecting the technocratic reforms. The debacle would have serious consequences – and stifle prospects for future reform for years, even as the continent grappled with the proper responses to the Eurozone debt crisis.

THE RIGHT TO VOICE

One alternative to playing Russian roulette at the ballot box is not to give stakeholders a vote, but instead to ensure that they have a voice in the rulemaking process and the opportunity to make arguments while policy decisions are being made.[15] Traditionally, this kind of "voice" has meant coordination with stakeholders and interest groups as decision makers went about making policy. So, especially after Seattle, Bretton Woods institutions have sought to institutionalize outreach programs. For instance, IMF officials may now meet occasionally with the Sierra Club to discuss the environmental impact of some lending decisions, just as WTO officials might participate in conferences with labor groups or field questions about new trade initiatives. Voice is also available in theory in non-binding referendums, where a country's citizenry may vote on an issue; however, politicians are often free to ignore the outcome of such votes. You can imagine how often that's been tried.

More recently, the tool of choice for facilitating voice has been more administrative procedure than ad hoc outreach. Minilateral organizations are, in short, adopting some of the notice-and-comment procedures discussed above in order to allow people and other market participants to offer their critiques of proposed international rules and regulations. In practice, this means that when important new rules are being contemplated, the public gets a chance to write regulators at the Basel Committee or IOSCO and let them know what they think of any proposals. Then, once rules are agreed to, the member regulators implement them locally – and will often open up the implementation process to further input and comment. In this way, virtually everyone – from foreign governmental bureaucracies to domestic market participants and consumer advocates – gets the opportunity to publicly offer their own assessment of the proposed policy.

Bureaucratic notice-and-comment procedures hold some real advantages over referendums and other ballot-box forms of governance. For the most part, notice-and-comment processes are a lot faster than many referendums. Referendums are costly and require polling stations to open, a national debate, and perhaps planned holiday time for voters. Administrative decision making can provide a means for stakeholders to get their two cents in and voice their opinion while circumventing the hazards of full-throttled politics. All along, when incorporated at the international level, well crafted policy making procedures can provide a real boost to legitimacy. By mimicking the forms of hoop-jumping that have long been practiced in many domestic systems, they allow international bodies to make their own claims to procedural integrity and widespread input that would otherwise not be credible.

This doesn't mean there is always a level playing field. Administrative procedure always carries the risk of death by a thousand cuts. Piece by piece, critique by critique, or reform after reform, legislative proposals can be gutted and lose their original power or effectiveness. Furthermore, well-organized interest groups tend to have the upper hand in engaging the regulatory process over individuals and associations of persons with less concentrated or overlapping interests.

On the other hand, administrative processes are useful in grabbing people's attention and acting as a focal point for engaging the public. At their best, they open up a simple, straightforward path to influencing debate and the decision-making process.[16] It's consequently easy, at least in principle, to improve international legislation as it is being both devised and implemented. This is a change of sorts from old-school treaties. The public may get the opportunity to let their elected representatives know their priorities at the outset of international treaty negotiations. But once a deal is inked, the practicalities of ratification usually leave little room for amendments, and even during the bargaining process, scrutiny over negotiators' acts and omissions can be negligible.[17]

Voice additionally tends to favor, and indeed require, reasoned debate. Politics is a rough-and-tumble business; the objective is to incite passions and widespread engagement in order to achieve goals that correspond with a nation's (or political party's) values or immediate interests. Administrative process, by contrast, is much more dispassionate. It requires that issues be analyzed systematically and rigorously. Parties are free to make arguments based on their own interests. But if they want to maximize their ability to influence the debate, their critiques have to be grounded in terms of societal welfare, or with regard to the overall objectives of the proposed rules. Policy arguments are thus more likely to be grounded in thoughtful analysis than would be the case in more heated electoral environments.

This is all important because managing international economic affairs is, as we've seen repeatedly, a complicated business. More often than not, new rules in one area like monetary cooperation can have important implications for banks, and by extension, international banking regulation (and vice versa). Trade, meanwhile, can affect current account surpluses and deficits of national governments in ways that can impact monetary policy. And this says virtually nothing about the unexpected consequences that fiscal policies can hold for foreign creditors and the stability of international capital markets. In an increasingly complicated economic world like today's, voice not only adds legitimacy, but it can also be an indispensable tool in raising the level of discourse and deliberation. Indeed, by providing an outlet for stakeholders to articulate their interests and preferences, smart administrative processes can help broaden the perspectives and information available to economic officials and authorities, and in doing so enable better decision making.

SHOULD JUDICIAL HUNCHES RULE?

A bit further along the technocratic spectrum, the entire issue of legitimacy could be outsourced from the people to the courts. Along these lines, international courts or panels could rule on the legitimate exercise of power by national and international regulatory authorities. An association of experienced financial officials could rule on whether or not standard-setting bodies are acting beyond their mandates. Or they could provide definitive rulings on matters of economic or regulatory best practices, and identify countries that have failed to abide by international commitments, as we already see in WTO dispute panels. Rulings could then be enforced through concerted actions by members of relevant international bodies, or through the use of existing arbitral treaties common in other areas of international economic law.

Establishing such a system is difficult, however. The long road from the ITO to the GATT and finally WTO took nearly a half century to complete. Other areas of international economic law will likely require just as much time and effort. Countries have to agree on the right institutional format – with an ever-growing number of stakeholders. Then, hard intellectual work has to be done to think through unprecedented issues of international law – such as how to make legal pronouncements out of explicitly non-binding soft-law standards. Would altogether new treaties have to be struck? Or would one try to convert existing informal arrangements into international obligations? Or, more modestly, should one try to directly import international rules through domestic legislative processes and then delegate power to international judges to arbitrate disputes?

And this brings up the additional challenge of judicial interpretation, whatever system arises: unlike many areas of the law, the wisdom of any particular financial regulation or monetary policy depends in part on the market or economy in which it is applied. When, for example, a country is experiencing a recession, more generous monetary policy or less onerous banking regulations may be warranted in order to achieve other policy gains – like economic growth and lower unemployment. How international judges would rule on such core matters of economic self-determination for any one country is hard to imagine. International dispute panels, for the most part, are not used to making analyses that consist of policy trade-offs across sectors or policy dimensions. Instead, they exist to implement particular goals and objectives of a particular sector – for instance, in the case of the WTO, the promotion of trade liberalization, often above all else. As a result, even if you could find the magic system that could accommodate these challenges, the institution you come up with will not necessarily be viewed as legitimate. After all, WTO dispute panels, for all of their effectiveness, are routinely criticized as prioritizing trade over other arguably more important social objectives. And the panels, like international courts more generally, suffer from the same Achilles' heel of far-flung, foreign officials making decisions that, in the eyes of many, should be left to local officials.

For these reasons, another, simpler option probably holds more appeal: just leave the question of legitimacy to local courts. In most well-run judicial systems, judges are educated (though not specialists), independent, and cordoned off from direct political pressure, making them good people to judge the merits of international administrative action. They're also usually citizens of the country in which they sit and charged under their national constitutions and conventions with ensuring that domestic laws are upheld – and by extension, that national agencies and political practices abide with domestic constitutional or administrative requirements. With such authority routinely asserted on local issues and procedures, courts could similarly rule on international economic practices as well.

There's certainly some precedence for it. Just recently, for example, the German Constitutional Court was required to determine the legality of the European Stability Mechanism (ESM) – and in very real ways, the very future of the euro. At issue was whether the ESM was constitutional under German law. The country's constitution declares that only the German government can determine fiscal policies. However, the terms of the ESM required Germany to participate in any properly constituted EU-level bailout operation. The problem was that as a kind of automatic pay system, the ESM potentially contravened Germany's constitutional provisions endowing the German parliament, or Bundestag, unfettered control over the national budget. If, in short, Germany were required to help bailout other countries, and if the funds for such a bailout came from the national budget, the parliament would no longer have a monopoly over the country's budgetary powers. Opponents to the ESM thus argued that the facility was unconstitutional.

Once a challenge was launched against the bailout, the German Constitutional Court, nestled in the quiet southwest town of Karlsruhe, became the focal point of the world's financial markets. Any contrary ruling would not only undermine already skittish markets, but also potentially doom the common currency by eviscerating what at the time was the only measure created to deal with the crisis. It wasn't, however, a decision that the court's founders remotely anticipated when the country's constitutional framework, the Basic Law, established the court in 1949. Instead, the primary function of the court was judicial review – to protect the postwar democracy and render any (mostly domestic) legislation null and void if it smacked of undermining the country's newly reinstated democratic principles. The euro hadn't even been created, and wouldn't be for nearly a half century. So wading into an issue of such economic importance to not only Europe, but also the world, was in many regards unprecedented.

Ultimately, the court ruled in favor of the German government, and supporters of the treaty won the day. For the court, the treaty was in itself lawfully entered into and a valid international obligation. Moreover, under the terms of the treaty, it was clear, at least in the court's view, that the Bundestag would regain substantial influence on the decisions of the German representatives in the decision-making bodies of the ESM. After all, the court reasoned, the treaty implied that German representatives to the ESM were effectively bound by the Bundestag's decisions. This meant that German technocrats needed the parliament's blessing for any decision with real budgetary relevance. As a result, the treaty was ruled constitutional, though with the understanding that both the upper and lower houses of the German parliament had be informed of and kept in the loop on any ESM decisions. Additionally, Germany had to limit its contributions to €190 billion unless both houses of parliament consented to a future increase.[18] That said, the decision implied that a full-blown parliamentary vote would not always be necessary for every ESM action.

Disappointment with the decision was widespread in some of the country's prominent legal circles. But in many ways, the court's ruling should have been expected. After all, it was made under considerable duress. The fate of the euro was in no uncertain terms hanging in the balance, and it was unlikely that the court would undo months of crisis management and planning by the continent's leading authorities and elected officials. Plus, the legal merits aside – and to be clear, the ESM was not obviously unconstitutional given its clear indications that parliaments would have to bless decisions made by their national representatives – the issue involved both technical issues and political questions that most courts feel are best left to other decision makers. On the one hand, the case involved a highly technical rescue plan that a court of generalist attorneys were not in the best position to second guess. Furthermore, it *had* been blessed by the country's key political actors. With that kind of institutional pedigree, there were practical limits as to just how assertive even a constitutional court could be. An unelected, non-specialized body overturning the work of the politicians and technocrats would smack not only of foolhardiness, but possibly of illegitimacy in its own right.

If the case of the ESM is any guide, it suggests that any policy unleashing judges as arbiters of legitimacy is certainly an attractive idea in theory, but in practice it probably won't get you far. Even when courts enjoy enough discretion to rule on the legitimacy of international regulatory or economic action, they probably will not want to use it – especially if their decisions speak to the actions of regulators in times of crisis and backed by the political establishment. Instead, courts will usually demure – and when pushed, might well be more comfortable with the administrative model of international policymaking discussed earlier in this chapter. Indeed, the German court's decision placed little emphasis on wholesale regional political processes. To the contrary, its reasoning focused, in true technocratic fashion, on voice. It queried the extent to which stakeholders – or at least their democratically elected representatives – enjoyed sufficient opportunity to participate in relevant decision-making processes when the ESM was created, and the extent that the consent of the legislature had been given. Concluding that they were, the court effectively held that the parliament's blessing would only be needed if Germany decided to increase funding in the future.

THE IMPORTANCE OF "MACRO" LEVEL LEGITIMACY

Whatever minilateral strategy is at work at any given time, its legitimacy can be tough to evaluate because in practice it requires assessing any potential democratic deficits from a wholesale, instead of retail, vantage point. The entire regulatory ecosystem has to be taken into account – the forest, in short, can't be overlooked for the trees.

One problem, however, with many commentators' criticisms of today's evolving economic statecraft is that all too often, people focus their fire on just one institution. And to be sure, at the micro-institutional level, virtually every player in the global economic system evinces some sort of democratic deficit if you look long and hard enough. The IMF, for example, is a rotten apple because rich countries have more voting power. Or the Basel Committee presumably must be illegitimate because no heads of state or nationally elected officials participate. Or the G-20, though for the most part democratic, is too exclusive. And so on.

The difficulty with bearing down on just one institution is that international institutions, and especially minilateral ones, don't act in a vacuum, but in a web of interconnected, and indeed overlapping, systems and strategies. A big picture or macro-level conception of legitimacy is required. Consider again the reformation of the international financial architecture in 2008. Prior to 2008, most international standard-setting bodies were relatively autonomous organizations that would set their own priorities with little guidance from G-groups in any formal sense. So, for example, the Basel Committee would promulgate standards on banks, and IOSCO would write reports on disclosure and securities firms, both more or less independently of one another. An institution called the Financial Stability Forum would then play the role of orchestrator between the various bodies. The G-8, meanwhile, focused for the most part on macroeconomic policy, while its interest in financial regulation was focused primarily on preventing bank runs and liquidity crises in developing countries.

The 2008 financial crisis changed things almost overnight. Besides leading to an expansion of the G-8 to the G-20, the G-20 – in contrast to the G-8 – assumed a comparatively more energized role in setting the agenda for financial market regulation through periodic leaders' summits that involve the heads of state from member countries. These meetings periodically address financial regulatory issues along with more traditional topics relating to monetary affairs. As a result, international standard-setting bodies, dominated by regulators and technocrats, now report at least indirectly to heads of state, thereby enabling greater accountability to political actors, most of which are democracies. In addition, the most important pieces of legislation, like the Basel Committee's rules for capital, are routinely routed back through the G-20 for a symbolic sign-off, or "ratification."

Additionally, as we saw above, the once-obscure Financial Stability Forum was renamed the Financial Stability Board and elevated to the status of a kind of technocratic counterpart to the G-20 to aid in setting the agenda and coordinating the activities of different regulatory agencies. When this happened, there was more than just a change in a complicated organizational chart. Unlike other organizations like the Basel Committee, which hosts central bankers, finance ministers participate in the FSB alongside a plethora of other regulatory officials (including securities and market regulators). What makes finance ministers interesting is that they are usually more politically sensitive political actors since they operate in executive agencies and, in some instances, may themselves be elected officials. Their participation in the FSB, along with the FSB's increasingly central role in agenda setting, has thus led to greater structural opportunities for political influence.

When you take a step back and look at the new international system, you notice a curious transformation of the international regulatory community after 2008. On the one hand, you have a more vertically regulated system, with the G-20 and FSB setting the agenda for other regulatory bodies like the Basel Committee. But you also have a more institutionally nested system where the expertise of standard setters is combined with more politically accountable authority represented by heads of state and their finance ministers. As such, the G-20 operates alongside technocratic standard setters as a kind of democracy-enhancing mechanism, just as standard setters can provide more technical and credible content for more political actors.

Similar kinds of observations can be made about a range of other institutions, too. For example, the EU, whatever its democratic deficits, is, at the very least, the product of treaties signed and delivered by heads of state. And many decisions still have to go through the EU Parliament, a body of elected officials that, though not nearly as high-profile as domestic legislatures, has an effective veto on the most significant policy proposals put forth by Brussels bureaucrats.

The lesson is that assessing legitimacy requires a close look at institutions at both a micro- and macro-level. You have to certainly look at who makes day-to-day decisions and what kind of input mechanism technocrats rely on. But you also have to examine the "big picture" of how an institution fits into a wider system of governance. However, such nuance is, unfortunately, rare. Ongoing debates are typically trapped, as law professor Bobby Ahdieh has observed, in unnecessarily binary conceptions of legitimacy/illegitimacy.[19] To escape this trap requires recognizing the "intersystemic" nature of economic statecraft – the fact that institutions and networks engage one another in at times overlapping and even interdependent ways in order to achieve their specific policy objectives. So you can't just look at the pieces; rather, you have to examine the system in its entirety when making judgments about effectiveness and legitimacy. Translating how the different pieces work will be an essential task of today's technocrats. When making decisions, they will have to appreciate and relate these larger-scale features to the same stakeholders that are on the receiving end of the decisions that may be coming from mere parts of the larger system. And only then will their claims to legitimacy be bolstered not only in theory, but also tangibly, on the ground, for the people and institutions from whom compliance is sought.

TOWARD A SMARTER MINILATERALISM

In sum, minilateralism is a toolset for surviving in a complex world. But it comes with tradeoffs for institutional governance and democracy itself, as economic integration and cooperation have outpaced anything remotely resembling a transnational political consensus.

Arguably, these challenges have only grown with the decline of post-war multilateralism. This is because even as Bretton Woods promoted a new institutional structure for global, rules-based cooperation – and even enabled today's globalized world – it reaffirmed hundreds of years of traditional state practice in which diplomacy was highly formalized. Under the largely Westphalian model of international relations, it embraced the notion that international obligations arise through legal custom and formal consent, with the latter usually involving the ratification of treaties and the participation of a range of domestic political elites.

We've seen, however, that these kinds of expectations and rituals don't go far in managing today's fast-paced world. Longstanding formalities and institutions are being increasingly shelved in the name of efficacy and necessity. In their place, new modes of cooperation are arising that can cavalierly sidestep treaties and global consensus while still intruding in the economic life and self-determination of sovereign states. So financial diplomats are under unprecedented pressure to prove to often-skeptical domestic audiences that they are doing everything possible to make themselves worthy of the authority they enjoy.

Fortunately, there is no single model of representative law-making that has to be applied to all international cooperation. No one approach will work all the time. Even going all out with a robust global government – with powers even beyond what we've seen with the IMF, World Bank, and WTO – would likely prove unsatisfactory over the long run. This is because the formal consent given by a government at any one point may not reflect the desires of its people. And it's something international law doesn't even try to figure out. Indeed, although international law requires consent, it gives little instruction as to how much transparency or inclusiveness should be required in order for a state to give its consent.[20] This means that even if you are able to secure a country's formal approval for international actions or rules, the consent given by its people might be quite shallow. And even if you could create a system whereby countries only sent elected officials to negotiate there would likely be occasional gaps between their actions and their publics' priorities. After all, international organizations routinely generate their own quirks and internal dynamics, and representatives may develop goals or objectives that do not always dovetail nearly with domestic politics. This makes it occasionally difficult for people to accept the judgments of international actors, no matter what their configuration, on issues that directly impact their economic lives.[21]

That said, one of the more interesting features of minilateralism is that just as countries are developing new tools to navigate an increasingly multipolar global economy, they are also deploying ever more innovative strategies to mitigate the democratic deficits that accompany their new financial statecraft. Indeed, these two activities in many ways run parallel to one another. Today's complex world requires action beyond the existing capabilities of individual nation states and traditional international organizations. Consequently, economic diplomacy routinely involves rethinking the means by which cooperation arises, and finding new means by which to balance the competing objectives of effectiveness (and more specifically, the goals of economic growth and financial stability) with overarching values of democratic participation and consent.

The trillion-dollar question is whether the evolving modes of representation and participation are enough to bolster minilateralism's claims of legitimacy for national and global publics. Although voting, voice, and inter-institutional cooperation all boost claims to legitimacy, none of these options will definitively solve democratic deficits. They may either merely mitigate earlier ones – for example, in the out growth of the G-20 from the G-7 – or redirect the means by which publics participate.

Still, several rules of thumb can be helpful in continually making the case for minilateralism, and keeping it at least on the path toward greater legitimacy. First, minilateralism and its practitioners must remain modest and open to change. Expertise and democratic legitimacy are not necessarily mutually exclusive; indeed, the two are necessary predicates to effective financial statecraft. Yet even where regulators strike some kind of agreement, either with regard to an institutional arrangement or an international rule, there needs to be both a culture and mechanisms available for periodically testing and evaluating the existing order. Such an approach differs considerably from past practice where there was an expectation of finality in international rulemaking. But today's global economy is characterized by constant change. This dynamism requires flexible institutions that embrace experimentation and regulatory innovation. Far from settling on any one institutional model, rule, or tactic, financial diplomats have to be willing to solicit and listen to a broad array of perspectives – and to review past assumptions and beliefs when necessary. The networks in which they operate must then be willing to update practices and approaches quickly and efficiently. New models must be revised by periodic updates and refinements – like the Basel III capital accord's revision of the old Basel II (and Basel I) rules – and revamped when they become obsolete, much like the G-7's displacement by the G-20.

At the same time, minilateral modesty also involves understanding the natural limits of minilateralism's institutional and regulatory innovations – and the technocracy driving it. Technocracy can help drive innovation in regulatory design forward in order to keep pace with financial innovation. Still, it can't do everything. Just consider Italy and Greece, the proverbial best-case scenarios for technocrats insofar as technocrats were installed as heads of state. In both cases, the unelected EU technocrats had little to show for their terms in office. From Prime Minister Mario Monti's difficulties in instituting deep reforms in Italy, to Prime Minister Papademos's failure to sustain support for austerity, technocrats more accustomed to leading armies of civil servants have found themselves unable to achieve and maintain the social consensus necessary for delivering meaningful economic reforms in their native countries. Even where they enjoy a broad mandate for change, they still have to navigate national on-the-ground political minefields to implement adjustment policies. Understanding that technocracy, even the most expert, will only be successful with significant political buy-in will be key to making minilateralism work in a multipolar world.

Towards this end, the smart minilateral diplomat will constantly work on reconciling multilateral, democratic principles of governance with the imperatives of the modern global economy, and vice versa. The best financial authorities will be able to relate decisions made in seemingly distant forums to the needs and interests of local citizens. In short, diplomacy at home will be as essential as diplomacy abroad. Technocrats will have to take the lead in informing domestic audiences about the global (or regional) economy, their country's place in it, and the trade-offs and often hard choices that have to be made about competing in an international marketplace. All the while, the new tools and strategies embraced to navigate a world of diffuse power should still be practiced in ways to maximize opportunities to enhance claims of legitimacy. Authorities shouldn't look for the *least* amount of representation to make things work. Instead, they should seek out the *most* legitimacy that can be accommodated in light of their economic and financial policy objectives.

Thus for minilateralism to work, engagement with both local and national politics is a must, as is engagement with new and old forums of interstate cooperation. Local-level concerns should be able to bubble up to the international sphere, just as international values and standards have to be digested and internalized domestically by countries that commit to them. Equally important, minilateral and multilateral tools must coexist in ways that draw on and enhance one another's strategic advantages, and not undermine them. Alliances can be useful tools for bypassing holdouts where widespread agreement or consensus exists, or where a band of states wants to take cooperation beyond that possible at a multilateral level. They should not, however, be used to keep others out of cooperative arrangements or to undermine global accords and nondiscrimination principles. Soft law is likewise best used to navigate uncertainty and govern quickly and effectively, but it should not be relied on in order to consistently sideline democratically elected officials. Even financial engineering, a useful tool in smoothing transitions to a multicurrency system, should not exacerbate existing exorbitant privileges or unwind decades of trade cooperation.

So in economic diplomacy as in life, balance is necessary. Minilateralism stands the best long-term chances of success when countries embrace it as a means for enhancing economic cooperation, not economic warfare. Of course, since minilateralism is itself the product of both diffuse power and disparate national agendas, this will be easier said than done. But only by teaming technocratic pragmatism with democratic norms and global aspirations will today's economic diplomats enjoy widespread support for their work – and begin to create a sustainable infrastructure for the twenty-first century economy.

Notes

Introduction: Rethinking Cooperation in a Multipolar World

1. PARAG KHANNA, HOW TO RUN THE WORLD: CHARTING A COURSE TO THE NEXT RENAISSANCE 10–14 (2011); Fareed Zakaria, *Stop Searching for an Obama Doctrine*, WASH. POST (Aug. 22, 2013, 5:10 PM), http://articles.washingtonpost.com/2011-07-06/opinions/35237315_1_foreign-policy-obama-doctrine-monroe-doctrine. *See generally* FRANCIS FUKUYAMA, THE END OF HISTORY AND THE LAST MAN (1992).
2. Ronald H. Coase, *The Problem of Social Cost*, 3 J.L. & Econ. 1 (1960); For an excellent summary of these issues and Coase's work, see JOHN CASSIDY, HOW MARKETS FAIL (2009).
3. CASSIDY, *supra* note 2, at 120.
4. GEORGE FRIEDMAN, THE NEXT 100 YEARS 10 (2009).
5. LOUIS HENKIN, HOW NATIONS BEHAVE: LAW AND FOREIGN POLICY 17 (1979).
6. THE SOCIAL SCIENCES AND RATIONALITY: PROMISE, LIMITS, AND PROBLEMS 51 (Axel van den Berg & Hudson Meadwell eds., 2004).
7. James A. Caporaso, *International Relations Theory and Multilateralism: The Search for Foundations*, 46 INT'L ORG. 599, 610 (1992).
8. *Id.*
9. LLOYD GRUBER, RULING THE WORLD: POWER POLITICS AND THE RISE OF SUPRANATIONAL INSTITUTIONS 23 (2000).
10. ROBERT COOPER, BREAKING OF NATIONS: ORDER AND CHAOS IN THE TWENTY-FIRST CENTURY (2004). Consequently, the best institutional approaches may involve varying degrees of market and bureaucratic tools to internalize costs and benefits. *See generally* JOEL TRACHTMAN, THE ECONOMIC STRUCTURE OF INTERNATIONAL LAW (2008).
11. ROBERT O. KEOHANE, AFTER HEGEMONY 33 (2005).
12. GRUBER, *supra* note 9, at 37.
13. *See* Moisés Naím, *Minilateralism*, FOREIGN POL'Y, July–Aug. 2009, at 136, *available at* http://www.foreignpolicy.com/articles/2009/06/18/minilateralism.
14. *See, e.g.*, Beth V. Yarbrough & Robert M. Yarbrough, *Cooperation in the Liberalization of International Trade: After Hegemony, What?*, 41 INT'L ORG. 1 (1987) (noting that "[l]iberalization can be unilateral, multilateral, or minilateral and can be accompanied by varying degrees of bargaining, threats, harmony, discord, and

explicit coordination"); Lawrence B. Krause, *The Pacific Basin: New Challenges for the United States*, 36 PROCEEDINGS ACAD. POL. SCI. 150, 154 (1986) (noting how "bilateral negotiations […] could evolve into so-called minilateral negotiations, that is, a joining together of several bilateral negotiations"); *see also* Ernest H. Preeg, *Next, a Free-Trade Pact With Japan?*, WALL ST. J., Aug. 12, 1988, at 1 (noting that "[t]he rewards of this agreement offer an incentive to other agreements. If possible, we hope this follow-up liberalization will occur in the Uruguay Round. If not, we might be willing to explore a 'market liberalization club' approach, through minilateral arrangements or a series of bilateral agreements.").

1. *Multilateralism's Rise and Fall*

1. *See* BENN STEIL & MANUEL HINDS, MONEY, MARKETS & SOVEREIGNTY 71 (2009).
2. *See* HENRY B. RUSSELL, INTERNATIONAL MONETARY CONFERENCES 2 (1898).
3. *See id.*
4. *See id.* at 5.
5. *See* CARL-LUDWIG HOLTFRERICH, FRANKFURT AS A FINANCIAL CENTRE 93–94 (J. A. Underwood trans., 1999).
6. *See* ANGELA REDISH, BIMETALLISM: AN ECONOMIC AND HISTORICAL ANALYSIS 13–105 (Cambridge, 2000).
7. JOHN THOM HOLDSWORTH, MONEY AND BANKING 16–23 (1917). One way to understand the arbitrage is through a simple example that the noted economist Francois Velde shared with me: Suppose that the legal ratio is 15.5, meaning that an ounce of gold in the form of coin has 15.5 the legal value of an ounce of silver in the form of coin. Suppose that the market ratio of prices is 15. Assuming there are no (or low) transaction costs, the arbitrage is to borrow 1000F in silver, melt it down into X ounces, use it to buy X/15 ounces of gold, go to the mint and turn those X/15 ounces into 15.5X/15 gold coins, which will be worth 1033F; reimburse the 1000F debt and clear a 33F profit.
8. RUSSELL, *supra* note 2, at 29.
9. Harold James, Opening Address at the Federal Reserve Bank of Boston's 43rd Economic Conference: A Historical Perspective on International Monetary Arrangements 35 (June 1999), *available at* http://www.bos.frb.org/economic/conf/conf43/33p.pdf.
10. *See* GIULIO M. GALLAROTTI, THE ANATOMY OF AN INTERNATIONAL MONETARY REGIME: THE CLASSICAL GOLD STANDARD 1880–1914, at 169 (1995).
11. BARRY J. EICHENGREEN, GLOBALIZING CAPITAL: A HISTORY OF THE INTERNATIONAL MONETARY SYSTEM 18 (2d ed. 2008).
12. *See, e.g., id.* at 24–25.
13. *See id.*
14. The mechanism by which this was often done was through discount rates. By manipulating its discount rate, the central bank could thereby affect the volume of domestic credit. It could increase or reduce the availability of credit to restore balance-of-payments equilibrium without requiring gold flows to take place. When a central bank anticipating gold losses raised its discount rate, reducing its holdings of domestic, interest-bearing assets, cash was drained from the market. The

money supply declined and external balance was restored without requiring actual gold outflows. *See* EICHENGREEN, *supra* note 11, at 27; *see also* Barry Eichengreen, *When Currencies Collapse*, 91 FOREIGN AFF., Jan.–Feb. 2012, at 117.

15. *See* EICHENGREEN, *supra* note 11, at 29.
16. *See* BERNARD SEMMEL, THE RISE OF FREE TRADE IMPERIALISM 19 (1970).
17. *See* HA-JOON CHANG, KICKING AWAY THE LADDER: DEVELOPMENT STRATEGY IN HISTORICAL PERSPECTIVE 52 (6th ed. 2007).
18. *See id.*
19. *See* SEMMEL, *supra* note 16, at 25.
20. *See* ALAN BEATTIE, FALSE ECONOMY: A SURPRISING ECONOMIC HISTORY OF THE WORLD 179 (2009).
21. DANI RODRIK, THE GLOBALIZATION PARADOX: DEMOCRACY AND THE FUTURE OF THE WORLD ECONOMY 28 (2011).
22. *Id.*
23. *Id.* at 33. *See generally* JULIA LOVELL, THE OPIUM WAR: DRUGS, DREAMS AND THE MAKING OF CHINA (2011).
24. *See* RODRIK, *supra* note 21, at 69.
25. *See* EICHENGREEN, *supra* note 11, at 45.
26. *See id.* at 78.
27. *See* RODRIK, *supra* note 21, at 43.
28. *See* Barry Eichengreen & Douglas A. Irwin, *The Slide to Protectionism in the Great Depression* 11 (Nat'l Bureau of Econ. Research, Working Paper No. 15142, 2009), *available at* http://www.nber.org/papers/w15142.pdf.
29. *See id.*
30. *See id.*
31. *See id.* at 12.
32. *See* DOUGLAS A. IRWIN, TRADE POLICY DISASTER: LESSONS FROM THE 1930S, at 102 (2011).
33. *The Bretton Woods Conference*, U.S. DEP'T OF STATE, OFFICE OF THE HISTORIAN, *available at* http://history.state.gov/milestones/1937–1945/BrettonWoods (last visited Sept. 20, 2012).
34. BENN STEIL, THE BATTLE OF BRETTON WOODS 185 (2013).
35. *See* Andreas F. Lowenfeld, *The International Monetary System Across Seven Decades*, 13 J. INT'L ECON. L. 575, 579 (2010).
36. *Id.*
37. *See* RODRIK, *supra* note 21, at 71.
38. *See* John H. Jackson, *GATT and the Future of International Trade Institutions*, 18 BROOK. J. INT'L L. 11, 17 (1992).
39. *See* Lowenfeld, *supra* note 35, at 579.
40. *See* EICHENGREEN, *supra* note 11, at 99.
41. *See* RODRIK, *supra* note 21, at 72.
42. *See generally* Rachel Brewster, *The Remedy Gap*, 80 GEO. WASH. L. REV. 102, 108–12 (2011). *See also* RODRIK, *supra* note 21, at 77.
43. *See* RODRIK, *supra* note 21, at 77.
44. *See id.* at 78.
45. *See* Lowenfeld, *supra* note 35, at 582.

46. *See id.* at 584.

47. *See* Susan C. Schwab, *After Doha: Why the Negotiations Are Doomed and What We Should Do About It*, 90 FOREIGN AFF., May–Jun. 2011, at 104, 106.

48. *See* G. John Ikenberry, *The Future of the Liberal World Order: Internationalism after America*, 90 FOREIGN AFF., May–Jun. 2011, at 56.

49. *See* Stewart Patrick, *Irresponsible Stakeholders? The Difficulty of Integrating Rising Powers*, 89 FOREIGN AFF., Nov.–Dec. 2010, at 44, 44–53.

50. *See id.* at 46.

51. *See* PARAG KHANNA, HOW TO RUN THE WORLD: CHARTING A COURSE TO THE NEXT RENAISSANCE 14 (2011).

2. *Playing the Numbers in Trade*

1. DAVID GREWAL, NETWORK POWER 235 (2009).

2. *See generally* MICHAEL E. PORTER, THE COMPETITIVE ADVANTAGE OF NATIONS (1998).

3. *See* DILIP K. DAS, REGIONALISM IN GLOBAL TRADE 9 (2004).

4. *See* Special Rapporteur on the Most-Favoured-Nation Clause, *First Rep. on the Most-Favoured-Nation Clause*, 159, Int'l Law Comm'n, U.N. Doc. A/CN.4/213 (Apr. 18, 1969) (by Endre Ustor), *available at* http://untreaty.un.org/ilc/documentation/english/a_cn4_213.pdf.

5. *See id.*

6. *See id.* at 160.

7. *See id.*

8. *See id.* at 162.

9. *See id.*

10. *See Work of the Committee on Regional Trade Agreements*, WORLD TRADE ORG. (2013), *available at* http://www.wto.org/english/tratop_e/region_e/regcom_e.htm.

11. *See* Stephen Walsh, *Addressing the Abuse of the WTO's Exemption for Regional Trade Agreements*, EUR. L. STUDENT ASS'N SELECTED PAPERS EUR. L., no. 1, 2004, at 62, 79, *available at* http://norway.elsa.org/fileadmin/user_upload/elsa_international/PDF/SPEL/SPEL04_1_WALSH.pdf.

12. *Id.*

13. *See id.*

14. *See* Appellate Body Report, *Turkey – Restrictions on Imports of Textile and Clothing Products*, WT/DS34/AB/R (Oct. 22, 1999), *available at* http://www.wto.org/english/tratop_e/dispu_e/34abr_e.pdf.

15. *See* Robert Z. Lawrence, *Regionalism and the WTO: Should the Rules Be Changed?*, THE WORLD TRADING SYSTEM: CHALLENGES AHEAD 41, 50 (Jeffrey J. Schott ed., 1996).

16. *See id.*

17. Andean Community, *Trade Integration, Customs Union, available at* http://www.comunidadandina.org/INGLES/comercio/customs_union.htm (last visited Sept. 25, 2013).

18. Jorge Creso-Velasco & Gonzales D. Bernal-Brito, *U.S.-Bolivia Trade and Investment Relations*, in THE ANDEAN COMMUNITY AND THE UNITED STATES: TRADE AND INVESTMENT RELATIONS IN THE 1990s, at 70, 70–71, (Miguel R. Mendoza et al.

eds., 1998), *available at* http://www.sedi.oas.org/DTTC/TRADE/Pub/Books/CAF/P3C6.pdf

19. *See* Maurice Schiff & L. Alan Winters, Regional Integration and Development 41 (2003).

20. *See* Dani Rodrik, The Globalization Paradox: Democracy and the Future of the World Economy 163 (2011).

21. *See* Das, *supra* note 3, at 62.

22. *See* Rodrik, *supra* note 20, at 168.

23. *See* Jeffrey D. Sachs & John Williamson, *External Debt and Macroeconomic Performance in Latin America and East Asia*, Brookings Papers on Econ. Activity no. 2, 523, 536 (1985).

24. *See* Alejandro Foxley, Regional Trade Blocs: The Way to the Future? 24 (2011).

25. *See* Das, *supra* note 3, at 60.

26. *See* Mark S. Manger, Investing in Protection: The Politics of Preferential Trade Agreements Between North and South 36 (2009).

27. *See id.* at 68.

28. *See id.*

29. *See id.* at 76.

30. *See id.* at 78.

31. David Williams, *Mexico's NAFTA Experience*, AgExporter Magazine 14 (Jan. 2, 2004), *available at* http://www.fas.usda.gov/info/agexporter/2004/January/pgs%20 14–15.pdf.

32. *Id.*

33. *Id.*

34. *See* Schiff & Winters, *supra* note 19, at 33.

35. *See id.*

36. *See id.* at 34.

37. *See* Kerry A. Chase, Trading Blocs: States, Firms, and Regions in the World Economy 265 (2005).

38. *See id.*

39. *See* Schiff & Winters, *supra* note 19, at 79–80.

40. *See* Lloyd Gruber, Ruling the World: Power Politics and the Rise of Supranational Institutions 162 (2000).

41. *See id.*

42. *See id.* at 166; *see also* Takashi Terada, *Competitive Regionalism in Southeast Asia and Beyond: Role of Singapore and ASEAN*, *in* Competitive Regionalism: FTA Diffusion in the Pacific Rim 161, at 167 (Mireya Solís et al. eds., 2009).

43. *See* Donald Crone, *Does Hegemony Matter?*, 45 World Pol. 501, 520 (1993).

44. Murray Hiebert, Meredith Broadbent, & Lindsay Roth, *The Significance of the Trans-Pacific Partnership Negotiations*, Ctr. Strategic & Int'l Studies, (Jan. 24, 2012), *available at* http://www.csis.org/publication/significance-trans-pacific-partnership-negotiations.

45. *See id.*

46. *See* Dana Gabriel, *Canada and Mexico to Join U.S. in NAFTA of the Pacific*, Infowars.com (Nov. 29, 2011), *available at* http://www.infowars.com/canada-and-mexico-to-join-u-s-in-nafta-of-the-pacific/.

47. *See* Peter Clark, *Is the Trans Pacific Partnership a Re-writing of NAFTA?*, iPolitics (Jan. 10, 2012), *available at* http://www.ipolitics.ca/2012/01/10/peter-clark-is-the-trans-pacific-partnership-a-re-writing-of-nafta/.
48. *See id.*
49. *See id.*
50. *Id.*
51. *See* Sherzod Shadikhodjaev, Retaliation in the WTO Dispute Settlement System 35 (2009).

3. *Soft Law in International Finance*

1. *See* Punam Chuhan, *Private Capital Flows in Historical Perspective, in* Global Development Finance 119 (World Bank ed., 2000), *available at* http://siteresources.worldbank.org/GDFINT/Resources/334952–1257197810941/CH6–118–139. pdf. Some of the arguments and excerpts found in this chapter can be found in my book, Soft Law and the Global Financial System (2012), which offers a more detailed overview of the institutions and actors driving international financial regulation.
2. Charles Roxburgh, Susan Lund & John Piotrowski, Mapping Global Capital Markets 18 (2011), *available at* http://www.mckinsey.com/insights/mgi/ research/financial_markets/mapping_global_capital_markets_2011.
3. *See* Review of the Competitiveness of London's Financial Centre, London: Winning in a Changing World (2008), *available at* http://legacy. london.gov.uk/mayor/economy/docs/london-winning-changing-world.pdf.
4. *See* Thomas P. DiNapoli, The Securities Industry in New York: New York State Comptroller Report 9–2013 (2012), *available at* http://s3.documentcloud. org/documents/459179/new-york-state-comptrollers-report-on-securities.txt.
5. Jose E. Alvarez, International Organizations as Law-makers 6 (2006) (citing Henry G. Schermers & Niels M. Blokker, International Institutional Law: Unity Within Diversity 32–33 (4th ed. 2003).
6. *Id.* at 9.
7. For example, Article 38(1) of the Statute of the International Court of Justice identifies international conventions, international custom, and general principles of law as primary sources, and in doing so implicitly raises treaties (conventions) to a higher status than custom or general principles of law. Harlan Cohen, *Finding International Law: Rethinking the Doctrine of Sources*, 93 Iowa L. Rev. 65, 76 (2007). The Restatement (Third) of International Law provides that "[t]he law of international economic relations in its broadest sense includes all the international law and international agreements governing economic transactions that cross state boundaries or that otherwise have implication for more than one state, such as those involving the movement of … funds." Restatement (Third) of Foreign Relations Law of the United States, Part VIII, intro. note (1987).
8. *See* Rob Davies, *Q & A: Basel Committee's Walter Outlines Basel II Reform Agenda*, Risk.net (June 17, 2009), *available at* http://www.risk.net/risk-magazine/ news/1518380/q-a-basel-committee-walter-outlines-basel-ii-reform-agenda.
9. *See* Press Release, Int'l Ass'n of Ins. Supervisors, IAIS Supports G-20 Declaration (Apr. 7, 2009), *available at* http://www.iaisweb.org/view/element_href.cfm?src=1/6782.pdf;

see also Press Release, Int'l Ass'n of Ins. Supervisors, IAIS Takes Action on G-20 and FSF Recommendations (Feb. 26, 2009), *available at* http://www.iaisweb.org/_temp/26_February_2009_IAIS_takes_action_on_G20_and_FSF_recommendations.pdf.

10. *See* JACK L. GOLDSMITH & ERIC A. POSNER, THE LIMITS OF INTERNATIONAL LAW 16–17 (2005) (noting that theorists have only recently considered international law to be "distinct from institutions embodied by international law").

11. *See* David Zaring, The Ubiquity of International Legal Process (working paper) (on file with author). Indeed, different flexibility-enhancing mechanisms can respond to different circumstances and generate varying opportunities for coordination. *See also* Timothy Meyer, *Soft Law as Delegation*, 32 FORDHAM INT'L. L.J. 888, 897 (2009).

12. *See* BASEL COMM. ON BANKING SUPERVISION, *Bank Failures in Mature Economies* 5 (Bank for Int'l Settlements, Working Paper No. 13, 2004), *available at* http://www.bis.org/publ/bcbs_wp13.pdf.

13. *See id.*

14. *See id.* at 67.

15. *See id.*

16. *See* DAVID A. SINGER, REGULATING CAPITAL: SETTING STANDARDS FOR THE INTERNATIONAL FINANCIAL SYSTEM 71 (2007).

17. *See id.* at 73.

18. *See id.* at 45.

19. *See id.* at 61.

20. *See* ABRAM CHAYES & ANTONIA HANDLER CHAYES, THE NEW SOVEREIGNTY: COMPLIANCE WITH INTERNATIONAL REGULATORY AGREEMENTS 2 (1995).

21. *See generally* Pierre-Hugues Verdier, *Transnational Regulatory Networks and Their Limits*, 34 YALE J. INT'L L. 113 (2009).

22. CHAYES & CHAYES, *supra* note 20, at 3.

23. *See* JACK GOLDSMITH, POWER AND CONSTRAINT: PRESIDENTIAL SYNOPTICON 206–07 (2012).

24. *Id.*

25. *See* Greg Schaffer & Mark A. Pollack, *Hard and Soft Law: What Have We Learned?* 15 (Minnesota Legal Studies Research Paper No. 12–17, 2012), *available at* http://papers.ssrn.com/sol3/papers.cfm?abstract_id=2044800 (discussing the opportunity to interpret opportunistically vague legal provisions that are not supported by dispute mechanisms).

26. *See* CHRIS BRUMMER, SOFT LAW AND THE GLOBAL FINANCIAL SYSTEM: RULE MAKING IN THE GLOBAL FINANCIAL SYSTEM (2012). It is possible that compliance could even be scored quantitatively, at least up to a point. That said, it could be unwise to do so in an absolute sense since ranking 173 countries on their compliance could heighten incentives to circumvent or short-circuit surveillance. Moreover, it would be hard, if not impossible, to create a robust or accurate hierarchy where regulatory systems are so diverse. But one could clearly envision a general schema of compliance like the ones used by credit-rating agencies to identify general levels of compliance with some of the most important standards. This approach is already being used by some forums like the FSB, but in what is often a haphazard (and random) way that in no way tracks the importance of various rules to financial stability.

4. *Hedging Bets in the Monetary System*

1. Indeed, when a central bank decides to pursue such a course of action, it is buying securities that – at least to some extent – will not be repaid. This injection of liquidity into the national economy will ultimately depreciate the national currency.

2. *See* Pierre-Hugues Verdier, *The Political Economy of International Financial Regulation, in* Public Law and Legal Theory Research Paper Series No. 2012–32, at 6 (2012).

3. *See id.* at 6–7.

4. *See id.*

5. Benn Steil, The Battle for Bretton Woods 132 (2013).

6. *See* Int'l Monetary Fund, International Financial Statistics Supplement on International Reserves xiii (1983).

7. Barry Eichengreen, *The Dollar Dilemma: The World's Top Currency Faces Competition*, 88 Foreign Aff., Sept.–Oct. 2009, at 53, 68.

8. *See id.* at 67.

9. *See* Gary A. Dymski, *Post-Hegemonic U.S. Economic Hegemony: Minskian and Kaleckian Dynamics in the Neoliberal Era*, J. Jap. Soc'y Pol. Econ., Apr. 2002, at 247, 247–49.

10. *See generally* Michael Dooley, David Folkerts-Landau & Peter Garber, *An Essay on the Revived Bretton Woods System* (Nat'l Bureau of Econ. Research, Working Paper No. 9971, 2003), *available at* http://www.nber.org/papers/w9971.pdf.

11. *See id.*

12. Daniel W. Drezner, *Will Currency Follow the Flag?*, 10 Int'l Rel. Asia-Pac. 389, 394 (2010).

13. *See* Benn Steil & Manuel Hinds, Money, Markets & Sovereignty 218 (2009).

14. Sebastian Edwards, *The U.S. Current Account Deficit: Gradual Correction or Abrupt Adjustment?*, 28 J. Pol. Modeling 629 (2006).

15. Congress of the United States Congressional Budget Office, Updated Budget Projections: Fiscal Years 2013 to 2023, *available at* http://www.cbo.gov/sites/default/files/cbofiles/attachments/44172-Baseline2.pdf. For an (even) more pessimistic editorial on this issue's implication for foreign policy, *see* Roger C. Altman & Richard N. Haass, *American Profligacy and American Power*, 89 Foreign Aff., Nov.–Dec. 2010, at 27.

16. *See* Barry Eichengreen, Exhorbitant privilege: the rise and fall of the dollar and the future of the international monetary system 71 (2010).

17. *See id.*

18. *See* Barry Eichengreen, Should the Maastricht Treaty Be Saved, at 29 (Princeton Studies in Int'l Fin., No. 74, 1992), *available at* http://www.princeton.edu/~ies/IES_Studies/S74.pdf.

19. *See* Danièle Nouy, *Is Sovereign Risk Properly Addressed by Financial Regulation?*, Banque Fr. Fin. Stability Rev., Apr. 2012, at 96, *available at* http://www.banque-france.fr/fileadmin/user_upload/banque_de_france/publications/Revue_de_la_stabilite_financiere/2012/rsf-avril-2012/FSR16-20-04.pdf#page=96.

20. *See* Mario Draghi, President, Eur. Cent. Bank, Introductory Statement to the Press Conference (Aug. 2, 2012), *available at* http://www.ecb.int/press/pressconf/2012/html/is120802.en.html.

21. Sideek M. Seyad, *A Legal Analysis of the European Financial Stability Mechanism*, 26 J. Int'l Banking. L. Reg. 421, 424 (2011).

22. *See id.*

23. *See* Victoria Cadman, *Eurozone's Firefight*, TheLawyer.com (Feb. 13, 2012), http://www.thelawyer.com/eurozone's-firefight/1011344.article.

24. For a general discussion, *see Casting a Spell: Has Mario Draghi Done What It Takes to Save the Euro?*, Economist, Sept. 15, 2012, *available at* http://www.economist.com/node/21562919.

25. *See* Ralph Atkins, *The Short View*, Fin. Times, Oct. 9, 2012.

26. *See* Peter Guest, *Eurozone Crisis: What Would Happen If Greece Left the Euro*, The Huffington Post (Aug. 12, 2011, 1:31 PM), http://www.huffingtonpost.co.uk/2011/12/07/eurozone-crisis-how-greece-can-leave-euro_n_1134384.html.

27. *See* Martin Wolf, *A Permanent Precedent*, Fin. Times, May 17, 2012.

28. *See* C. Randall Henning, East Asian Financial Cooperation 16 (2002). For this reason, swaps are distinct from loans. Loans involve one party lending money to another with an expectation of interest. Currency swaps, by contrast, involve the mutual exchange of assets in the future. That said, in the world of international finance, they can and often do create liabilities for a country to the extent to which a sought after, convertible currency is exchanged for one that is nonconvertible or one that loses its value in times of crisis.

29. European banks had found themselves short of dollars necessary to repay some of the loans they took out in international money markets. Consequently, the Federal Reserve had to come to the rescue to approve major transactions with major central banks, including the ECB, to the tune of over a half trillion dollars.

30. *See, e.g.*, Qu Hongbin, *From Greenbacks to Redbacks*, *in* The Rise of the Redback: A Guide to Renminbi Internationalisation 13 (HSBC Global Research ed., 2010).

31. Arvind Subramanian, *Renminbi Rules: The Conditional Imminence of the Reserve Currency Transition* 1 (Peterson Inst. for Int'l Econ., Working Paper 11–14, 2011), *available at* http://www.piie.com/publications/interstitial.cfm?ResearchID=1918.

32. *See* Sebastian Mallaby & Olin Wethington, *The Future of the Yuan: China's Struggle to Internationalize Its Currency*, 91 Foreign Aff., Jan.–Feb. 2012, at 135, 135–36, *available at* http://www.foreignaffairs.com/articles/136778/sebastian-mallaby-and-olin-wethington/the-future-of-the-yuan.

33. *See* Eichengreen, *supra* note 16, at 143–144. Until recently, the RMB's use was only permitted with its immediate neighbors, or with select trustworthy companies chosen to settle transactions in the Chinese currency.

34. *See* Mallaby & Wethington, *supra* note 32.

35. *See id.*

36. *See id.*

37. Editorial, *China's Real Monetary Problem*, Wall St. J., Sept. 17, 2010, http://online.wsj.com/article/SB10001424052748703743504575493120916038074.html.

38. *See id.*

39. *See id.*

40. *See id.*

41. *See* John Greenwood, *The Costs and Implications of PBC Sterilization*, 28 Cato J. 205, 209 (2008), *available at* http://www.cato.org/pubs/journal/cj28n2/cj28n2-4.pdf.

42. *See id.* at 210.

43. *See Chinese President Hu Jintao Meets with British Prime Minister Brown*, MISSION OF THE PEOPLE'S REP. OF CHINA TO THE EUR. UNION (Apr. 2, 2009), http://www. fmprc.gov.cn/ce/cebe/eng/zxxx/t555804.htm.

44. Peter B. Kenen, *Currency Internationalisation: An Overview, in* BIS PAPERS NO. 61, at 11 (2012).

45. Qu Hongbin, *supra* note 30, at 13.

46. *See* Haihong Gao & Yongding Yu, *Internationalisation of the Renminbi, in* BIS PAPERS NO. 61, at 109 (2012).

47. *See* Joshua Aizenman & Rajeswari Sengupta, *The Financial Trilemma and a Comparative Analysis with India*, at 3 (Working Paper, Nov. 2011), *available at* http://economics.ucsc.edu/research/downloads/The_Trilemma_in_China-Draft_Nov_Final.pdf.

48. *See* Kenen, *supra* note 44, at 12.

49. *See* Samuel Shen & Pete Sweeney, *China Investment Quota Granted to Foreigners Exceeds $30 Bln*, REUTERS (Sept. 24, 2012, 4:26 PM), http://in.reuters.com/article/2012/09/24/china-qfii-idINL4E8KO5NR20120924.

50. *See id.*

51. *U.S./China Media Brief: Currency Revaluation*, UCLA ASIAN AM. STUDIES CENT., http://www.aasc.ucla.edu/uschina/trade_currencyrevaluation.shtml (last visited Oct. 16, 2012).

52. *See* Robert Cookson, *China Revs Up Renminbi Expansion*, FIN. TIMES (July 28, 2010), http://www.ft.com/intl/cms/s/0/2ff1d6ea-9a65-11df-87fd-00144feab49a.html#axzz22Fil9bkz.

53. J. P. MORGAN, *Chinese Takeaway: What Every Corporate Needs to Know About RMB*, THE ASSET (Apr. 2011), *available at* http://www.jpmorgan.com/cm/BlobServer/10_Things_You_Should_Know_About_RMB.pdf?blobkey=id&blobnocache=true&blobwhere=1320534215246&blobheader=application%2Fpdf&blobcol=urldata&blobtable=MungoBlobs.

54. *See id.*

55. *See* Nasser Saidi et al., *The Redback Cometh: Renminbi Internationalisation and What to Do About It, in* DUBAI INT'L FIN. CTR. ECON. NOTE NO. 18, at 14–15 (2011).

56. *Id.*

57. *See id.* at 21.

58. *See* Cookson, *supra* note 52.

59. *See* Arvind Subramanian & Martin Kessler, *The Renminbi Bloc Is Here: Asia Down, Rest of the World to Go?*, at 2 (Peterson Inst. for Intl Econ., Working Paper No. 12–19, 2012), *available at* http://piie.com/publications/wp/wp12–19.pdf.

60. INT'L MONETARY FUND, STRATEGY, POLICY, AND REV. DEPT., ENHANCING INTERNATIONAL MONETARY STABILITY – A ROLE FOR THE SDR? (Jan. 7, 2011), *available at* http://www.imf.org/external/np/pp/eng/2011/010711.pdf.

61. *See* Ettore Dorrucci & Julie McKay, *The International Monetary System After the Financial Crisis, in* OCCASIONAL PAPER SERIES NO. 123, at 35 (Eur. Ctr. Bank, 2011), *available at* http://www.ecb.europa.eu/pub/pdf/scpops/ecbocp123.pdf.

62. *See* EICHENGREEN, *supra* note 16, at 137; *see also* Eichengreen *supra* note 7, at 53, 67–68 ("The emergence of a reserve system based on multiple currencies should

not be alarming .... [I]f anything, the lesson is that reserve-currency competition ratchets up the market discipline felt by policymakers. The more alternatives central banks and other international investors possess, the more pressure policymakers will feel to take the steps needed to maintain those investors' confidence.").

63. Barry Eichengreen, *When Currencies Collapse*, 91 FOREIGN AFF., Jan.–Feb. 2012, at 117, 132.

64. Mallaby & Wethington, *supra* note 32.

65. Banyan, *Internationalising the Yuan: Redback Mountain*, THE ECONOMIST, Dec. 8, 2010, http://www.economist.com/blogs/banyan/2010/12/internationalising_yuan.

66. *See* Policy Letter from Charles H. Dallara, Managing Dir., Inst. for Int'l Fin., to François Baroin, Minister for Econ., Fin. and Indus., Fr. (Sept. 14, 2011).

67. IGNAZIO ANGELONI ET AL., GLOBAL CURRENCIES FOR TOMORROW: A EUROPEAN PERSPECTIVE 7 (2011), *available at* http://www.bruegel.org/publications/publication-detail/publication/592-global-currencies-for-tomorrow-a-european-perspective/#.UUCrmo6Pdao.

5. *Managing Minilateralism*

1. *See generally* JOSEPH S. NYE, THE FUTURE OF POWER 208 (2011); Suzanne Nossel, *Smart Power*, 83 FOREIGN AFF., Mar.–Apr. 2004, at 131–143, *available at* http://www.foreignaffairs.com/articles/59716/suzanne-nossel/smart-power.

2. NYE, *supra* note 1, at 208.

3. *Id.*

4. JOSEPH E. STIGLITZ, GLOBALIZATION AND ITS DISCONTENTS 96 (2002).

5. *See id.*

6. *See id.*

7. *See* Duncan McDonnell, *With Mario Monti's Technocratic Government, It Is Not Just the Idea of Party Government Which Is Being Damaged in Italy, but the Very Idea of the Political Party's Role as an Indispensable Agent of Democracy*, EUROPP BLOG, LONDON SCH. OF ECON. & POL. SCI. (Apr. 16, 2012), http://blogs.lse.ac.uk/europpblog/2012/04/16/italy-monti-democrac.

8. John R. Hibbing & Elizabeth Theiss-Morse, *Voice, Validation and Legitimacy*, *in* COOPERATION: THE POLITICAL PSYCHOLOGY OF EFFECTIVE HUMAN INTERACTION, at Part III No. 8 (2007), *available at* http://www.polisci.unl.edu/dept/hibbing/Minnesota_rev2.pdf.

9. *See* David A. Super, *Are Rights Efficient? Challenging the Managerial Critique of Individual Rights*, 93 CAL. L. REV. 1051, 1074–76 (2005).

10. *See id.*

11. WORLD ECONOMIC OUTLOOK UPDATE: JANUARY 2012, at 2 (Int'l Monetary Fund ed., 2012), *available at* http://www.imf.org/external/pubs/ft/weo/2011/update/01/pdf/0111.pdf.

12. *See China Overview*, WORLDBANK.ORG (2012), http://www.worldbank.org/en/country/china/overview; *see also* D'Vera Cohn, *Revising the Past, Using 2010 Census Data*, PEWSOCIALTRENDS.ORG (Sept. 20, 2012), http://www.pewsocialtrends.org/2012/09/20/revising-the-past-using-2010-census-data/.

13. *See Country at a Glance: South Africa*, WORLDBANK.ORG (2012), http://www.worldbank.org/en/country/southafrica; *see also Country at a Glance: Brazil*,

WorldBank.Org (2012), http://www.worldbank.org/en/country/brazil; *Country at a Glance: China*, WorldBank.Org (2012), http://www.worldbank.org/en/country/china.

14. Byron Williams, *I Am Tired of California's Legislating by Ballot Box*, The Huffington Post (Oct. 19, 2006, 3:55 PM), http://www.huffingtonpost.com/byron-williams/i-am-tired-of-californias_b_32080.html.

15. *See* Hibbing & Theiss-Morse, *supra* note 8.

16. *See* Eyal Benvenisti, *Exit and Voice in the Age of Globalization*, 98 Mich. L. Rev. 167, 168 (1999).

17. *Id.* at 200.

18. *See* Szu Ping Chan, *Debt Crisis: As It Happened*, Telegraph.co.uk (Sept. 12, 2012), http://www.telegraph.co.uk/finance/debt-crisis-live/9537151/Debt-crisis-as-it-happened-September-12-2012.html.

19. *See* Robert B. Ahdieh, *Dialectical Regulation*, 38 Conn. L. Rev. 863, 868–69 (2005).

20. Informal International Lawmaking 525 (Joost Pauwelyn, Ramses A. Wessel & Jan Wouters eds., 2012).

21. *See* Nye, *supra* note 1.

Index